Older Workers, Active Ageing, and the Future of Work

Studies in Employment and Social Policy

VOLUME 59

Editors

Objective

Studies in Employment and Social Policy series seeks to provide a forum for highlighting international and comparative research on contemporary areas of significance for evaluation and regulation of the world of work.

Introduction

Launched in 1997, the Studies in Employment and Social Policy Series now boasts over fifty titles, addressing key policy and development issues in the fields of industrial relations, labour law, social security, and international labour regulation.

Content

With contributions from leading figures in the field, the series brings together key policymakers, academics, and regulators, providing a unique context in which to analyse and evaluate the rapid and dramatic work and social policy developments taking place around the globe.

The titles published in this series are listed at the end of this volume.

Older Workers, Active Ageing, and the Future of Work

Discourses and Legal Advancements

Edited by

Jenny Julén Votinius
Mia Rönnmar

Wolters Kluwer

Published by:
Kluwer Law International B.V.
PO Box 316
2400 AH Alphen aan den Rijn
The Netherlands
E-mail: lrs-sales@wolterskluwer.com
Website: www.wolterskluwer.com/en/solutions/kluwerlawinternational

Sold and distributed by:
Wolters Kluwer Legal & Regulatory U.S.
920 Links Avenue
Landisville, PA 17538
United States of America
E-mail: customer.service@wolterskluwer.com

ISBN 978-94-035-1047-7

e-Book: ISBN 978-94-035-1057-6
web-PDF: ISBN 978-94-035-1067-5

Editors

Jenny Julén Votinius, Professor of Private Law, Faculty of Law at Lund University, Sweden.

Mia Rönnmar, Professor of Private Law, Faculty of Law at Lund University, Sweden.

Contributors

Takashi Araki, Professor of Labour and Employment Law, Graduate Schools for Law and Politics at the University of Tokyo, Japan.

Martina Axmin, Swedish General Ombudsman for Social Security and Associate Senior Lecturer, Faculty of Law at Lund University, Sweden.

Núria Pumar Beltrán, Professor of Labour Law and Social Security Law, Faculty of Law at the University of Barcelona, Spain.

Alysia Blackham, Associate Professor, Melbourne Law School at the University of Melbourne, Australia.

Eusebi Colàs-Neila, Associate Professor of Labour and Social Security Law, Faculty of Law at Pompeu Fabra University, Spain.

Ana Virginia Moreira Gomes, Professor of Labour Law, Faculty of Law at University of Fortaleza, Brazil (on leave).

Xavier Groussot, Professor of EU Law, Faculty of Law at Lund University, Sweden.

Julia López López, Professor of Labour Law and Social Security Law, Faculty of Law at Pompeu Fabra University, Spain.

Alezini Loxa, Post-doctoral Researcher in EU Law, Faculty of Law at Lund University, Sweden.

Ann Numhauser-Henning, Professor Emerita of Private Law, Faculty of Law at Lund University, Sweden.

Birgitta Nyström, Professor of Private Law, Faculty of Law at Lund University, Sweden.

Sophie Robin-Olivier, Professor of Law at the Sorbonne School of Law, University Paris 1 Panthéon Sorbonne.

Afonso de Paula Pinheiro Rocha, Labour Public Prosecutor and PhD in Constitutional Law, Faculty of Law at Uni7 University, Brazil.

Summary of Contents

Table of Contents

PART I Introduction

CHAPTER 1

Ageing in the World of Work

Jenny Julén Votinius & Mia Rönnmar[*]

1 INTRODUCTION TO THE BOOK

An ageing population, in the Member States of the EU and in many other countries around the world, is a major trend with important implications for economic performance, intergenerational solidarity, social cohesion, and the sustainability of welfare systems.

This book focuses on the ageing of the workforce and specific challenges and potentials for labour law, industrial relations, and collective bargaining. With its interdisciplinary approach and multitude of theories, conceptual frameworks, methodologies, and materials, the book provides a multifaceted and comparative analysis of discourses and legal advancements related to older workers, active ageing, and the future of work. It engages with issues of great societal and practical importance and global reach and focuses on three themes:

(1) fundamental rights developments,
(2) dynamics in non-discrimination and employment protection, and
(3) advancements in active ageing.

Distinguished international scholars provide expert examination of current societal, policy, legislative, and case law developments and core issues in labour law, non-discrimination law, elder law, and EU law, as well as of synergies and possible

* This research is carried out within the research project 'Prolonged Working Lives, Older Workers, and Dismissals', funded by the Swedish Research Council for Health, Working Life, and Welfare (*Forte*). We are also grateful for the support of the Faculty of Law at Lund University, which, *inter alia*, enabled us to organize a research workshop at the Faculty of Law, where draft chapters for this book were presented and discussed. The research project has received ethical approval by the Swedish Ethical Review Authority (dnr 2021-05026).

conflicts between these areas of law, to advance our understanding of the law and current challenges and potentials.

The discussion also addresses the topic of older workers and active ageing from the broader perspectives of sustainability and just transition, technological advancements, and fundamental rights and informal work in times of challenges and crises, including the COVID-19 pandemic and economic crisis.

The analysis in this book is comparative and policy-relevant and relates to developments in the European Union, Asia, Australia, and Latin America and to the multilevel regulation of the world of work in the Global North and the Global South.

The outline of this book is as follows. Part I encompasses this introductory chapter. Part II explores the theme of fundamental rights developments in three chapters, Part III covers the theme of dynamics in non-discrimination and employment protection in five chapters, and Part IV addresses the theme of advancements in active ageing in three chapters.

2 FUNDAMENTAL RIGHTS DEVELOPMENTS

Part II of the book examines the development of fundamental rights and older workers in international, European, and EU law, with each of the three chapters taking a different perspective.

In the chapter 'Human Rights Protection of Older Persons: The Case for a New Convention?' *Martina Axmin* explores and discusses human rights protection for older persons from an elder-law perspective in relation to evolving legal frameworks and policies on international and regional levels, and specifically the process to establish a new UN convention on the rights of older persons. Acknowledging the significant legal and political challenges that have characterized this area, the chapter interestingly identifies and analyses three discursive strands: first, whether there is a need for specific human rights protection for older persons or whether the impact of the current human rights framework should instead be strengthened; second, the understanding and delimitation of the term 'older persons', and the persons who should be included in this category; and, third, concerns that increased protection of the rights of older persons will generate new costs that cannot be easily estimated. The complexity of this area and the strong (in some respects) political efforts to advance the legal process make for a field where future developments are far from certain and where crucial legal and societal questions and potential conflicts will inevitably need to be addressed.

In the subsequent chapter, 'The European Social Charter and Rights for Older Workers', *Birgitta Nyström* provides an insightful study of the existing and emerging protections for older workers under the European Social Charter, setting the scene for an initiated discussion on the potential for more comprehensive Charter protection in this area. Based on the European Social Charter provisions on the right to work, employment protection, social protection, and non-discrimination, the chapter provides a comprehensive analysis of the European Committee of Social Rights' case law development of in age-related labour law cases. The author finds that despite the relatively low number of assessments carried out thus far by the Committee in this area, and when viewed against the background of commitments to older people made by the Council of Europe and bearing in mind the dynamic nature of some of the rights in the Charter, the European Social Charter has strong potential to protect older workers.

The final chapter in this part of the book, *Fundamental Social Rights and the EU Charter in Times of Crisis: Reality and Prospects* by *Xavier Groussot* and *Alezini Loxa*, examines the EU Charter of Fundamental Rights and its potential in developing social protection, particularly during what the authors characterize as periods of poly-crisis – intervals of multiple, interconnected crises at local, regional, and EU policy levels. Focusing on recent legislative and policy developments as well as case law from the Court of Justice of the European Union (CJEU) on social rights, the chapter explores how poly-crisis situations create instability and affect the interpretation of the EU Charter and EU law. In analysing the legal argumentation related to the protection of social rights, the authors stress that, in parallel with the 'dignity model' often proposed in EU law, a 'solidarity model' or solidarity narrative also has a place in EU law, as evidenced by CJEU case law on 'Budget Conditionality'. Taking such a more comprehensive understanding of the regulatory theoretical basis more seriously could potentially reduce the negative impact of future crises on the extent to which fundamental social rights are consolidated.

3 DYNAMICS IN NON-DISCRIMINATION AND EMPLOYMENT PROTECTION

Part III analyses aspects of national and EU labour law; more specifically, the five chapters in this part of the book examine the protection of older workers provided through the prohibition against age discrimination, the employment protection regulation, and collective bargaining and the interaction between these regulatory frameworks.

Jenny Julén Votinius addresses the use of courts to advance discrimination law in 'Strategic Litigation, Discrimination Law, and Older Workers' and explores the increased use of strategic litigation in discrimination law in the EU and the Member States. Using Sweden as the main national example, the chapter interestingly discusses the current promotion at EU level for equality bodies and interest groups in the Member States to increasingly push political demands for social change by bringing court cases based on supranational fundamental rights regulation. The important implications of such a development are analysed in relation to both discrimination law in general and the particular outcomes for older workers. Over time, strategic litigation initiated by civil society organizations has proven powerful in pushing legal rights, including the right to protection against discrimination. However, the current trend – whereby EU-level policymakers are encouraging the inclusion of strategic litigation in the 'toolbox' for managing Member States' compliance with EU law – represents a radically different development which, according to the author, risks undermining the legitimacy of discrimination law and can be detrimental to older workers.

The development of discrimination law is also the topic of the thought-provoking chapter by *Sophie Robin-Olivier*, 'Modernizing EU Anti-discrimination Law to Better Combat Discrimination Against Older Workers in the Context of "Just Transition"', on possible evolutions in anti-discrimination law that could provide better ways of addressing discrimination against older workers. Following a rich analytical examination of age-discrimination case law, thoroughly pinpointing the problems resulting from the way that the Court of Justice applies the proportionality test, the chapter explores the intersectionality perspective and then examines the potential of the Green Deal Programme in its capacity as a global framework for legal development at EU level. The author argues that the notion of 'just transition' at the heart of this framework – and its associated commitment to leave no one behind – is altering the wider legal interpretative context outside matters relating to climate change. Against this backdrop, the chapter explores how a re-examination of the concept 'reasonable accommodation' in the light of the Green Deal Programme would challenge the established understanding of the EU rules for preventing age discrimination.

The next three chapters examine various aspects of the interaction between discrimination law and employment protection.

In her chapter, 'Dismissed Older Workers at Conceptual and Legal Crossroads: An Interplay Between Employment Protection, Non-discrimination, and Collective Bargaining', *Mia Rönnmar* focuses on dismissed older workers and explores the legal protection offered to older workers in dismissal situations and the conceptual and legal interplay of employment protection, non-discrimination, and collective bargaining in this context. The discussion is focused on Swedish labour law and industrial relations within an EU law context and includes recent major statutory and collective bargaining reforms of employment protection. Employment protection is the primary protective regulation to which non-discrimination protection and collective bargaining relate. The analysis illustrates how non-discrimination law in this context can both reinforce existing and provide new and extended protection for older workers in dismissal situations, for example, by way of reference to discrimination on grounds of disability and/or age in the context of dismissals for reasons of redundancy and the application of rules for selection of employees. In turn, collective bargaining can both reinforce and weaken the protection of older workers as a result of the Swedish labour market model and its emphasis on collective autonomy and collective bargaining and scope for derogations from statutory individual rights.

In the chapter 'Older Workers, Unfair Dismissal, and Age Discrimination Law: Strengthening Employment Protection? Comparative Perspectives from Australia and the UK', *Alysia Blackham* carries out a comprehensive study of claims and cases of unfair treatment of older workers in Australia and the UK. Drawing on a mixed-method, multi-year comparative study of the enforcement of age-discrimination law in the UK and Australia, this chapter interrogates the relationship between age-discrimination law and unfair dismissal, particularly in the way it affects older workers. Through the integration of statistical evidence from a large number of reported decisions in UK Employment Tribunal and Australian cases, qualitative expert interviews with more than a hundred experts, and a survey of a large number of lawyers working in this field, the chapter provides a sophisticated analysis of various ways in which age discrimination and unfair dismissal are linked in practice. This empirical evidence is then used to identify gaps in enforcement and the legal framework, revealing a need for new approaches to promote protection of employment; here, the author convincingly argues that collective action and collective bargaining have a particular potential to strengthen employment protection in practice.

The late stage of working life and the crucial matter of compulsory (or mandatory) retirement is the topic of the chapter '*The Capability Approach, Compulsory Retirement, and the* Hörnfeldt *Case Revisited*' by *Ann Numhauser-Henning*. The general acceptance of compulsory retirement as a traditional means of terminating employment in the case law of the European Court of Justice is an important expression of the fact that EU law allows a wider scope for exceptions to the prohibition of age discrimination than is the case for other grounds of discrimination. For a developed understanding of the prohibition of age discrimination and its interpretations, the chapter turns to the theoretical and methodological framework of capability, developed by Amartya Sen and later by Martha Nussbaum, which emphasizes the importance of institutional conditions for meaningful social development in terms of economic self-sufficiency for the individual. Drawing on the capability framework, the chapter revisits the high-profile *Hörnfeldt* case and extends the conceptual lines from the case to recent Swedish legislative reforms.

4 ADVANCEMENTS IN ACTIVE AGEING

Part IV is devoted to the theme of advancements in active ageing. The rich variation in content and approach between the chapters in this part of the book aptly illustrates the range of realities that might be attributed to the conceptual and policy areas of active ageing and existing challenges and practices in various countries around the globe.

In the insightful chapter 'Slavery of Aging Domestic Workers: An Analysis of the Policies in Brazil', *Ana Virginia Moreira Gomes* and *Afonso de Paula Pinheiro Rocha* explore the situation of older persons who are not only workers but also – often lifelong – victims of the crime of slavery. The chapter analyses the main characteristics of this form of exploitation along with the intersections between forced labour, informality, gender, and race and examines the legal norms designed to combat domestic slave labour internationally and in Brazil. Although the state authorities' monitoring and eliminating working conditions analogous to slavery belong to the policy domain of working life, interventions aimed at workers in domestic slavery involve measures that are far from the realm of traditional labour law, including rescue operations, police interventions, and criminal trials. Normally, such workers require long-time support to live as free persons and cope with the trauma of a life in slavery. The latter is particularly crucial for workers who have spent the greater part of their lives in the enslaving family and do not have any other familial and social bonds; this is the case for many older domestic workers who have been held in slavery by their employers.

Very differently, in the chapter 'Japan's Elderly Employment Promotion Policy Without Anti-age Discrimination Law: Experiments in a Most Rapidly Ageing Country', *Takashi Araki* draws on long national experience of population ageing to provide a comprehensive analysis of Japanese elderly employment policies. In contrast to many countries, including those represented in this book, Japan has not relied on a ban on age discrimination to protect older employees. Instead, given the non-litigious character of Japanese society, measures to actively promote employment for older people have been considered more effective. The chapter examines the development of these employment policies over the past five decades, where increases in the mandatory retirement age have been combined with government interventions targeted at employers to promote employment among older people. While these policies have been successful in terms of the share of older people in employment, the analysis reveals how the unique Japanese policy of not regulating age discrimination has also given rise to challenges in terms of the quality of older people's employment. These challenges are elaborated on and discussed with a comparative outlook on employment policies for older people in the US and the EU.

The final chapter of the book 'Telework, Sustainability of Pensions, and Synergies with Market Institutions: Constructing a Theory of Fundamental Rights' by *Julia Lopéz Lopéz*, *Eusebi Colàs-Neila*, and *Nuria Pumar Beltrán*, creatively examines how part-time teleworking in the home could positively promote active ageing and provide opportunities to influence one's personal economic situation through continued employment after retirement age. The chapter explores this possible path of development, focusing on how labour market arrangements could be structured to protect the fundamental rights of older workers while also promoting social inclusion and continued labour market involvement. Identifying the principles of voluntary work and non-discrimination in part-time and teleworking as key factors, the analysis shows that these principles alone are not sufficient. To respond to the needs of older employees and secure gender equality, the governance of pension systems must also integrate policies related to care and training. If approached carefully and in its full complexity, the authors argue, teleworking adapted to individuals' respective needs has a strong potential for extending working lives, addressing the sustainability of pensions, and improving opportunities for older workers who might otherwise rely solely on pensions.

PART II Fundamental Rights Developments

CHAPTER 2

Human Rights Protection of Older Persons: The Case for a New Convention?

Martina Axmin

1 INTRODUCTION

In recent years, the topic of ageing has transformed, evolving from a matter primarily concerned with demographics and welfare to a central issue regarding rights. Instead of being perceived as mere recipients of passive welfare, older persons are increasingly recognized as legitimate rights holders. This shift represents a significant change in perspective – a transition that is moving older persons from invisibility into sharper focus, from a climate of ageism to an environment that upholds dignity and respect.[1] Prominent international organizations including the United Nations (UN), the World Health Organization (WHO), and the European Union (EU) have unequivocally denounced all forms of age-based discrimination while also underscoring the need to ensure equality and preserve human dignity.

Recently, there has been a growing recognition that providing sufficient support for older persons requires a human rights-centred approach. To date, no human rights instrument dedicated specifically to older persons has been introduced. In 2011, the UN took a significant step by establishing the Open-Ended Working Group on Ageing (OEWGA). This group's primary objective is to protect older persons' rights through a comprehensive review of how prevailing human rights instruments encompass these rights, identification of any deficiencies in protection, and investigation of the feasibility of new instruments. Moreover, in 2013, the Human Rights Council designated an 'Independent Expert on the enjoyment of all human rights by older persons'. The

1. Bill Mitchell, *Towards a Convention on the Rights of Older Persons*, ADA Australia National Conference, 23–24 March 2017.

appointed Independent Expert shall identify exemplary practices in this domain and highlight existing legal frameworks concerning the human rights of older persons.

An ongoing academic discourse revolves around whether it is time to classify older persons as a distinct category within human rights law. In tandem with this, a global social movement has gained momentum, advocating for establishing an international convention that specifically addresses the rights of older persons. Various non-governmental organizations and committees are also advocating for a new convention. Some proponents contend that a new treaty is imperative to increase awareness of the challenges that older persons face; sceptics counter by claiming that the existing framework of international human rights already encompasses protections for the rights of older persons and assert that any discernible gaps in protection are primarily due to inadequacies in implementing these existing provisions. Still, others argue that a convention is unlikely to yield substantive changes. Ultimately, the efficacy of such initiatives hinges upon the political will driving their implementation.

While a dedicated human rights treaty specifically focused on older persons does not exist today, numerous instruments address older persons' concerns. Over the years, the UN has adopted several non-binding principles aimed at safeguarding the rights of older persons, including the 1982 Vienna International Plan of Action on Ageing,[2] the 1991 UN Principles for Older Persons,[3] and the 2002 Madrid International Plan of Action on Ageing (MIPAA).[4] Furthermore, regional organizations have embraced extensive legal frameworks concerning the rights of older persons.

This chapter aims to explore and discuss human rights protection for older persons from an elder-law perspective. Initially, the discussion focuses on evolving legal frameworks and policies with a view to charting the issue of ageing on both international and regional levels. Thereafter, the chapter addresses ongoing efforts for a new UN convention on the rights of older persons. In this context, special attention is devoted to two pivotal entities within this process: OEWGA and the Independent Expert on the enjoyment of all human rights by older persons. The final section reflects on the significant challenges within a broader legal and political context, explores potential future developments, and presents concluding remarks.

2 SETTING THE SCENE: THE MATTER OF AGEING ON INTERNATIONAL AND REGIONAL LEVELS

2.1 The International Level

Human rights are inherent to all individuals and are universal, extending to every human being. The International Covenant on Economic, Social and Cultural Rights (ICESCR) and the International Covenant on Civil and Political Rights (ICCPR) lack

2. UN Vienna International Plan of Action on Ageing, 26 July–6 August 1982.
3. UN General Assembly, United Nations Principles for Older Persons, Resolution 46/91 of 16 December 1991.
4. Report of the Second World Assembly on Ageing, Madrid, 8–12 April 2002, UN Doc A/CONF.197/9.

direct mentions of older persons. However, as elucidated below, General Comment No. 6 on the Economic, Social and Cultural Rights of Older Persons legally interprets how the ICESCR should encompass older persons. Moreover, in the context of conventions targeted at specific groups, only a handful refer to age; examples include Article 25(b), on the right to health and Article 28, paragraph 2(b), on the right to an adequate standard of living, of the Convention on the Rights of Persons with Disabilities.[5]

While a dedicated international human rights treaty specifically safeguarding older persons is not in place, the UN has, over time, adopted a series of non-binding principles and documents. These aim to address the protection of older persons, focusing on equitable treatment and preservation of autonomy.

In 1982, the first world conference on ageing was held, the World Assembly on Ageing. This conference resulted from the adoption of Resolution 33/52 in 1978, which acknowledged the 'need to draw worldwide attention to the serious problems besetting a growing portion of the global population'.[6] With this recognition, the General Assembly decided to convene a World Assembly in 1982. The primary objective was to initiate an international action programme to ensure both economic and social security for older persons while contributing to national development. In line with the same resolution, the General Assembly called upon the Secretary General to collaborate with Member States, relevant specialized agencies, and concerned organizations to formulate a draft programme for the World Assembly on the Elderly. Furthermore, recommendations were requested regarding the organization and objectives of the World Assembly.

After the conference, the World Assembly on Ageing sanctioned the Vienna International Plan of Action. This Plan of Action stands as the first international instrument on ageing, delineating the steps to be undertaken by Member States to protect older persons' rights. Comprising 62 actionable recommendations, it encompassed domains such as research, data collection and analysis, training and education, and sector-specific spheres such as health and nutrition, safeguarding older consumers, housing and environment, family, social welfare, income security and employment, and education. This marked the initial response to the rights of older persons.

The subsequent advancement occurred in 1991, with the UN General Assembly's establishment of the UN Principles for Older Persons.[7] This instrument delineates 18 principles clustered into 5 fundamental themes: independence, participation, care, self-fulfilment, and dignity. These principles have provided the foundation for numerous subsequent UN initiatives.[8] Notably, however, scholars have pointed out that

5. *See also* the Convention on the Elimination of All Forms of Discrimination against Women which mentions 'age' in Art. 11 with regard to the right to social security, the International Convention on the Protection of the Rights of All Migrant Workers and Members of Their Families (Art. 7 includes 'age' in the list of prohibited grounds for discrimination).
6. UN General Assembly, *World Assembly on the Elderly*, A/RES/33/52, 14 December 1978.
7. UN General Assembly, *United Nations Principles for Older Persons*, Resolution 46/91 of 16 December 1991.
8. Mitchell, *supra* n. 1.

despite being encompassed within a resolution, these principles do not employ the explicit 'language of rights'.[9]

Another pivotal document addressing older persons is General Comment No. 6 on the Economic, Social and Cultural Rights of Older Persons. This comment was adopted in 1995 by the UN Committee on Economic, Social and Cultural Rights (CESCR).[10] The comment provides an interpretative framework for the ICESCR concerning older persons. Additionally, it observes that the Covenant does not expressly forbid age-based discrimination. Nevertheless, it asserts that the prohibition of discrimination based on 'other status' could conceivably encompass age as a protected category.[11]

In 2022, 20 years after the first World Conference on Ageing, the MIPAA was established.[12] MIPAA was embraced as a revised and significantly expanded iteration of the Vienna International Plan of Action on Ageing, introduced during the Second World Assembly on Ageing. MIPAA serves as the primary policy framework for addressing the opportunities and challenges that an ageing population presents. It has steered the global discourse on the rights of older persons.[13] In addition, MIPAA offers a comprehensive foundation based on three key points: the intersection of older persons with development, the progression of health and well-being throughout the ageing process, and the establishment of nurturing and accommodating environments. Along with having specific responsibilities, states are urged to cultivate a positive perspective among employers concerning the continued productive potential of older workers. Additionally, they are called upon to facilitate the sustained engagement of older persons in the workforce for as long as these persons want to work and are capable of doing so. Moreover, the document provides recommendations for states to champion initiatives that extend basic social protection and social security to all employees, encompassing relevant provisions for pensions, disability insurance, and healthcare benefits. The framework thus reaffirms the dedication to eradicating age-based discrimination and underscores the significance of enhancing the integration of older persons within society.

While the document lacks legal binding, it holds significant authoritative weight. The UN General Assembly oversees the execution of MIPAA. To enhance the well-being of older persons, MIPAA also calls for a systematic review of its implementation every five years. As of now, four such reviews have been conducted. The latest evaluation of MIPAA centres on the ramifications of population ageing, addressing

9. Annie Herro & Andrew Byrnes, *Transcending the Framing Contests over the Human Rights of Older Persons*, 38 Aust. Year B. Int. Law, 253–284 (2020) https://doi.org/10.1163/26660229_03801012.
10. UN Committee on Economic, Social and Cultural Rights (CESCR), *General Comment No. 6: The Economic, Social and Cultural Rights of Older Persons*, 8 December 1995, UN Doc E/1996/22.
11. *Ibid.*, para. 12.
12. Report of the Second World Assembly on Ageing, Madrid, 8–12 April 2002, UN Doc A/CONF.197/9.
13. Marthe Fredvang & Simon Biggs, *The Rights of Older Persons: Protection and Gaps under Human Rights Law*, Social Policy Working Paper No. 16, Centre for Public Policy & Brotherhood of St. Laurence. Melbourne: University of Melbourne (2012).

emerging concerns such as the future of work.[14] The report delves into strategies for ensuring financial security during one's later years while emphasizing challenges and prospects of employment for older adults. It culminates with pivotal recommendations, including the imperative of measures that counter age-related bias and detrimental employment stereotypes. Additionally, the report advocates the establishment and advancement of lifelong learning systems, facilitating skill acquisition, upskilling, and reskilling throughout an individual's lifespan.

Efforts to safeguard the human rights of older persons on the international stage have been underway for many years. Nevertheless, despite the growing demand for a universally binding instrument concerning the human rights of older persons, more progress has been achieved at the regional level.

2.2 The Regional Level

In recent years, regional instruments addressing the protection of human rights for older persons have been established. Regional entities have assumed leadership roles in this regard, adopting legally binding treaties at the regional level to address the rights of older persons.

In 2015, the Organization of American States adopted the Inter-American Convention on the Protection of Human Rights of Older Persons.[15] This convention, comprising 41 articles, came into force in January 2017 and stands as the inaugural instrument devoted to safeguarding the human rights of older persons. The convention encompasses an array of rights that impose the responsibility upon states to protect and advance human rights for older persons. These rights encompass the right to equality and non-discrimination based on age (Article 5), the right to experience a dignified existence in one's later years (Article 6), the entitlement to social security to ensure their dignified living (Article 17), and the right to pursue work (Article 18).

Another development was the passage in 2016 of the African Union Protocol to the African Charter on Human and Peoples' Rights on the Rights of Older Persons in Africa.[16] This Protocol encompasses a broad spectrum of rights, including provisions for access to healthcare services (Article 15), the entitlement to freedom from discrimination and the right to pursue employment (Article 6), and the assurance of social protection (Article 7). This framework sets out guidelines for governments to effectively safeguard these rights. The Protocol is set to attain the status of a legally binding instrument upon ratification by 15 of the 55 Member States.[17]

Currently, no specific European instrument addresses the human rights of older persons. Nevertheless, the rights of older persons are delineated in various European human rights instruments. One particularly significant instrument in this regard is the

14. UN Secretary General, *Follow-up to the International Year of Older Persons: Second World Assembly on Ageing*, UN Doc A/75/218, 22 July 2020.
15. OAS (Organization of American States), Inter-American Convention of protecting the human rights of older persons, A-70, adopted 15 June 2015.
16. AU (African Union), Protocol to the African charter on human and people's rights on the rights of older persons in Africa, adopted 31 January 2016.
17. As of 25 March 2022, only six countries have ratified the Protocol.

European Social Charter (ESC).[18] The protection of older persons' rights is outlined in Article 23 of the ESC, which pertains to 'the right for elderly persons to social protection'. Furthermore, the Council of Europe has adopted several resolutions and recommendations addressing diverse aspects of the rights of older persons.[19]

The Charter of Fundamental Rights of the EU (the Charter) encompasses a range of rights relevant to older persons. Article 25 of the Charter pertains to the rights of older persons and stipulates that 'the Union recognizes and respects the rights of the elderly to lead a life of dignity and independence and to participate in social and cultural life'. The Explanations accompanying the Article indicate that this provision draws inspiration from Article 23 of the ESC. Due to the Article's broad applicability – it is not limited to specific domains – discussions have arisen suggesting its potential application in any instance where EU law is being enforced.[20] Additionally, Article 21, which addresses non-discrimination, explicitly safeguards against age-based discrimination.

3 TOWARDS A CONVENTION ON THE RIGHTS OF OLDER PERSONS: THE BROADER CONTEXT

Over the years, various groups of vulnerable individuals have gained heightened protection through conventions designed to safeguard their human rights. However, as noted, no specific convention is dedicated to the rights of older persons. The earliest endeavour to create such a convention dates back to 1948 when Argentina submitted a Draft Declaration of Old Age Rights to the UN General Assembly.[21] The preamble of this Draft Declaration asserted that, just like other protective measures, ensuring rights in old age is crucial for enhancing the quality of life for workers and promoting their well-being. However, the proposal failed to garner sufficient backing among the Member States.

A pivotal moment in the discourse regarding adopting a human rights-centred approach to assist older persons was the formation of the UN OEWGA in 2010.[22] The primary objective of this initiative was to enhance the safeguarding of older people's rights. This was pursued through a comprehensive assessment of how current instruments address these rights, pinpointing areas where protection falls short and examining the viability of introducing novel instruments.

In 2012, the UN General Assembly adopted Resolution 67/139, 'Towards a comprehensive and integral international legal instrument to promote and protect the

18. *See* the chapter by Birgitta Nyström in this book.
19. *See*, for example, Council of Europe (2011a) Resolution 1793 *Promoting active ageing – capitalizing on older people's working potential*, Council of Europe (2013) Resolution 1958 *Combating discrimination against older persons on the labour market* and Council of Europe (2012) Resolution 1882 *Decent pensions for all*.
20. Colm O'Cinneide, *The Rights of Elderly*, in *The EU Charter of Fundamental Rights: A Commentary*, 693–708 (Steve Peers, et al., eds, Hart Publishing 2014).
21. A/C.3/213 30 September 1948.
22. UN General Assembly, 65th Session, *Follow-up to the Second World Assembly on Ageing*, A/RES/65/182, 4 February 2011.

rights and dignity of older workers'.[23] This resolution marked a pivotal moment: it prompted a shift in the working group's mandate to encompass the examination of proposals for an international legal instrument aimed at championing and safeguarding the rights and dignity of older persons. The OEWGA was tasked with formulating a proposal outlining key components to be included within this international legal instrument. This decision may be seen as the more formal inception of the drafting process for a novel human rights convention centred on older persons, even though discussions on the matter had been in progress for some time.

UN Member States, national human rights institutions, non-governmental organizations, and other stakeholders actively engage in the group's activities. Since 2011, annual sessions have been convened, serving as platforms for cooperating international, regional, national, and non-governmental representatives. Each annual agenda focuses on two specific areas concerning the protection of the rights of older persons. Throughout the year, these deliberated-upon areas encompass a broad spectrum of challenges confronted by older persons, including aspects such as non-discrimination, equality, social protection, and social security. Ahead of each session, the working group solicits normative and substantive insights regarding the pertinent topics.

A central matter extensively deliberated by the OEWGA is whether it should propose to the UN General Assembly the adoption of a new normative instrument regarding the human rights of older persons and, if so, delineate the components of such an instrument. A unified stance among Member States has not yet been achieved. The OEWGA has been a forum of contention since its inception, hosting both proponents and opponents of a new human rights convention.[24]

A global social movement advocating for a new international Convention on the Rights of Older Persons has emerged.[25] Establishing the OEWGA has empowered civil society to actively participate in developing a proposal for this new human rights convention. Through its mandate, OEWGA has created a platform to exchange experiences highlighting the inadequate protection of the current legal frameworks in safeguarding the human rights of older persons.[26]

While non-governmental organizations and committees display considerable engagement by participating in OEWGA sessions, the same level of commitment is not observed among Member States. In the 13th Working Session, only 23 of the 193 UN Member States, including the EU, submitted substantial inputs; only 14 Member States provided normative inputs.[27]

Another step towards formulating a new convention addressing the concerns of older persons was taken in 2013. During that time, the Human Rights Council

23. UN General Assembly, 67th Session, *Towards a comprehensive and integral international legal instrument to promote and protect the rights and dignity of older persons*, A/RES/67/139, 13 February 2013.
24. Léon Poffé, *Towards a New United Nations Human Rights Convention for Older Persons?*, 15 Hum. Rights Law Rev, 591–601, 593 (2015) https://doi.org/10.1093/hrlr/ngv022.
25. *See*, for example, the Global Alliance for the Rights of Older People, https://rightsofolderpeople.org/ (13 June 2023).
26. Claudia Martin, Diego Rodrígues-Pinzón & Bethany Brown, *Human Rights of Older People. Universal and Regional Legal Perspectives*, 16 (Springer 2015).
27. *See* https://social.un.org/ageing-working-group/Thirteenthsession-govts.shtml (13 June 2023).

designated an 'Independent Expert on the enjoyment of all human rights by older persons'.[28] This move was supported by Resolution 24/20, which established the mandate of the Independent Expert to raise awareness about promoting and safeguarding the rights of older persons.

The mandate involves several key aspects: evaluating adherence to national, regional, and international standards related to the rights of older persons; identifying, exchanging, and advocating for exemplary practices linked to promoting and safeguarding these rights; reporting on progress, obstacles, and areas lacking protection in the realization of older persons' rights, and making pertinent recommendations. To fulfil these responsibilities, the Independent Expert submits an annual report to the Human Rights Council and the UN General Assembly. Furthermore, the Independent Expert's role encompasses evaluating the implementation of the MIPAA.

The mandate of the Independent Expert on the human rights of older persons has brought both focus and depth to the realm of older persons' human rights. A crucial facet of this mandate involves the identification of best practices. This is achieved by soliciting input from Member States, international and regional organizations, and civil society. Regular reporting to the Human Rights Council and the UN General Assembly is a fundamental aspect of this role, encompassing a wide range of subjects from addressing ageism and age discrimination to exploring the repercussions of social exclusion experienced by older persons. Additionally, the Independent Expert's reports incorporate insights from country visits. Through these comprehensive reports, a prevailing theme emerges: the widespread discrimination and neglect that older persons confront across the globe.

The Independent Expert is also an active participant in the work of OEWGA.[29] The current Independent Expert is a strong voice in the ongoing discourse surrounding a potential new UN convention focused on older persons. Several of her reports contain a critical observation: the current legal framework falls short in establishing comprehensive and specific obligations to effectively safeguard the human rights of older persons.[30] Moreover, the Independent Expert has pointed out that the absence of a universal convention addressing the human rights of older persons renders assurance of older persons' dignity impossible. In 2016, she called on states to intensify their efforts to determine optimal methods to protect these rights. She also prompted them to consider the development of a convention dedicated to the rights of older persons.[31]

The next section examines current debates on creating a new Convention on the Rights of Older Persons and prospects for future developments.

28. UN Human Rights Council, The human rights of older persons, UN Doc A/HRC/RES/24/20.
29. UN Human Rights Council, The human rights of older persons, A/HRC/RES/42/12.
30. Report of the Independent Expert on the enjoyment of all human rights by older persons, Claudia Mahler, *Older persons deprived of liberty*, A/HRC/51/27, 13 September 2022.
31. UN Human Rights Council, *Report of the Independent Expert on the enjoyment of all human rights by older persons*, A/HRC/33/44, 8 July 2016.

4 CURRENT DEBATES AND PROSPECTS FOR DEVELOPMENT

4.1 Advocacy for a Convention on the Rights of Older Persons

The discourse regarding the necessity of adopting a human rights-based approach to assuring rights for older persons began in 1948 and has continued for more than seven decades. In this timeframe, perceptions regarding older persons have undergone noteworthy transformations across numerous societies; this can be attributed in part to the increasing significance of this demographic segment. Our existence is now characterized by extended lifespans and improved well-being.

Whether a new human rights treaty is necessary, along with an efficient mechanism for safeguarding the human rights of older persons, has been a topic of discourse during the OEWGA's sessions. Concurrently, an academic dialogue persists regarding adopting a human rights-based approach to support older persons. Numerous scholars have meticulously scrutinized the assertions presented within this debate.[32] However, it is important to note that this discourse is intricate and lacks unanimous consensus.[33]

Advocates for the convention underscore its necessity, pointing to the dearth of provisions on the human rights of older persons within existing norms. The foremost argument centres on the glaring fact that no binding international instrument currently addresses the rights of older persons. A new treaty is deemed essential for raising awareness about the challenges older persons face and establishing an international monitoring mechanism. Furthermore, a targeted convention addressing older persons holds the potential to combat and mitigate ageism within society. This framework would impose obligations on states to respect, protect, and fulfil the realization of older persons' rights, thereby emphasizing dignity and autonomy rather than mere necessity. Ultimately, the aim is to portray older persons more positively, accentuating their societal contributions while also countering ageist rhetoric and discriminatory practices. Such a convention could also serve as a valuable tool for litigation in both national and international courts.[34]

Those who oppose the notion of a convention on the human rights of older persons assert that existing human rights conventions already encompass this group. They emphasize that introducing a new convention might inadvertently lead to paternalistic tendencies and a heightened emphasis on age-based distinctions.[35] In essence, this convention could exacerbate the situation. Furthermore, concerns have been raised regarding the strain on the UN body system, positing that a new convention would demand substantial resources when states grapple with reporting responsibilities to monitoring bodies. Financial concerns also form a recurring line of argumentation. States harbour reservations about the prospect of a novel human rights treaty that

32. *See*, for an overview, Israel Doron & Itai Apter, *The Debate Around the Need for an International Convention on Rights of Older Persons*, 50 Gerontologist, n. 5, 586-593 (2010) https://doi.org/10.1093/geront/gnq016, Poffé, *supra* n. 24, and Herro and Byrnes, *supra* n. 9.
33. Doron and Apter, *supra* n. 32.
34. *See* the chapter by Jenny Julén Votinius in this book.
35. Doron and Apter, *supra* n. 32.

will impose financial obligations to support older persons. This, in turn, could result in fewer ratifications.

Furthermore, opponents of a new convention contend that older persons already benefit from robust soft-law protections at the international level. As noted earlier, the Vienna International Plan of Action was adopted in 1983. The UN Principles for Older Persons underscore the significance of dignity, independence, participation, care, and self-fulfilment. Moreover, the MIPAA offers extensive recommendations to foster a society inclusive of all age groups. This is complemented by annual national reports and a review system associated with the MIPAA. Likewise, the UN General Comment No. 6 is often highlighted as a noteworthy instance of soft law.

Securing political backing for formal negotiations has presented a significant challenge in its own right.[36] The outbreak of the COVID-19 pandemic has been a pivotal juncture in this discourse.[37] The pandemic shed a spotlight on human rights concerns related to older persons. Numerous reports note that the pandemic underscored the exclusion of older persons as genuine bearers of rights, highlighting the urgency of counteracting stigmatization and age-based discrimination.[38] In one of her reports issued during the pandemic, the Independent Expert emphasized the emergence of ageist attitudes manifested through unfavourable portrayals of older persons in global media and public discussions, which often depicted older persons as unproductive and burdensome to society.[39]

It has been argued that the pandemic could be considered a case study that highlights the limitations of the legal systems available for safeguarding the human rights of older persons. It has been suggested that the pandemic could even catalyse the development of new legal rights for older persons and move the ongoing debate in a progressive direction.[40]

The preceding discussion highlights existing disagreements across various issues. This chapter will now examine three distinct challenges within the discourse surrounding the pros and cons of formulating a new Convention on the Rights of Older Persons: the gap challenge, the concern about old age, and the discourse around

36. Annie Herro, *The Human Rights of Older Persons: The Politics and Substance of the UN Open-Ended Working Group on Ageing*, 23 Aust. J. Hum. Rights, n. 1, 90–108 (2017) https://doi.org/10.1080/1323238x.2017.1314806.

37. Andrew Byrnes & Titti Mattsson, *Background Paper 20th Informal ASEM Seminar on Human Rights Human Rights of Older Persons*, Informal ASEM Seminar on Human Rights Human Rights of Older Persons Virtual/ Seoul Republic of Korea, 22–24 February 2021 and United Nations, Secretary-General's Policy Brief: *The Impact of COVID-19 on Older Persons* 1 May 2020.

38. *See*, for example: Report of the Independent Expert on the enjoyment of all human rights by older persons, Claudia Mahler, *Impact of the Coronavirus Disease (COVID-19) on the Enjoyment of All Human Rights by Older Persons*, A/75/20, 21 July 2020 and OHCHR, *Update to the 2012 Analytical Outcome Study on the Normative Standards in International Human Rights Law in Relation to Older Persons*, March 2021.

39. Report of the Independent Expert on the enjoyment of all human rights by older persons, Mahler, *supra* n. 38.

40. Susan McGrath, *COVID-19, Human Rights and Older People*, 39 Australas. J. Ageing, 328–330 (2020) https://doi.org/10.1111/ajag.12887 and Benjamin Mason Meier, Victoria Matus & Maximillian Seunik, *COVID-19 Raises a Health and Human Rights Imperative to Advance a UN Convention on the Rights of Older Persons*, 6 BMJ Global Health, e007710 (2021) https://doi.org/10.1136/bmjgh-2021-007710.

economic aspects. The first two challenges, gap and old-age, revolve around tackling – through a human rights lens – the hurdles that older persons encounter. These perspectives consider older persons as bearers of rights, which imposes a legal obligation upon states to respect, protect, and fulfil these rights. On the contrary, the third challenge – the discourse centred on economics – adopts an alternative stance. This viewpoint perceives older persons as recipients and thus adopts an economic approach towards ageing.

4.2 The Gap Challenge

Among its various mandates, OEWGA's primary task is to scrutinize how current instruments encompass the human rights of older persons and pinpoint deficiencies in their protection. Since its inception, the discourse surrounding the necessity of a human rights convention for older persons has predominantly been fuelled by the 'gap challenge': does a normative gap exist within the present international human rights frameworks, or is it a matter of gaps in monitoring and implementation? A significant portion of OEWGA has expended significant efforts on determining whether the human rights of older persons are adequately safeguarded within the existing human rights framework.[41]

The gap challenge becomes apparent in the report stemming from the thirteenth session of OEWGA, during which numerous delegations underscored that in its previous efforts, the working group had already established evidence of prevailing normative gaps. Moreover, it was contended that even in instances where specific provisions exist, they often possess limited applicability – typically with regard to particular situations, such as the area of employment. Other representatives corroborated the presence of shortcomings in safeguarding the human rights of older persons; nevertheless, it was suggested that a more productive approach would involve scrutinizing potential normative gaps before delving into consideration of whether new instruments might be required.[42] It seemed that this discourse had reached an impasse.

The existence of rights gaps, whether normative or implementation-related, has spurred a debate about the necessity for a new convention. In its 2021 updated study, the Office of the High Commissioner for Human Rights (OHCHR) criticized the gap debate and emphasized the need for fundamental change. The OHCHR stressed that merely urging existing mechanisms to increase efforts and incorporate the viewpoints of older persons with a view to fulfilling their mandates falls short of the true goal. The study concludes by asserting that a new instrument addressing the rights of older persons is necessary to effectively rectify the shortcomings of current instruments.[43]

41. William Johan Mitchell, *Making the Case for a Convention on the Human Rights of Older Persons*, 27 Aust. J. Hum. Rights, n. 3, 532–553 (2021) https://doi.org/10.1080/1323238x.2021.2009634.
42. Open-ended Working Group on Ageing, thirteenth session, *Report of the Open-ended Working Group on Ageing*, A/AC.278/2023/2, 26 April 2023.
43. OHCHR, *supra* n. 38.

In response to the 'gap debate', Herro and Byrnes have presented the 'relative invisibility' argument.[44] They contend that while current human rights treaties theoretically encompass older persons, these persons are significantly overlooked on the global stage. This oversight subsequently extends to the execution of human rights at the domestic level. As a result, these researchers posit that a key approach to enhancing the prominence of older persons within international and national legal frameworks is to establish a UN convention specifically addressing older persons' rights. Such a convention would also entail the creation of a related monitoring body, which would go far in eliminating this invisibility.

4.3 The Old-Age Challenge

A crucial question here is how a future convention will conceptualize the notions of 'older age' and 'older person'. There is no all-encompassing definition for older persons on either the international or the regional level. The categorization of older persons as a collective presents challenges in terms of precise definition.

Life expectancy and cultural perceptions of old age exhibit cross-country variation and temporal fluctuations. Within ageing studies, the classifications of 'younger old' (aged 65–75), 'old' (aged 75–85), and 'oldest-old' (aged 85 and above) are frequently employed.[45] In gerontology, age is typically examined and approached from four distinct angles: (1) chronological age, determined by one's birthdate; (2) biological age, associated with physical transformations; (3) psychological age, which pertains to mental and personality changes throughout the lifespan; and (4) social age, denoting individual transitions within the societal context.[46]

The category of *older persons* is frequently determined based on chronological age. National, regional, and international policies and legal frameworks frequently adopt chronological age as a criterion for defining older persons. During the pandemic, chronological age gained heightened significance and was often used to guide decisions. It is common to define older persons as individuals aged 65 and above – the traditional retirement age in numerous developing nations. However, as is widely recognized, demographic shifts have compelled countries to alter existing pension systems and adjust retirement ages, frequently sparking substantial resistance.[47]

When the EU designated 2012 as 'The Year of Active Ageing', the term encompassed persons 'in their late 50s and over'.[48] Conversely, within a human rights

44. Herro and Byrnes, *supra* n. 9.
45. Lawrence A. Frolik, *The Developing Field of Elder Law Redux: Ten Years After*, 10 Elder L.J, 1–14 (2002).
46. *See*, for example, Vern L. Bengtson & Richard Settersten (eds), *Handbook of Theories of Aging* (Springer 2016).
47. Giuseppe Carone, et al., *Pension Reforms in the EU since the Early 2000's: Achievements and Challenges Ahead*, Discussion Papers 42, 8 (Brussels 2016).
48. Article 2 of Decision 940/2011/EU.

context, older persons are typically defined as those aged 60 and above.[49] Consequently, the point at which an individual is considered 'old' varies considerably, depending on the context.[50]

Further complexities arise from the inherent heterogeneity within the older-person demographic. Broadly diverse attributes characterize this group. The circumstances of older persons can differ significantly based on an array of factors, including sex, gender, disability, race, nationality, employment status, health condition, caregiving responsibilities, and socio-economic standing. Effectively encompassing the breadth of experiences among older persons poses a notable challenge for any forthcoming convention focused on these persons' rights.

Present proposals involve creating a convention to safeguard 'older persons'' human rights. However, an alternative perspective posits that a more effective approach would be to devise a treaty that safeguards and fulfils all human rights, devoid of discrimination stemming from 'older age'. Advocates of this view contend that employing the term 'older age' more accurately captures the group's diversity and the societal construction of ageing. Notably, the Independent Expert has underscored the significance of framing older persons as a social construct rooted in customs, practices, and communal roles.[51]

Regardless of the approach chosen, a certain level of definition or characterization about 'older age' or an 'older person' becomes necessary. Such clarity is essential in defining the scope of state parties' responsibilities and identifying those eligible for the treaty's assurances during specific life stages.

4.4 The Economic-Discourse Challenge

The two challenges mentioned earlier stem from the premise that the rights of older persons are being infringed upon. The proposed solution entails adopting a human rights perspective. While the matter of 'the gap challenge' revolves around determining whether the solution is a new convention or reinforcement of existing human rights frameworks, the 'old age challenge' has embraced, so to speak, the path of a 'new convention', aiming to define the scope of coverage under such an agreement. However, despite the discernible shift towards a human rights-based approach, the discourse remains tinged with an economically centred narrative focusing on monetary aspects, cost-benefit analyses, and economic considerations.

Older persons continue to be depicted as unfavourable; they are often viewed as a potential threat or burden to the workforce and essential systems such as healthcare

49. UN Committee on Economic, Social and Cultural Rights, General Comments No 6: The Economic, Social and Cultural Rights of Older Persons, UN Doc. E/1996/22, 8 December 1995, paras 1 and 9 and Art. 2 The Inter-American Convention on Protecting the Human Rights of Older Persons.
50. Corinna E. Löckenhoff et al., *Perceptions of Aging Across 26 Cultures and Their Culture-Level Associates*, 24 Psychol. Aging, n. 4, 941–954 (2009) https://doi.org/10.1037/a0016901.
51. Report of the Independent Expert on the enjoyment of all human rights by older persons, Mahler, *supra* n. 38.

and pensions.[52] The 'grey tsunami' and similar expressions are used to paint a dire picture of the social challenges and financial complexities linked to the ageing population. These adverse beliefs are at the core of ageism, with stereotypes, biases, and/or discrimination directed at older persons based on either their age or perceptions of them as old or elderly.[53] The 2021 report from the Independent Expert called for nations to implement measures that encourage the media to refrain from portraying older persons in stereotypical ways, including framing them as frail and as societal burdens.[54]

A frequently voiced concern is that societies undergoing ever-increasing ageing processes could face substantial pressure on their national budgets, particularly if tasked with ensuring sufficient welfare services for their populations. Among the prominent apprehensions surrounding a convention addressing the rights of older persons is the inclusion of a segment concerning economic security.[55] States argue that doing so could obligate states to furnish welfare benefits to a rapidly expanding older populace. Simultaneously, as the demographic makeup shifts towards older age groups, the birth rate is declining – leading to a projected increase in what is known as the dependency ratio. This ratio denotes the proportion of individuals either too young or too old to participate in the workforce (persons within 'working age'). To illustrate, in 2019, and considering the EU as an example, there were approximately three individuals of working age for every dependent person; by 2070, this is expected to decrease to fewer than two working-age individuals for each dependent person. The major portion of this escalation is attributed to the 80-and-above age bracket compared to the 20–64 age group, with the former projected to surge by 15.8 percentage points (from 9.9% to 25.7%) between 2019 and 2070.[56]

Moreover, the global economic downturn that commenced in 2008 has been identified as a factor that renders any financial commitments a formidable proposition.[57] The repercussions of the global financial crisis have prompted nations to emphasize potential fiscal ramifications.[58] This trend is particularly pronounced among European countries.[59] Furthermore, numerous states have encountered substantial and unforeseen financial burdens in implementing the Convention on the Rights of Persons with Disabilities, making it challenging for them to fulfil the

52. Liat Ayalon, *Are Older Adults Perceived as a Threat to the Society? Exploring Perceived Age-Based Threats in 29 Nations*, 74 J. Gerontol: Series B, n. 7, 1246–1265 (2019) https://doi.org/10.1093/geronb/gbx107.
53. Robert N. Butler, *Dispelling Ageism: The Cross-Cutting Intervention*, 53 the Annals of the American Academy of Political and Social Science, 138–147 (1989).
54. Report of the Independent Expert on the enjoyment of all human rights by older persons, Claudia Mahler, A/HRC/48/53, 4 August 2021.
55. Jennifer Dabbs Sciubba, *Securing Rights in the Twenty-First Century: A Comparison of the Disability and Older Persons' Rights Conventions*, 15 Int. J. Hum. Rights, n. 4, 533–549 (2016) https://doi.org/10.1080/14754835.2015.1103162.
56. European Commission, *The 2021 Ageing Report: Economic and Budgetary Projections for the EU Member States (2019–2070)* (2021). The figures are based on this report.
57. Dabbs Sciubba, *supra* n. 55.
58. Poffé, *supra* n. 24, at 600.
59. Dabbs Sciubba, *supra* n. 55.

obligations of the convention.[60] This circumstance could influence the political backing for a new convention as well.

5 CONCLUDING REMARKS

This chapter explores and discusses human rights protection for older persons from an elder-law perspective. Awareness is increasing regarding the need to safeguard human rights for older persons. At the same time, a dynamic human rights discourse is unfolding, engaging diverse stakeholders in discussions of how to frame a new human rights convention dedicated to the rights of older persons. This discourse is witnessing a shift from a predominantly economic viewpoint to matters of ageism, discrimination, and equality. Moreover, the COVID-19 pandemic has brought the human rights of older persons to the forefront, highlighting the need to protect their rights. As a result, the need for human rights safeguards for older persons has gained visibility on many different levels.

The advancement examined within this chapter pertains to soft law and other outputs from international organizations and entities. These instruments collectively share the objective of averting age-based discrimination while fostering the dignity and equality of older persons. They establish a robust foundation for upholding the human rights of older persons on both a global and regional scale. However, in this domain, binding legal measures - that is, hard law - remain conspicuously absent.

Older persons are protected to some degree by their human rights through various general and thematic human rights treaties. The UN has begun in earnest to contemplate the creation of a Convention on the Rights of Older Persons, and this has been facilitated by the OEWGA. Concerns about the effectiveness of international human rights frameworks in enhancing the quality of life for older persons prompted the UN General Assembly to establish this working group in 2010. The group is expecting to identify gaps in the international frameworks and explore proposals for an international legal instrument aimed at promoting and safeguarding the rights and dignity of older persons.

Another important measure has been the 2013 designation by the Human Rights Council of an 'Independent Expert on the enjoyment of all human rights by older persons'. The Independent Expert's role involves identifying exemplary practices and illuminating deficiencies within existing legislation concerning the human rights of older persons. Since the role's establishment, Independent Experts have furnished comprehensive reports concerning the rights status of older persons. These reports indicate that despite advancements regarding their rights, older persons continue to encounter numerous barriers to the full enjoyment of these human rights. Therefore, the situation requires prompt attention, particularly with regard to discrimination and ageism.

The rights of older persons have emerged as a significant political and legal concern over the past decade. OEWGA's sessions have been subject to extensive

60. *Ibid.*

deliberation as to whether establishing a human rights convention dedicated to older persons is an effective solution for safeguarding and reinforcing their rights. Academic discourse persists regarding the necessity for a human rights-centred approach to support older persons.

While some observers contend that this issue arises from a gap in international law, others assert that it is tied to the inability to implement appropriate human rights instruments. Another obstacle lies in the endeavour to guarantee that individuals are not subjected to discrimination based on their advanced age, which raises the question of how 'older age' or 'older persons' should be defined. Furthermore, the demographic of older persons is exceptionally varied. States are concerned about the implications of a new human rights treaty in terms of financial support for older persons. The most formidable challenge to progress in this area is that the current discourse focuses heavily on economic considerations.

As mentioned earlier, certain arguments are not exclusive to the discourse surrounding human rights for older persons; on the contrary, similar concerns have surfaced in debates regarding initiatives such as the Convention on the Rights of Persons with Disabilities. Scholars have also emphasized that insights garnered from the negotiation and enactment of other human rights instruments designed to safeguard the rights of specific groups could serve as valuable guidance. Notable lessons that come to mind are those acquired from the advocacy culminating in the Convention on the Rights of Persons with Disabilities. A comparative analysis of this convention process with the approach for assuring older persons' rights may illuminate how the prevailing international economic, social, and political landscapes influence the formulation of rights instruments.[61]

In conclusion, in recent years, the continuing discussion regarding a new UN convention to address the human rights of older persons has intensified. A factor in this development is the COVID-19 pandemic, which has brought older persons into new focus. The goal of this chapter has been to outline several processes that are progressing towards the establishment of a convention. However, no firm decision is in place to embark on developing a new instrument. While the case for a new convention is consistently gaining traction, numerous challenges remain, and a significant journey appears to lie ahead.

61. *Ibid.* and Gerard Quinn, *The Anatomy of the Treaty Drafting Process: Lessons for the Age Treaty from the Drafting of the UN Disability Treaty,* at 4, in Ralph Ruebner, Teresa Do & Amy Taylor (eds), *International and Comparative Law on the Rights of Older Persons* (Vandeplas Publishing 2015).

CHAPTER 3

The European Social Charter and Rights for Older Workers

Birgitta Nyström[*]

1 INTRODUCTION

This chapter is aimed at discussing how the European Social Charter protects and potentially may protect older workers. Developments concerning the interpretation of the concept of 'discrimination' when it comes to age will be investigated, as well as the interaction of the right to work, non-discrimination, and employment protection of older persons. A few comments on the relationship between the Charter and EU law will be given along with a discussion of whether the Charter provides additional, as-yet untested opportunities to provide older workers with rights. The chapter begins with a brief overview of the Charter, how it is monitored, and how its content is interpreted.

2 THE EUROPEAN SOCIAL CHARTER

The European Social Charter, adopted in 1961 and radically revised in 1996, represents one of the Council of Europe's most important and influential treaties.[1] The rights of the Charter have their origin in the Universal Declaration of Human Rights. The European Social Charter complements the European Convention on Human Rights (ECHR) by guaranteeing economic and social rights. The Charter is at the forefront of international

* I would like to thank Henrik Kristensen, Deputy Head of the Department of the European Social Charter, Council of Europe, who has been so kind to provide comments on an early draft of this chapter. Any mistakes or errors are of course on my part.

1. The 1961 Charter and the 1996 Charter are separate documents and coexist as autonomous international treaties. In this chapter, if nothing else is indicated, references refer to the Revised Charter.

instruments protecting labour and social rights in international law, yet compared to the ECHR, the Charter occupies the 'back seat'.[2]

The Charter not only gives special weight to the protection of workers but also gives protection to vulnerable groups such as children, young persons, the disabled, and older persons. Rights beyond the labour rights guaranteed by the Charter concern, *inter alia*, health, social security, social and medical assistance, legal protection, and housing. The rights of the Charter must be guaranteed to everyone concerned, including foreigners lawfully residing and/or working in a country that has signed the Charter (a State Party), without discrimination.[3]

States may decide to accept only a limited number of articles and paragraphs of the Charter, according to a kind of *à la carte* system. The revised Charter consists of 31 substantive articles and 98 numbered paragraphs. A States Party must accept at least 16 articles or 63 paragraphs. Furthermore, the state must accept at least six out of nine 'core' articles.[4]

3 THE EUROPEAN COMMITTEE OF SOCIAL RIGHTS, MONITORING AND INTERPRETATION OF THE CHARTER

The European Committee of Social Rights is the Charter's regulatory body and assesses whether the situation of the States Parties complies with the European Social Charter. The Committee is a quasi-judicial body comprising 15 independent and impartial experts. The Committee is the only institution competent to legally assess whether the requirements of the Charter have been met. The Governmental Committee and the Committee of Ministers of the Council of Europe constitute the final political power, and the Committee of Ministers can issue a recommendation to a state, inviting the state to bring its rights situation into compliance with the Charter.[5]

The Committee examines national situations according to two different procedures: examination of national reports and processing of collective complaints. The Committee assesses the situation in the states based on reports submitted at regular intervals by State Parties; this is the *reporting procedure*. The Committee adopts

2. An example: in Bridget Lewis, Kelly Purser & Kirsty Mackie, *The Human Rights of Older Persons, A Human Rights-Based Approach to Elder Law* 38–39 (Springer 2020), the ECHR is mentioned among other international instruments and treaties as a regional inter-governmental treaty adopted by the Council of Europe, but the Social Charter is not mentioned.
3. Barbara Mikolajczyk, *The Council of Europe's Approach towards Ageism*, Chapter 20, 323–324, 329–331 (Liat Aylon & Clemens Tesch-Römer eds, *Contemporary Perspectives on Ageism*, International Perspective on Ageing 19, Springer, 2018).
4. The core articles cover the right to work (Art. 1), right to organize (Art. 5), right to collective bargaining (Art. 6), protection of children and young persons (Art. 7), right to social security (Art. 12), right to social and medical assistance (Art. 13), right of the family to social legal and economic protection (Art. 16), right of migrant workers and their families to protection (Art. 19), right to equal opportunities in employment and occupation without discrimination on the grounds of sex (Art. 20).
5. Birgitta Nyström, *The European Social Charter and Labour Rights in Times of Crisis*, 78 and footnote 10 (Laura Carlson, Örjan Edström & Birgitta Nyström eds, *Globalisation, Fragmentation, Labour and Employment Law. A Swedish Perspective*, Iustus 2016).

Conclusions regarding the conformity of each State's measures to the specific articles of the Charter.

The *collective complaints procedure* was introduced in 1995 in an Additional Protocol to the Social Charter. This instrument allows non-governmental organizations (NGOs) and organizations of employers and workers to seek a decision, finding that certain legislation and/or policies of a States Party are not compatible with the state's obligations according to the Charter. Complaints may only raise questions concerning non-compliance of a state's law or practice with one or more of the provisions in the Charter. Individual situations may not be submitted. It is important to understand that complaints may be lodged without domestic remedies having been exhausted, and the complaining organization does not have to be directly affected by the matter about which the complaint has been lodged. When the Committee finds a complaint admissible, it adopts a decision on the merits of the complaint. Up to now, only 16 states have accepted the collective complaints procedure. The number of collective complaints has increased in recent years, and until now (autumn 2024), over 240 collective complaints have been filed. The procedure has made the Charter more visible and gives a practical illustration of how rights in the Charter can be used and transferred into concrete obligations for States Parties.[6]

The Committee assesses both whether existing laws and regulations are consistent with the Charter rights and whether these laws and regulations are properly applied in practice. The Committee has emphasized that as a human rights protection instrument, the Charter's aim and purpose is to protect rights both theoretically and in fact.[7] The Committee's 'case-law' comprises all the sources in which the Committee sets out its interpretation of the Charter's provisions. The Committee's interpretation of Charter provisions is presented in Digest of the Case Law of the European Committee of Social Rights, with the latest version released in June 2022.[8] The interpretations presented in the Digest are not binding for the Committee.[9]

When interpreting the Charter, the Committee takes its basis in the 1969 Vienna Convention on the Law of Treaties, and the Charter is interpreted to give life and meaning to fundamental social rights. The rights guaranteed by the Charter are seen in the context of other international standards, in particular, ILO Conventions and the ECHR. In relation to EU law, the Committee does not presume conformity with the Charter based solely on compliance with EU law.[10]

6. Nyström, *supra* n. 5, at 86.
7. *International Commission of Jurists (ICJ) v. Portugal*, Collective complaint No. 1/1998, para. 32. (This was the first collective complaint that the Committee assessed after the collective complaints procedure had entered into force.) *See also European Federation of National Organisations Working with the Homeless (FEANTSA) v. Slovenia*, Collective complaint No. 53/2008, para. 28.
8. https://rm.coe.int/digest-ecsr-prems-106522-web-en/1680a95dbd.
9. Detailed descriptions of the monitoring procedure and the various actors can be found in Andrzej Marian Swiatkowski, *Charter of Social Rights of the Council of Europe* 375–398 (Kluwer, 2007), *see also Against Ageism and Towards Active Social Citizenship for Older People. The Current Use and Future Potential of the European Social Charter*, Study by Gerard Quinn and Israel (Issi) Doron, 84–100 (Council of Europe, August 2021).
10. *See* Nyström, *supra* n. 5, at 78–79 with references.

4 RIGHTS FOR OLDER WORKERS UNDER THE CHARTER

4.1 Right to an Occupation (Article 1 § 2)

According to Article 1 § 2, States Parties shall effectively protect the rights of workers to earn their living in an occupation freely entered into.[11] Article 1 § 2 protects workers of all kinds, including self-employed persons and those seeking employment.[12]

Article 1 § 2 is one of the so-called core articles (*see supra* section 2). The article has developed through the years in the European Committee of Social Rights' case law.

Very early on, the Committee decided that the elimination of all forms of discrimination was a particularly important matter under Article 1 § 2.[13] Any form of employment discrimination should be removed.[14] The Committee has interpreted Article 1 § 2 as requiring states to introduce legislation that imposes a comprehensive and effective prohibition on age discrimination that cannot be shown to be objectively justified within the field of employment and occupation. In 2002, the Committee stated that the case law on prohibition of discrimination on the ground of sex should apply to any ground of discrimination, including age, when interpreting Article 1 § 2.[15]

4.2 Right to Social Protection (Article 23)

Article 4 of the Additional Protocol to the 1961 Charter and Article 23 of the Revised Charter give older persons the right to social protection.[16] The Charter was the first international human rights instrument to protect this right.[17]

Article 23 is dynamic in the sense that the appropriate measures it calls for may change over time in line with new and progressive notions of what life should be for older persons.[18]

States Parties that accept to be bound by Article 23 are, *inter alia*, obliged to adopt appropriate measures that enable older persons to remain full members of society for as long as possible, choose their lifestyle, and live independent lives.[19] The wording of Article 23 is primarily aimed at giving social protection to older persons who have left

11. About Art. 1 §2, *see* Swiatkowski, *supra* n. 9, at 59 ff.
12. Swiatkowski, *supra* n. 9, at 65 and references.
13. Conclusions II (1971).
14. Conclusions I p. 15.
15. Conclusions XVI-1 (2002) Statement of interpretation of Art. 1 §2, *see also Fællesforbundet for Sjøfolk (FFFS) v. Norway*, Collective complaint No. 74/2011, paras 105 ff. and references.
16. These provisions are identical.
17. An empirical study of the Committee's work concerning Art. 23 during the period 1995–2015 is presented in Benny Spanier & Israel (Issi) Doron, *The European Social Charter and the Rights of Older Persons*, Chapter 7, 146–173 (Israel (Issi) Doron & Nena Georgrantzi eds, *Ageing, Ageism and the Law*, Edward Elgar, 2018).
18. Digest of the case law of the European Committee of Social Rights, 2018, 270. Conclusions XIII-3 (1995) Statement of interpretation Art. 23.
19. *See* Swiatkowski, *supra* n. 9, at 319 ff.

the workforce. It concerns subject such as pensions, which will not be dealt with here.[20]

To enable older persons to remain full members of society, as Article 23 prescribes, is interpreted as ensuring the right to take part in society's various fields of activity to all active or retired persons, including measures to allow or encourage older persons to remain in the labour force.[21] The Committee does not specify any limit for being active in professional life.

4.3 Termination of Employment (Article 24)

Article 24 of the Charter protects the right not to have employment terminated without a valid reason; valid reasons are connected to the capacity or conduct of the employee and certain economic aspects. The Appendix to Article 24 lists reasons for which it is prohibited to terminate employment. Among the invalid reasons, we find discrimination and temporary absence from work due to illness. Grounds for discrimination, Appendix to Article 24 § 3.d, are defined as race, colour, sex, marital status, family responsibility, pregnancy, religion, political opinion, national extraction, and social origin. Age is not mentioned, but the specific reasons mentioned are examples - and age is included in the article. An employee whose employment is terminated without valid reason should have the right to appeal to an impartial body and to receive adequate compensation.[22]

According to the Appendix to Article 24, States parties are authorized to exclude some categories of workers from protection: those employed under a temporary, probational or casual basis. This list is exhaustive. States Parties are not allowed to expand the list. In 2003, the Committee found that Italy was not in conformity with Article 24 because it had expanded the list of excluded categories to workers aged 60 years or older who were entitled to social-security benefits for old age.[23]

According to the Committee's case law, an employer's termination of the employment relationship on the sole ground that the employee has reached a pensionable age is not justified.[24] In 2012, the Committee adopted the following statement of interpretation[25] on age and the termination of employment:[26]

> The Committee recalls that according to the Appendix to the Charter, for the purposes of Article 24 the term 'termination of employment' means termination of employment on the initiative of the employer. Therefore, situations where a mandatory retirement age is set by statute, as a consequence of which the

20. *See*, for example, *International Federation of Associations of the Elderly (FIAPA) v. France*, Collective complaint No. 145/2017, assisted decision-making for the elderly guaranteeing their right to make decisions for themselves. Statement of interpretation of Art. 23, Conclusion 2013. Spanier & Doron, *supra* n. 17, at 146–173.
21. Conclusions XIII-5, Finland, 305.
22. *See* Swiatkowski, *supra* n. 9, at 166 ff. Although Art. 24 is separated into three paragraphs, these are not separated in nature, and states must accept Art. 24 in its entity.
23. Conclusions 2003, Italy, Vol. 1, 111; Swiatkowski, *supra* n. 9, at 168–169.
24. Collective complaint No. 74/2011, *see* paras 86, 89, 97, 99.
25. The statements of interpretation signal a development in the jurisprudence of the Committee.
26. Conclusions 2012, General Introduction.

> employment relationship automatically ceases by operation of law, do not fall within the scope of this provision.
>
> The Committee further recalls that Article 24 establishes in an exhaustive manner the valid grounds on which an employer can terminate an employment relationship. Two types of grounds are considered valid, namely on the one hand those connected with the capacity or conduct of the employee and on the other hand those based on the operational requirements of the enterprise (economic reasons).
>
> The Committee holds that under Article 24 dismissal of the employee on the initiative of the employer on the ground that the former has reached the normal pensionable age (age when an individual becomes entitled to a pension) will be contrary to the Charter, unless the termination is properly justified with reference to one of the valid grounds expressly established by the provisions of the Charter.

The statement of interpretation clarifies that the prohibition of termination of employment is applicable only when it is initiated by the employer. Furthermore, situations where a mandatory retirement age is set by statute, resulting in the automatic cessation of the employment relationship, do not fall within the scope of Article 24. Legislation that makes retirement mandatory for the employee but allows the employer to retain and continue employing the worker is not considered to be a statutory exception to the Charter.[27]

4.4 Non-discrimination (Article E)

Article E of the Charter prescribes that the rights in the Charter shall be secured without discrimination on any ground such as race, colour, sex, language, religion, political or other opinion, national extraction or social origin, health, association with a national minority, birth, and other status.[28] Both direct and indirect discrimination are covered.[29] Article E must be read in conjunction with another (substantive) article of the Charter. The Committee has found that Article E has been violated in conjunction with another article, even though the latter article was not violated independently. If the alleged discrimination falls within the scope of a substantive article, this is sufficient. Article E is placed outside the numbered articles of the Charter and is not an opt-in article. This means that all States Parties are bound by Article E.[30]

Article E of the Social Charter is modelled on Article 14 of the ECHR, but the grounds covered by Article E of the Charter are more extensive than those covered by Article 14 ECHR. Age is not explicitly included as one of the prohibited grounds of discrimination in Article E. However, the European Committee of Social Rights has interpreted Article E to include a prohibition of discrimination on the ground of age,

27. Csilla Kollonay Lehoczky, *Who, Whom, When, How? Questions and Emerging Answers on Age Discrimination*, The Equal Rights Review 88 (Vol. 11, 2012).
28. Article E was added in the Revised Charter of 1996. The 1961 Charter does not contain a general non-discrimination provision but nevertheless affirms the principle of non-discrimination in the Preamble.
29. *International association Autism (IAAE)Europe v. France*, Collective complaint No. 13/2002, para. 52.
30. The Committee's interpretation concerning Arts 23 and E, *see* Kollonay Lehoczky, *supra* n. 27, at 69–98, especially at 87–89.

under the category 'other status'. (In addition, Article 14 ECHR has been interpreted to prohibit discrimination on the ground of age.)[31]

Article E prohibits two categories of discrimination. The first category concerns differential treatment of persons or groups of people despite an identical situation. The second category concerns situations where persons or groups in different situations are treated identically. Under the first category, discriminatory behaviour can be justified by an objective and reasonable justification if it pursues a legitimate aim or if there is a reasonable relationship of proportionality between the means employed and the aim sought to be realized. State Parties have a certain margin of appreciation in assessing whether differences in similar situations justify differential treatment. Under the second category, discrimination may arise through failure to take due and positive account of relevant differences or failure to take adequate steps to ensure that rights that are open to all are genuinely accessible by and to all.[32]

A difference in treatment is not discriminatory if it is supported by an objective and reasonable justification. If the Committee finds that there is a legitimate aim behind the differences in treatment, the Committee will then analyse whether there is a proportionate relationship between the desired aim and the means chosen (see *infra* section 5 and the collective complaints referred to there). Finally, differential treatment must have some statutory basis (the principle of legality).

5 CASE LAW FROM THE EUROPEAN COMMITTEE OF SOCIAL RIGHTS

In 2013, in the important *Collective complaint Fællesforbundet for Sjøfolk (FFFS) v. Norway*, Article 1 § 2 and Article 23 were connected.[33] The Committee stated that the right to earn one's living in an occupation freely entered upon (Article 1 § 2) is also consistent with one of the primary objectives of Article 23 that include measures to allow or encourage older persons to remain in the labour force.[34] Such measures include delaying retirement age or taking early retirement to take up another job or become self-employed.[35]

In *Collective complaint Fællesforbundet for Sjøfolk (FFFS) v. Norway*, the complainant trade union alleged that Norwegian legislation stipulating retirement for seamen upon reaching the age of 62 years was an unjustified prohibition of employment and discriminatory denial of seamen's right to work as such. According to the Committee's case law, dismissal on grounds of age does not constitute a valid reason

31. Disability has been interpreted in the same way, *see International Association Autism-Europe (IAAE) v. France*, collective complaint No. 13/2002, para. 51. Cf. the Universal Declaration of Human Rights 1948, which does not specifically mention age, but which covers age under 'other status' in Art. 2.
32. *See European Roma Rights Centre (ERRC) v. France*, Collective complaint No. 51/2008, paras 81–83 and references. *See also Confédération Démocratique Francaise du Travail (CFDT) v. France*, Collective complaint No. 50/2008, paras 38–39.
33. *Fællesforbundet for Sjøfolk (FFFS) v. Norway*, Collective complaint No. 74/2011.
34. Collective complaint No. 74/2011, para. 116, *see also* Conclusions XIII-5 Finland.
35. Collective complaint No. 74/2011, para. 116.

for termination of employment unless the termination, within the context of national law, is objectively and reasonably justified by a legitimate aim such as employment policy, labour market objectives, or the operational requirements of the undertaking, and provided that the means of achieving the aim are appropriate and necessary.[36] In this case, the Committee held that even when based on a legitimate aim (employment policy, operational requirements, health and security of those at sea), an age limit must also be necessary for the attainment of the policy's aims. There was no evidence on degeneration of seamen's health on reaching 62 years of age; seamen with a certificate of medical fitness may be re-employed regardless of age, and the age limit was not considered necessary for obtaining the desired goals. The Committee found that the age limit was not founded on objective grounds. It had not been shown that the desired aims could not be attained by less intrusive means. The Committee found a violation of Article 24 of the Charter because dismissals directly on the grounds of age were permitted, thereby not effectively guaranteeing the seamen's right to protection in cases of termination of employment.[37] This was the situation irrespective of whether the seamen in question would be entitled to a pension following the termination of the employment relationship. Further, the difference in treatment because of the age limit was considered to constitute discrimination contrary to Article 1 § 2 of the Charter.[38,39]

In the *Collective complaint International Federation of Associations of the Elderly (FIAPA) v. France*, the complainant organization alleged that an age limit was a violation of Article 23 of the Charter.[40] In France, the public health code prescribed a maximum age limit of 71 years for candidates for a council or a chamber of health professions. The Committee recalled that Article 23 requires States Parties to 'combat age discrimination, through the adaption of an adequate legal framework, as a fundamental measure to eliminate age discrimination of older persons'. The age limit in the case 'amounted to an obstacle for the persons concerned in enjoying their right, enshrined in the Article 23 of the Charter, to remain full members of society as long as possible, taking into account their own physical, psychological and intellectual capacities (Appendix to Article 23)'.[41] The Committee further found a violation of Article E in conjunction with Article 5. Article 5, which guarantees the right for workers and employers to organize, also covers persons who exercise rights resulting from work, such as pensioners. The 71-year age limit constituted differential treatment of persons in this age group as compared to other persons – with respect to their right to organize. The aim of the age limit was to reduce overrepresentation by inactive members and support the renewal of leadership. The Committee found that the means chosen were

36. Collective complaint No. 74/2011, para. 84.
37. Collective complaint No. 74/2011, para. 99.
38. Collective complaint No. 74/2011, paras 115–117.
39. Norway has since raised the age limit, and the Committee now considers the problem remedied, https://rm.coe.int/follow-up-cc-2019-fr-findings-2019-on.the-follow-up-to-collective-comp/16809cf9a5, 41–42.
40. *International Federation of Associations of the Elderly (FIAPA) v. France*, Collective complaint No. 162/2018.
41. Collective complaint No. 162/2018, para. 68.

neither reasonable nor proportionate to this aim and that the age limit represented direct discrimination.[42]

6 OTHER ARTICLES IN THE CHARTER WITH POSSIBLE GROUNDS TO PROTECT OLDER WORKERS

Anti-discrimination rules are not the only means by which older persons' rights to remain active in the labour force could be encouraged. Other articles in the Charter than those mentioned above could be used to strengthen and protect older workers' rights. The following list of articles is not intended to be exhaustive.[43]

According to Article 1 § 1, the States Parties' primary aims and responsibilities should include the achievement and maintenance of a high and stable level of employment with a view to the attainment of full employment. Concerning the obligations under Article 1 § 1, the efforts made by states must be adequate in the light of the economic situation and the level of unemployment. In the past, the absence of both a declaratory commitment to full employment and a concerted employment policy has led to a national situation being held to be in breach of the Charter.[44] It is important to include older workers in such national policies and strategies.

Availability of education and training are important for promoting the right to work for older persons. Older workers may need upskilling or reskilling late in their careers, and lifelong learning is a precondition for longer participation in the workforce. To support older persons who want to continue working, it is essential that they can access appropriate education and training. This is particularly important in the context of today's rapid changes in the labour market as a result of digitalization and technological developments. Under Article 1 § 4 of the Charter, States undertake to provide or promote appropriate vocational guidance, training, and rehabilitation. Article 1 § 4 guarantees the right to vocational guidance, continuing vocational training for employed and unemployed, and specialized guidance and training for persons with disabilities. States must provide these services, grant access to these services for all interested persons, and ensure equality in the treatment of nationals of other States Parties and for persons with disabilities.[45] The right to vocational training, Article 10, states in 10 § 3.a that States Parties shall provide or promote adequate and readily available training facilities for adult workers. Under Article 10 § 3.b, the States Parties undertake to promote special facilities for the retraining of adult workers as a result of technological development or new trends in employment. The main indicators of compliance with Article 10 § 3 are the types of continuing vocational training and education available on the labour market, training measures for certain groups such as

42. Collective complaint No. 162/2018, paras 87–89.
43. The right to social and medical assistance (Art. 13), freedom from poverty and social exclusion (Art. 31), the right to protection of health (Art. 11) are examples of articles that could also be of interest when discussing protection of older workers.
44. Conclusions XVI-1 Netherlands (Netherlands Antilles and Aruba), 464.
45. Conclusions XII-1 (1991) Statement of interpretation of Art. 1 §4, 67. Vocational training for persons with disabilities is dealt with under Art. 15 of the Charter for States that have accepted Art. 15.

women, the overall participation rate of persons in training and the gender balance, the percentage of employees participating in continuing vocational training, and the total expenditure.[46] Training measures for certain groups can also mean training for older workers.

For older workers, the right to work and the right to good working conditions are two closely related rights. Some older workers will experience more fragile health, and in this case, Article 3 of the Charter concerning safe and healthy working conditions becomes even more important. The quality of the work environment can directly affect the extent of a person's participation in working life. Additionally, Article 15 § 2, which obliges states to promote access to employment for persons with disabilities, can play a role here. In the future, there might be a possibility to use the concept of 'reasonable accommodation', used in respect of workers with disabilities, in the assessment of good working conditions for older workers.[47]

Article 12 concerning the right to social security not only encompasses old-age pensions but also includes many other benefits such as unemployment benefits. States Parties that exclude older workers from unemployment benefits can be seen as discriminatory and in contravention with Article 12 in conjunction with Article E.

In Article 26, which concerns the right to dignity at work, one aim is to prevent sexual harassment in the workplace and recurrent reprehensible or distinctly negative and offensive actions directed against individual workers in the workplace or in relation to work. Here, States Parties shall take measures to encompass actions aiming at protecting, among others, older workers against various kinds of unacceptable employer or coworker behaviour.

Measures aiming at protecting older workers can entail costs for the States Parties. In the *Collective complaint European Federation of National Organisations Working with the Homeless (FEANTSA) v. France*, Article 31 on the right to housing and Article E were tested.[48] The Committee stated that the rights in the Charter must take a practical and effective form rather than a purely theoretical one; this means that for the situation to be compatible with the Charter, a States Party must adopt the necessary legal, financial, and operational means of ensuring steady progress towards achieving the goals laid down by the Charter. Furthermore, the Committee emphasized that implementation of the Charter requires States Parties not only to take legal action but also to furnish the resources and introduce the operational procedures necessary to give full effect to the rights specified in the Charter.[49]

46. Conclusion XIV-2 (1998) Statement of interpretation of Art. 10 §3, 61.
47. Conclusions 2007, Statement of interpretation of Art. 15 §2. Conclusions (2008) Czech Republic 'under article 15 § 2, anti-discrimination legislation must include the adjustment of working conditions (reasonable accommodation)'. *See also* Quinn & Doron, *supra* n. 9, at 157.
48. *European Federation of National Organisations Working with the Homeless (FEANTSA) v. France*, Collective complaint No. 39/2006.
49. Collective complaint No. 39/2006, paras 55–57.

7 RELATIONSHIP BETWEEN THE EUROPEAN SOCIAL CHARTER AND EUROPEAN UNION LAW

A brief comparison of the European Social Charter and EU law concerning the protection of older workers reveals some differences.[50]

Age discrimination is explicitly forbidden under EU law, irrespective of the age concerned. Article 1 of Directive 2000/78/EC[51] bans discrimination in working life due to age, and Article 21 of the Charter of Fundamental Rights forbids discrimination based on (among other grounds) age. Article 6 of Directive 2000/78/EC admits several possible deviations from age discrimination and opens for the justification of direct age discrimination. Article 6.1 provides a non-exhaustive list of examples of legitimate aims that can allow differences in treatment on the ground of age. Legitimate aims shall be related to employment policy, labour markets, and vocational training objectives. The measure at issue must also be both appropriate and necessary. Member States are given a considerable margin of appreciation when it comes to differential treatment on the grounds of age.[52]

Under the European Social Charter, the general anti-discrimination rule in Article E must be used in conjunction with another (substantive) article in the Charter. Discrimination on the ground of age is not explicitly prohibited according to Article E, but this article has been interpreted to include age. Several articles under the Social Charter protect older workers in certain respects. Some articles are applicable to all ages and some only to older persons.

Directive 2000/78/EC applies only to the labour market. Several of the European Social Charter Articles dealt with earlier in this chapter are also applicable to age discrimination outside the labour market.

Under the European Social Charter, age discrimination is (so far) rather undeveloped in case law. Compared to the cases and case law involving the European Social Charter and discrimination of older workers, there are a considerable number of cases and case law from the Court of Justice of the European Union (CJEU) concerning age discrimination.

Situations where employment automatically ceases when employees reach a mandatory retirement age set by law are not covered by the Social Charter. Termination of employment initiated by the employer, because the employee has reached pensionable age, is prohibited according to Article 24 of the European Social Charter. Under Directive 2000/78/EC, a series of judgments has been delivered by the CJEU concerning termination of the employment relationship at a pensionable age or at a

50. For an overview of age discrimination and EU law, *see* Frank Hendrickx, *Age and European Employment Discrimination Law* 3-30 (Frank Hendrickx, ed., *Active Ageing and Labour Law*, Intersentia 2012). Concerning EU law and discrimination of older workers, *see also* Chapters 4 and 6 in this book.
51. Council Directive 2000/78 of 2 December 2000 on establishing a general framework for equal treatment in employment and occupation.
52. Colm O'Cinneide & Kimberly Liu, *2000/78/EC: Framework Equality Directive* 101-102 (Monika Schlachter ed., *EU Labour Law: A Commentary*, Wolters Kluwer 2015); Monika Schlachter, *Mandatory Retirement and Age Discrimination*, The International Journal of Comparative Labour Law and Industrial Relations 27, 287-299 (2011) https://doi.org/10.54648/ijcl2011019.

certain age. The retirement age as such is outside the scope of the Directive, but under the Directive, compulsory retirement at a fixed age constitutes direct discrimination. In many cases, the CJEU has accepted compulsory retirement rules and found them justifiable under Article 6.1 of the Directive.[53]

Protection against age discrimination seems to be treated more uniformly and comprehensively under EU law, while protection under the Social Charter seems more point-orientated and linked to a specific Article of the Charter. Additionally, one must take into account that the States Parties can choose to accept only a limited number of articles of the European Social Charter, although Article E applies to all States Parties. EU law is supranational, and all Member States must accept it in its entirety.[54]

8 CONCLUSIONS AND THOUGHTS ON FUTURE DEVELOPMENTS

Age discrimination in the workforce is a barrier to older persons' full enjoyment of their human rights. Age discrimination creates divisions between generations, and discrimination can prevent older persons from realizing their full potential. The steady increase in life expectancy in most countries entails rising costs for society. The sustainability of future pension claims is one of the world's great challenges in relation to an ageing population. At the same time, older persons are enjoying increasingly better health; many physically demanding jobs have been phased out, and in general the working environment has improved. Addressing issues associated with older workers is still a fairly new and underdeveloped phenomenon. This also applies to the rights of older workers under the European Social Charter. The concept of discrimination under the European Social Charter has developed over the years, and gradually, the European Committee of Social Rights' interpretation has come to include age discrimination in the list of prohibited grounds. As has been shown above, the Charter contains a number of articles that could be relevant in this regard; there are several grounds that presumably could be used to protect older workers, but so far, few concrete assessments have been made.

According to O'Cinneide, 'The human rights body that has perhaps the most demanding approach in respect of age discrimination is the European Committee of Social Rights.'[55] O'Cinneide concludes that although the jurisprudence under the European Charter of Social Rights in respect of age discrimination is of 'recent vintage', it 'adopts a more demanding standard of scrutiny than has been applied in other systems of fundamental rights protection at national or international level'.[56]

53. Ann Numhauser-Henning, *Pension Norms and the EU Ban on Age Discrimination*, 129 f. (Ann Numhauser-Henning & Mia Rönnmar eds, *Age Discrimination and Labour Law*, Wolters Kluwer, 2015); Schlachter, *supra* n. 52.
54. Colm O'Cinneide, *Constitutional and Fundamental Rights Aspects of Age Discrimination*, 51–69 (Ann Numhauser-Henning & Mia Rönnmar eds, *Age Discrimination and Labour Law*, Wolters Kluwer, 2015), provides some reflections concerning EU age-discrimination law and age discrimination under the European Social Charter.
55. O'Cinneide, *supra* n. 54, at 62.
56. O'Cinneide, *supra* n. 54, at 63.

In 2014, the Committee of Ministers of the Council of Europe issued a Recommendation to Member States on the Promotion of Human Rights of Older Persons.[57] The Recommendation affirms that older persons shall fully enjoy the rights guaranteed in the ECHR and the Revised Social Charter. According to paragraphs 26–28 of the Recommendation, Member States should ensure that older persons do not face discrimination in employment, including aspects such as conditions for access to employment, initial and continuous vocational training, working conditions (including dismissal and remuneration), membership in trade unions, and retirement. Any difference in treatment should be justified by a legitimate aim of employment policy and proportionate to achieve that aim. Promotion of older persons' participation in the labour market should be included in national employment policies. Specific attention should be paid to safety and health problems of older workers.

Looking at future developments and a possibility for a progressive interpretation of the European Social Charter when it comes to the protection of older workers, we can see that the Charter contains some rights of a more dynamic nature. Such provisions require the States Parties to actively progress relevant legislation and improve the situation for people.[58] One example is Article 12 § 3 concerning social-security systems, where States Parties undertake to progressively raise the system of social security to a higher level.[59] There is also possibly room for 'progressive realization' under other articles.[60] Signs of this can be detected in the Committee's case law. In *Collective complaint European Federation of National Organisations Working with the Homeless (FEANTSA) v. France*[61] concerning Article 31 (right to housing), the Committee stated that States Parties must 'adopt the necessary legal, financial and operational means of ensuring steady progress towards achieving the goals laid down by the Charter'.[62] In *Collective complaint Centre for Housing Rights and Evictions (COHRE) v. Italy,*[63] the Committee mentioned the progressive character of many rights in the Charter: 'realisation of the fundamental social rights recognised by the Revised Charter is guided by the principle of progressiveness, which is explicitly established in the Preamble…'.[64,65]

57. Council of Europe: Committee of Ministers, CM/Rec(2014)2 on the protection of human right of older persons and Explanatory Memorandum, 19 February 2014. *See also* Mikolajczyk, *supra* n. 3, at 335–336.
58. *See* General Introduction, p. XIV, 1973.
59. Another example is Art. 2 §1 of the Charter, which contains a dynamic dimension regarding the right to fair working conditions: 'reasonable daily and weekly working hours, the working week to be progressively reduced to the extent that increase of productivity and other relevant factors permit'.
60. The International Covenant on Economic Social and Cultural Rights, Art. 2.1. prescribes that States Parties shall take steps to the maximum of their available resources, with a view to progressive achievement of the full realization of the rights in the Covenant. There is no equivalent to this article in the European Social Charter.
61. *European Federation of National Organisations Working with the Homeless (FEANTSA) v. France,* Collective complaint No. 39/2006.
62. Collective complaint No. 39/2006, para. 56.
63. *Centre on Housing Rights and Evictions (COHRE) v. Italy,* Collective complaint No. 58/2009.
64. Collective complaint No. 58/2009, para. 27.
65. Quinn & Doron, *supra* n. 9, discuss progressive realization under the Charter with references to the Committee's case law.

The European Social Charter has strong potential; there is room for further developments of the Committee's jurisprudence concerning age discrimination and protection of older workers. Considering the ageing of populations, these questions will become more topical, and we can expect new and interesting developments.

CHAPTER 4

Fundamental Social Rights and the EU Charter in Times of Crisis: Reality and Prospects

Xavier Groussot & Alezini Loxa

1 INTRODUCTION

The core aim of this chapter is to explore the potential of the EU Charter in developing social protection in times of poly-crisis. In the past, EU Member States have gone through a number of events that have been termed as crises, calling for a paradigm shift in EU governance (economic, migration, and, more recently, health crises). While the effects of these crises are still felt, the EU is faced with a war at its borders, a rule-of-law crisis within the EU, and an energy crisis. Looking ahead, it becomes hard to imagine that EU will soon return to 'normal' – that is, to the adoption of policies and legislation that will not be framed around a prevailing crisis discourse. Against this background, we use the term '*poly-crisis*' to refer to the situation of multiple crises taking place in parallel at local and regional European levels and which are interlinked with EU policy making. By understanding the present through the lens of a poly-crisis, we want to explore how social rights protection appears in current EU law and policy and offer alternative theoretical models to drive change that can foster stronger protection of social rights.

More precisely, section 2 looks at what has been achieved (but also not achieved) in terms of recent legislation and case law as regards social rights. Regarding case law, we focus on the Court of Justice of the European Union (CJEU) judgments on working conditions. It is important to do so because EU law doctrine often sees the new legislation and the case law of the CJEU as the key elements for developing the protection of social rights in EU Law. At the same time, Fritz Sharpf's theory on 'constitutional asymmetry' has significantly impacted the debate on the possibility of a positive evolution.[1] On top of that, the poly-crisis situation creates instability and influences the interpretation of the EU Charter and the making of EU legislation.

Section 3 analyses the various 'models of changes' that can be used to extend the protection of social rights, and we look at the situation in three different fields: EU law, international law, and legal theory. The doctrine in EU law often proposes a model of change based on the rationale of dignity (the 'dignity model'). In this chapter, we question the relevance of this model in light of international law and legal theory. We argue that the 'dignity model' should not be the only model used in developing the protection of social rights in the EU. The 'solidarity model', or solidarity narrative, should also be relied on in EU Law. The cases of the CJEU regarding 'budget conditionality' delivered by the plenary Court in February 2022 relied significantly on this narrative of solidarity.[2] Can this case – delivered in a field other than social rights – be of relevance for the protection of social rights in EU law? Finally, section 4 offers our conclusions. As we reflect on the analysis of this chapter, we suggest that the type of future crisis can affect the extent to which social rights will be consolidated.

2 SOCIAL RIGHTS IN EU LAW

Social rights are protected under Title IV of the EU Charter of Fundamental Rights. Scholars have commented extensively on the shortcomings of the Charter when it comes to reinforcing the protection of social rights.[3] On a doctrinal level, these shortcomings relate to the cryptic distinction between rights and principles, the applicability of the Charter only within the scope of application of EU law, and the direct applicability of different provisions of the Charter.[4] In this section, we explore the ways in which social rights make their appearance in more recent EU law and policy (section 2.1) and in the case law of the Court with a focus on working conditions (section 2.2)

1. Fritz Scharpf, *The European Social Model*, 40 Journal of Common Market Studies 645 (2002) https://doi.org/10.1111/1468-5965.00392.
2. Case C-156/21, *Hungary v. Parliament and Council*, 16.2.2022, ECLI:EU:C:2022:97; Case C-157/21, *Poland v. Parliament and Council*, 16.1.2022, ECLI:EU:C:2022:98.
3. Maribel González Pascual, *Social Rights Protection in the EU: Unlocking the Social Content of the EU Charter*, in *Social Rights and the European Monetary Union: Challenges Ahead* 36–41 (Maribel González Pascual & Aida Torres Pérez eds, Edward Elgar Publishing 2022) especially on Charter silence during the Eurocrisis; Pieter Pecinovsky, *EU Economic Governance: A Tool to Promote or Threaten Social Rights? The Example of the Right to Collective Bargaining*, in *Law, Solidarity and the Limits of Social Europe* 62 (Ann-Christine Hartzén, Andrea Iossa & Eleni Karageorgiou eds, Edward Elgar Publishing 2022) on the right to collective bargaining during the economic crisis and the potentials after the health crisis.
4. For a more general overview, *see* the anthology edited by Sybe de Vries, Ulf Bernitz & Stephen Weatherill, *The EU Charter of Fundamental Rights as a Binding Instrument, Five Years Old and Growing* (Hart Publishing 2015).

2.1 The 'Social' in New Legislation

The economic crisis and the Baroso Commission's emphasis on the economy side-tracked social rights from the EU agenda for some time.[5] Nevertheless, EU policy adopted under both the Juncker and the von der Leyen Commission points towards a potential for reinforcing social rights in the EU legal system.

Specifically, in 2017, the European Pillar of Social Rights (the Pillar) was launched as an interinstitutional, soft-law agreement aimed at promoting social rights.[6] The Pillar contains 20 principles that are more broadly construed than the social rights protected in Title IV of the Charter, and a whole chapter of it is devoted to fair working conditions. Specifically, under Chapter II of the Pillar, secure and adaptable employment, wages, information about employment conditions and protection in case of dismissals, social dialogue and involvement of workers, work-life balance, and health and safety at work are addressed. Following the pandemic, the Commission presented the Pillar Action Plan in order to guide its implementation at Member-State level.[7]

According to the Commission, the Pillar principles 'are the beacon guiding us towards a strong Social Europe'.[8] The extent to which the Pillar has a real potential for shaping a true social Europe remains to be seen. So far, positive steps can be seen in the context of coordination of the Pillar goals with financing instruments at EU level. Specifically, since 2018, the social aspect came under the European Semester cycle, when Member States were required to report on the implementation of the Pillar in their national reform programmes. Authors reacted in various ways to this evolution, from identifying the progressive 'socialization' of the European Semester[9] to criticizing the policy as subordinating social objectives to the goal of financial stability.[10]

Indicatively, Dawson has suggested that this turn to the social aspect can be criticized for the very same deficiencies characterizing past EU social policy. Specifically, Dawson stated that:

> The very notion of re-stating social rights (some of which have well-established juridical form) as principles seems an indication of how far the logic of policy coordination has reached into the very fabric of EU social policy. If part of the problem of Social Europe is its reliance on soft law instruments, which are too often outweighed by harder economic procedures, the Pillar of Social Rights

---

5. For an analysis of the effects on the right to collective bargaining, *see* Pecinovsky, *supra* n 3.
6. Interinstitutional Proclamation on the European Pillar of Social Rights OJ C 428, 13.12.2017.
7. Communication from the Commission to the European Parliament, the Council, the European Economic and Social Committee and the Committee of the Regions, 'The European Pillar of Social Rights Action Plan', COM(2021)102 final. *See also* endorsement of the plan in Porto Social Commitment and European Council, Porto Declaration 8 May 2021.
8. Action Plan, p. 2.
9. Jonathan Zeitlin & Bart Vanhercke, *Socializing the European Semester: EU Social and Economic Policy Co-ordination in Crisis and Beyond,* 25 Journal of European Public Policy 149 (2018) https://doi.org/10.1080/13501763.2017.1363269. *See also* Elise Muir, *Drawing Positive Lessons from the Presence of 'The Social' Outside of EU Social Policy Stricto Sensu,* 14 European Constitutional Law Review 75, 86 (2018) https://doi.org/10.1017/s1574019618000020.
10. Mark Dawson, *New Governance and the Displacement of Social Europe: The Case of the European Semester,* 14 European Constitutional Law Review 191 (2018) https://doi.org/10.1017/s1574019618000081.

replicates this phenomenon, with much of its content deliverable only via soft law, including the European Semester itself.[11]

From a different perspective, some authors have emphasized the potential of the Pillar to catalyse social rights protection in the EU.[12] In this regard, Garben has commented on the Pillar as an indication that the political landscape at EU level has shifted towards a more social outlook that could ensure its implementation.[13] Muir has also suggested that the impact of EU economic law on social values 'invites us to rethink both the political opportunities that the EU may offer to advance social rights'.[14]

Moreover, following the COVID-19 crisis, and under the NextGenerationEU, the national Recovery and Resilience Facility became the first instrument linking financial support to the Pillar by making its implementation one of the goals of the Recovery and Resilience Facility. In this respect, González Pascual noted that 'the NGEU[NextGenerationEU] is nothing short of a historic milestone' but that it still did not represent 'a radical shift away from the economically oriented priorities of the EU'.[15] In any case, we can see that the COVID-19 crisis pointed to a need for transformation of European Economic Governance, which so far has shown a potential to strengthen social rights in the EU.[16] In general, the incorporation of the Pillar in financing instruments should be welcomed as an opportunity to consolidate social rights by mainstreaming them in other areas of EU law and as a step towards the creation of a stronger social Europe.[17]

In addition, a second positive evaluation of the potential of the Pillar to shape a stronger social Europe appears in relation to concrete legislative initiatives. Specifically, in 2020, the Commission put forward a proposal on adequate minimum wages which resulted in the Minimum Wage Directive adopted in 2022.[18] The preamble of the Directive refers to Articles 23, 27, 28 and 31 of the Charter, the European Social Charter, and the Pillar as sources of fundamental rights protection guiding the adoption of the Directive.[19] Moreover, in 2021, the Commission put forward a proposal on a Directive for platform workers in order to ensure that labour and social rights would also be

11. *Ibid.*, 208.
12. Muir, *supra* n. 9, at 83; Sacha Garben, *Chapter 3: Balancing Fundamental Social and Economic Rights in the EU: In Search of a Better Method*, in *Social Policy in the European Union 1999–2019: The Long and Winding Road* 58 (Bart Vanhercke & others, European Trade Union Institute (ETUI) European Social Observatory (OSE) 2020) calls the European Pillar of Social Rights a catalyst for implementing social rights.
13. Sacha Garben, *The European Pillar of Social Rights: Effectively Addressing Displacement?*, 14 European Constitutional Law Review 210, 222 (2018) https://doi.org/10.1017/s1574019618000093.
14. Muir, *supra* n. 9, at 77.
15. González Pascual, *supra* n. 3, at 44 and 46.
16. *Ibid.*, at 47.
17. Muir, *supra* n. 9, at 83 and González Pascual, *supra* n. 3, at 43.
18. Proposal for a Directive of the European Parliament and of the Council on adequate minimum wages in the European Union, COM/2020/682 final; Directive (EU) 2022/2041 of the European Parliament and of the Council of 19 October 2022 on adequate minimum wages in the European Union OJ L 275, 25.10.22.
19. Recitals 3–5 of Directive 2022/2041. Recital 5 also mentions the specific Pillar principles, principle nos 6 and 8 on worker's right to fair wages and consultation rights, respectively.

protected in the digital environment.[20] Political agreement on this proposal was reached in March 2024 and was presented as another step for reinforcing the social dimension of the EU.[21] The preamble of the compromise text refers to Articles 8, 12, 16, 21, 27 and 31 of the Charter and the Pillar as sources of fundamental rights protection behind the adoption of this Directive.[22] Next to these two Directives, the Pay Transparency Directive, the Work Life Balance Directive and the Directive on Transparent and Predictable Working Conditions all include references to the Pillar in general and to specific principles thereof specifically, thereby indicating that the Pillar is added to the sources which should guide more concrete social protection in Europe.[23]

Finally, the Commission also published an Interpretative Communication and an Implementation Report on the current Working Time Directive, with the aim of increasing legal certainty and ensuring better implementation. This initiative has also been linked to the implementation of the Pillar and thereby the strengthening of Article 31 of the Charter.[24]

These evolutions show the potential of reinforcing social rights in binding instruments in allaying fears of dilution of social rights in soft law.

We continue by elaborating on how the Court has addressed the social content of the Charter in relation to working conditions. Preliminarily, it should be noted that as González Pascual has stated, 'secondary law is the main key to unlocking the social content of the EU Charter, whereas the European Pillar of Social Rights (and the European Social Charter) might help the EU institutions to consolidate genuine progress of social rights both in terms of legislative proposals and judicial decisions'. Muir has also emphasized the opportunities for advocacy and regulatory innovation of social policy through the developments in EU economic governance, despite the stagnation in the traditional social acquis.[25] Indeed, the Pillar and its use following the COVID-19 crisis could have a powerful potential for the consolidation of social rights in the EU.

20. Proposal for a Directive of the European Parliament and of the Council on improving working conditions in platform work COM(2021) 762 final 2021/0414 (COD).
21. Council of the EU Press Release, Platform workers: Council confirms agreement on new rules to improve their working conditions, 11.3.2024.
22. Council of the EU, 7212/24 ADD 1 Note, Proposal for the Directive of the European Parliament and of the Council on improving working conditions in platform work – Analysis of the final compromise text with a view to agreement, 8.3.2024 Recitals 2 and 3, 2021/0414 (COD).
23. *See* Recital 9 Directive (EU) 2023/970 of the European Parliament and of the Council of 10 May 2023 to strengthen the application of the principle of equal pay for equal work or work of equal value between men and women through pay transparency and enforcement mechanisms, OJ L 132, 17.5.2023; Recital 9 Directive (EU) 2019/1158 of the European Parliament and of the Council of 20 June 2019 on work-life balance for parents and carers and repealing Council Directive 2010/18/EU OJ L 188, 12.7.2019 and Recitals 2 and 3 Directive (EU) 2019/1152 of the European Parliament and of the Council of 20 June 2019 on transparent and predictable working conditions in the European Union OJ L 186, 11.7.2019.
24. Directive 2003/88/EC of the European Parliament and of the Council of 4 November 2003 concerning certain aspects of the organisation of working time OJ L 299, 18.11.2003. *See also* p. 1 Interpretative Communication.
25. Muir, *supra* n. 9, at 95.

2.2 Social Rights of Workers in Working Conditions Case Law

The strength of the Charter on the protection of social rights depends on the scope of application of EU law. This is especially true in areas of social policy where – as Safradin, de Bryes, and de Heer note – the limited legislative powers of the EU can mean that in practice, citizens often cannot invoke their EU Charter rights in courts.[26] What is more, the issue of horizontal applicability of different provisions of the Charter is even more important in the case of labour disputes between private parties.[27]

In *Mangold* and *Kücükdeveci,* the Court held that fundamental rights (in these cases, the principle of non-discrimination) can have a horizontal direct effect if they find specific expression in secondary legislation.[28] These cases pointed to the potential of using fundamental rights as specified in various EU law instruments to impact the outcome of private disputes.[29]

In similar cases concerning the overlap between a Charter social right and the provisions of secondary law, the Court did not continue on this path. Specifically, in *AMS*, the Court engaged with the potential of applying Article 27 (worker's right on information and consultation) of the Charter of itself or in conjunction with Directive 2002/14 to a private dispute.[30] In that case, Advocate General Cruz Villalón suggested that there is 'a strong presumption' that the rights set out under the Solidarity title of the Charter belong to the category of 'principles' so that these rights could only be claimed provided that there is secondary legislation that gives them expression.[31] The Court held that Article 27, by virtue of its wording, does not suffice to confer direct effect on individuals, even when considering the more specific provisions of Directive 2002/14.

Contrary to the confusion created by *AMS*, the case law of the Court on the Working Time Directive has shown more potential for consolidation of social rights.[32] The early case law of the Court has given flesh to the right to paid annual leave as protected in Article 31(2) of the Charter. Specifically, and already since *BECTU* in the context of Directive 93/104, the predecessor of the Working Time Directive, the right to paid annual leave was recognized as a principle of EU social law from which there can be no derogation and which national authorities must implement within the limits laid

26. Barbara Safradin, Sybe de Vries & Simona de Heer, *Fundamental Social Rights Protection and Covid-19 in the EU: Constraints & Possibilities*, 17 Utrecht Law Review 103, 111 (2021) https://doi.org/10.36633/ulr.679.
27. *Ibid.*, 113.
28. Case C-144/04 *Mangold*, 22.11.2005, ECLI:EU:C:2005:709; Case C-555/07, *Kücükdeveci*, 19.1.2010, ECLI:EU:C:2010:21.
29. Muir, *supra* n. 9, at 91.
30. Case C-176/12, *Association de médiation sociale* (AMS), 15.1.2014, ECLI:EU:C:2014:2; Directive 2002/14 of the European Parliament and of the Council of 11 March 2002 establishing a general framework for informing and consulting employees in the European Community OJ L 80/29, 23.2.2002.
31. Opinion of Advocate General Cruz Villalón in Case C-176/12, *AMS*, C-176/12, 18.7.2013, ECLI:EU:C:2013:491 para. 55.
32. Directive 2003/88/EC of the European Parliament and of the Council of 4 November 2003 concerning certain aspects of the organisation of working time OJ L 299, 18.11.2003.

down by EC law.[33] Later, in its case law, the Court established the link to Article 31 of the Charter as an expression of this general principle and also recognized the potential of direct effect of Article 31(2).[34]

Then, in *Bauer*, the Court found that Article 31(2) of the Charter can have horizontal direct effect and acknowledged the obligation of national courts to safeguard the Charter by ensuring the conforming interpretation of national law, and where this is not possible, to disapply national legislation in order to guarantee the effective protection of individuals under EU law.[35] In *Max Planck*, the horizontal direct effect of this provision was confirmed.[36]

While this case law points to a consistent consolidation of Article 31 of the Charter to the extent to which its provisions are specified via secondary law, the case law in *TSN* and *Coca-Cola* creates questions as to the potential of strengthening the protection of social rights via litigation.[37]

In these cases, the Court emphasized the scope of the Charter in order to exclude its application in cases of more favourable treatment of workers under domestic law. *TSN* concerned national rules that provided the granting of days of paid annual leave exceeding the minimum period of four weeks laid down in Article 7(1) of the Working Time Directive but which excluded the carrying over of those days on grounds of illness. In *TSN*, the Court drew on the conferral of competences in the area of social policy[38] and highlighted that the purpose of the Working Time Directive is to lay down minimum standards on working conditions.[39] In light of this, the Court suggested that Member-State action, which is more favourable to the protection of workers, does not fall in the scope of EU law; rather, it is an expression of Member States' powers in the field of social policy in line with the national protective clause of Article 15 of the Directive.[40] As a consequence, the Charter was not deemed applicable in this case.[41]

This finding was contrary to the Opinion of Advocate General Bot.[42] The Advocate General suggested that the adoption of national measures in the context of a

33. Case C-173/99, *BECTU*, 26.6.2001, ECLI:EU:C:2001:356 para. 43. As to WTD for the first time in Case C-277/08, *Vicente Pereda*, 10.9.2009 ECLI:EU:C:2009:542.
34. And in connection with the CFR, as expressly protecting that principle, *see* Case C-155/10, *Williams and others*, 15.9.2011, ECLI:EU:C:2011:588. *See also* Case C-214/10, *KHS*, 22.11.2011, ECLI:EU:C:2011:761 and repeated in a series of case law. Indicative Case C-178/15, *Sobczyszyn*, 30.6.2016, ECLI:EU:C:2016:502, para. 20; Case C-337/10, *Neidel*, 3.5.2012, ECLI:EU:C:2012:263 para. 40. In Case C-316/13, *Fenoll*, 26.3.2015, ECLI:EU:C:2015:200, the Court rejected horizontal direct effect of the Charter *rationae temporis*. In principle, the possibility of horizontal direct effects of Art. 31(2) was not excluded, but the claim concerned periods before the Lisbon treaty entered into force. *See also* Opinion of Advocate General Mengozzi in Case C-316/13, *Fenoll*, 12.6.2014, ECLI:EU:C:2014:1753, paras 48–52.
35. Joined Cases C-569/16 and C-570/16 *Bauer*, 6.11.2018, ECLI:EU:C:2018:871 para. 91.
36. Case C-684/16, *Max-Planck-Gesellschaft zur Förderung der Wissenschaften*, 6.11.2018, ECLI: EU:C:2018:874.
37. Joined Cases C-609/17 and C-610/17, *TSN*, 19.11.2019, ECLI:EU:C:2019:981; Joined Cases C-257/21 and C-258/21, *Coca-Cola European Partners Deutschland*, 7.7.2022, ECLI: EU:C:2022:529.
38. Joined Cases C-609/17 and C-610/17, *TSN*, paras 46–47.
39. *Ibid.*, para. 48.
40. *Ibid.*, para. 49.
41. *Ibid.*, paras 53–55.
42. Opinion of AG Bot in Joined Cases C-609/17 and C-610/17, *TSN*, 4.6.2019, ECLI:EU:C:2019:459.

clause allowing for it in a Directive is a domestic extension of the provisions laid down in that Directive and should be considered an implementation of EU law. The argument was based on *Alemo-Herron*, where the Court found that freedom to conduct a business should be ensured in the context of the interpretation of Directive 2001/23 on safeguarding employees' rights in the event of transfers of undertakings.[43]

A similar finding of the Court can be seen in *Coca-Cola*, where the Court held that the provision of a collective agreement providing a higher supplementary allowance for irregular night work than the allowance established for regular night work is not implementing the Working Time Directive; as a result, this provision falls outside the scope of EU law and cannot be examined in light of compliance with the Charter.

So, while we see a positive perspective in the consolidation of the right set out in Article 31 of the Charter when tied to the provisions of secondary law specifying its application, the Court does not seize the opportunity to take social rights a step forward. This is in line with the Court's general approach to extend the protection of social rights when supported by secondary law and to be more restrictive when it comes to decisions related to more sensitive fields, which require a permanent dialogue between Member States.[44] Instead of relating the protection of the Charter to more favourable policies for workers, by reviewing national measures as domestic implementations of the relevant secondary law, the Court denies that such favourable measures are within the scope of EU law to begin with. As a result, the Court misses the opportunity to move away from the protection of workers' rights under a minimum-standards logic and chooses instead to put forward a positive vision on the protection of workers' rights in the EU in light of the demands of Article 3 TEU, the Charter, and (now) the Pillar.

The question remains open regarding the extent to which the Court can draw on other areas of its case law to reinforce the protection of social rights. A brief analysis of Articles 27–33 of the EU Charter shows that in proceedings at national level, many provisions have been relied on directly or that these provisions boast a potential for such direct reliance. Examples include Articles 28, 29, and 32(2) of the Charter. It is true that the wording of the provisions referring to 'national law and practice', for example, in Article 30 of the Charter on unjustified dismissal, may be difficult for an individual to rely on directly in national proceedings. But what about the scope of Articles 31(1) and 33 of the Charter? Do these provisions boast a potential for increasing the protection of social rights in Europe?

While the potential of the specific provisions remains to be seen, the finding of the Court in *KL* connects social rights to procedural rights under EU law with important implications.[45] This recent case concerned the termination of a fixed-term employment under Polish law and its compliance with the framework agreement on fixed-term

43. Case C-426/11, *Alemo-Herron and others*, 18.7.2013, ECLI:EU:C:2013:521.
44. González Pascual, *supra* n. 3, at 32.
45. Case C-715/20, *K.L.*, 20.2.2024, ECLI:EU:C:2024:139. *See* for developments on the importance of procedural rights in EU law, Darren Harvey & Xavier Groussot (eds), *Process-Oriented Federalism in EU Law* (EU Law Live Press, forthcoming).

work annexed to the Fixed-Term Work Directive.[46] Under national law, the dismissal of fixed-term workers did not require the statement of reasons for termination, while this was not the case for workers with indefinite employment. KL, the worker in the present case, claimed that this constituted discrimination under Article 21 of the Charter which deprived him of the rights granted under Article 30 of the Charter. The referring court asked to what extent this differentiation was in compliance with the framework agreement and if the agreement could have a horizontal direct effect. In a groundbreaking finding, the Court held that the agreement, as an annex to a Directive, cannot have a horizontal direct effect; however, Article 47 of the Charter requires from the national court to partially disapply national law in order to ensure the worker's right to effective remedy. The Court did not engage with the demands of Article 30 of the Charter, but it did employ Article 47 in order to extend the horizontal direct effect of Directives and thereby extend the protection of workers from unjustified dismissal as a byproduct.

González Pascual has suggested that the development of the Court's case law on social rights depends on the consensus within the EU on the balance of economic and social goals. Such consensus is normally expressed through secondary law, but it can also be derived from other shared commitments.[47] To González Pascual, this explains the timid role of the Charter during the Eurocrisis and its heightened potential during the health crisis.[48] In such case, the consensus expressed via the adoption of the Pillar and its connection to the NextGenerationEU and the Recovery and Resilience Facility could drive a potential extension of the Charter's scope to cover provisions of domestic law adopted under the national protective clause. At the same time, we see the beginning of a new era after *KL*, where the protection of social rights enters through the backdoor of procedural rights.

3 MODEL OF CHANGES AND SOLIDARITY

With this section, we would like to provide an alternative way to look at the expansion of social rights. If one considers the present doctrinal debate in EU law as to the protection of social rights, this debate reveals that two central arguments are often used to expand social-rights protection: an argument based on EU Legislation on the one hand[49] and an argument based on the expansion of the social rights enshrined in the EU Charter via reliance on the rationale of dignity on the other hand.[50]

46. Council Directive 1999/70/EC of 28 June 1999 concerning the framework agreement on fixed-term work concluded by ETUC, UNICE and CEEP, OJ L 175, 10.7.1999, pp. 43-48.
47. González Pascual, *supra* n. 3, at 36.
48. *Ibid.*
49. *See, e.g.*, González Pascual, *supra* n. 3 and Safradin, de Vries & de Heer, *supra* n. 26.
50. *See, e.g.*, Sacha Garben, *Dignity and Reciprocity Based Solidarity as the Normative Framework of the EU Constitutional Settlement*, in *Law, Solidarity and the Limits of Social Europe* 160 (Ann-Christine Hartzén, Andrea Iossa & Eleni Karageorgiou eds, Edward Elgar Publishing 2022); Niilo Jääskinen, *Fundamental Social Rights in the Charter: Are They Rights? Are They Fundamental?*, in *The EU Charter of Fundamental Rights: A Commentary* 1703-1714 (Steve Peers & others eds, Bloomsbury Publishing 2021).

As discussed previously, EU legislation is naturally crucial in expanding social rights while simultaneously respecting the competence and consensus dilemma.[51] This path is certainly the best model if compared to a right-based model founded on a progressive interpretation of the EU Charter. In this latter scenario, the expansion of EU social rights (especially through the EU Charter) is often linked to the debate on human dignity and equality. As put by Jääskinen: '[p]hilosophically and historically the need to afford some kind of protection to certain social rights can be justified with reference to human dignity and equality. Both of these values are equally recognized by the Charter'.[52]

However, one should not forget that the EU Charter also includes the value of solidarity, which is defined as foundational in the Charter preamble. Our view is that the EU law debate on the expansion of social rights is too heavily based on the 'dignity narrative'.[53] This 'dignity narrative' is closely linked to all civil and political rights while being linked to very few of the social rights enshrined in the EU Charter.[54] In this narrative, the most significant legal mechanism to ensure respect for dignity is based on the 'recognition and protection of fundamental human rights',[55] i.e., the Charter in EU law.

Now, if we look specifically at this second line of argumentation based on dignity, it is worth comparing it with the recent debates in the fields of international law and legal theory and the principle of solidarity. Our position is that the 'dignity narrative' which is often relied on in EU law literature in order to develop the protection of social rights could be replaced (or at least supplemented) by a 'solidarity narrative'. Because the EU Charter of Fundamental Rights considers in its preamble that the principle of solidarity is a 'founding principle' of EU law, it would also be appropriate for the CJEU to rely on this principle of solidarity when recognizing or applying the EU Charter in its adjudicative process. When analysing the CJEU case law and EU law doctrine as we did in the previous sections, it appears that too often, the expansion of social rights is based on a 'dignity narrative'.

The recent debate in international law provides, for instance, a counternarrative to the 'dignity narrative' using a historical perspective by showing how the 'solidarity narrative' was undermined in the Universal Declaration of Human Rights. A 2022 book edited by Steven Jensen and Charles Walton on the history of social rights challenges the concept of social rights as second-generation rights.[56] The authors also explain why social rights have become the 'Cinderella of the human rights corpus', subordinated to

51. Catherine Barnard, *EU Citizenship and the Principle of Solidarity*, in *Social Welfare and EU Law* (Eleanor Spaventa & Michael Dougan eds, Hart Publishing 2005).
52. *See* Jääskinen, *supra* n. 50, at 1708.
53. *See, e.g.*, Garben, *supra* n. 50, at 160, where she looks at the interaction of competition, cooperation, and solidarity while adding a dignity as a fourth crucial piece to the puzzle. European integration remains dominated by a focus on competition. Garben also underlines the complex relationship between solidarity and dignity.
54. This mostly covers the rights related to protection of workers (but in contrast to rights protecting the whole society as a collective, for example, social-security rights).
55. *See* Garben, *supra* n. 50, at 174.
56. Steven Jensen & Charles Walton, *Social Rights and the Politics of Obligation in History* (Cambridge University Press 2022).

civil and political rights and overlooked in favour of charity.[57] The book's main thesis is that the concept of 'three generations of human rights' that is embedded in scholarship and legal education fails to recognize the deeper history of social rights.[58]

Among the authors of chapters in this book, Samuel Moyn[59] and Philip Alston[60] engage in analysis that could provide arguments to challenge the 'dignity model' behind the development of fundamental rights protection. Specifically, Moyn and Alston offer different views to explain the failure to consolidate protection of social rights. Samuel Moyn sees inherent flaws in social rights as protected by the Universal Declaration of Human Rights.[61] By contrast, Philip Alston considers that this failure is due to contingent choices made by the United Nations and probably influenced by robust neoliberal forces. For Alston, the United Nations' 1952 decision to divide the Universal Declaration of Human Rights into two distinct covenants formed the key momentum that ensured the failure of social rights.[62] Is the weakness of social rights in EU law due to inherent weaknesses or contingent choices? It is not the purpose of this chapter to provide an answer to this thorny question in the EU law context. Yet, it is common knowledge that the solidarity chapter of the EU Charter (Chapter IV) was the one facing the deepest criticism at the time of its negotiation.[63] The reaction was notably by the UK government, which was known for its neoliberal views and its explicit rejection of the principle of solidarity. The principle of solidarity was pushed forward in the negotiations and explicitly recognized at national level by some continental EU Member States such as Italy, France, and Spain. This view of 'historical weaknesses' of EU social rights may explain the CJEU's difficulties in making those rights powerful tools of adjudication in Europe via the application of the Charter in the case law.

Legal theory is another field that provides a fertile ground for developing counternarratives to the 'dignity narrative'. Theories based on a sociological approach to law are important in this respect, such as those of the French institutional school, which has developed a strong 'solidarity narrative' following the path opened by Durkheim.[64] This narrative is studied in detail in the recent works on solidarity by Alain

57. *Ibid.*, p. 9 citing also Sandra Fredman, *Human Rights Transformed: Positive Rights and Positive Duties* (Oxford University Press 2008).
58. Jensen & Walton, *supra* n. 56, at 3.
59. Samuel Moyn, *The Spirit of Social Rights*, in *Social Rights and the Politics of Obligation in History* (Steven Jensen & Charles Walton, Cambridge University Press 2022).
60. Philip Alston, *The Past and Future of Social Rights*, in *Social Rights and the Politics of Obligation in History* (Steven Jensen & Charles Walton eds, Cambridge University Press 2022).
61. For a criticism of Moyn's position, *see* Alston, *supra* n. 60, at 317–322. According to Moyn, human rights instruments are too weak to achieve social justice.
62. *See* Alston, *supra* n. 60, at 310.
63. This resulted in the opt-out protocol signed by Poland and the United Kingdom. *See* Consolidated Version of the Treaty on the European Union, Protocol (No. 30) on the Application of the Charter of Fundamental Rights of the European Union to Poland and to the United Kingdom, OJ C 202, 7.6.2016, pp. 312–313.
64. *See, e.g.*, in that respect, Jürgen Habermas, *Between Facts and Norms* (1992); *see also* by the same author *Why Europe Needs a Constitution*, New Left Review (2001). Habermas' theory is useful in the EU context also in its consideration of its use of 'cosmopolitan solidarity'. *See also* Alston, *supra* n. 60, 322–323.

Supiot[65] and Karine Abderemane.[66] Supiot's and Abderemane's works are of particular interest because they connect to the principle of solidarity and EU law. Here, solidarity is studied outside the 'dignity narrative' and within its 'collective meaning' that forms an integral part of its social and legal sense in French scholarship.

In EU law, the narrative of solidarity is undervalued and 'under-used'. EU law could well be considered to provide and foster only a liberal vision. Taken to its extreme, liberalism and its ideology may in fact hamper (and even eliminate) the application of the principle of solidarity. To counter such a probable development, Alain Supiot has invited the CJEU to securely anchor the principle of solidarity in EU constitutional law.[67] Similar problems exist in the field of labour law. Recently, Julia López López examined the challenges related to the enforceability of solidarity in a labour law context and pointed to the opportunities created by linking solidarity to equality and opting for an inclusive solidarity as happened in the EU's response to the pandemic.[68] Karine Adberemane has also noted, rightly, that manifold crises lead to a decrease in social liberties and the growth of inequalities – both of which call for a reinforcement of the principle of solidarity in EU law.[69]

Are the *Budget Conditionality* cases a step in that direction? Certainly, as in these cases, the CJEU relied explicitly on solidarity as a fundamental principle with normative force. The two cases, where Poland and Hungary turned against the Budget Conditionality Regulation,[70] allowed the CJEU to place the solidarity principle in the limelight of EU law in relation to the application of the rule of law based on Article 2 TEU.[71] As a consequence of this turn of events, we should then ask the following question: can and should CJEU judges use the principle of solidarity as a new narrative to protect social rights? As seen before, EU social fundamental rights are part of Title IV of the Charter, which is entitled 'Solidarity'. The preamble of the EU Charter considered the principle of solidarity to be among the 'foundational principles' of EU law. One of the proposed mottos of the EU during the making of the Constitutional Treaty was 'Peace, Liberty and Solidarity'. But what is the rightful place of the principle of solidarity in CJEU case law? Is it a legal principle? And perhaps more importantly: can it be used for what Georges Gurvich has called 'transpersonalism', i.e., a model that

65. Alain Supiot (ed.), *La Solidarité: Enquête Sur Un Principe Juridique* (Odile Jacob 2015).
66. Karine Abderemane, *Le mot solidarité en droit de l'Union européenne,* in *Solidarité et droit de l'Union européenne: un principe à l'épreuve* 28 (Rostane Mehdi & Nathalie Rubio eds, DICE Éditions 2021).
67. Supiot, *supra* n. 65.
68. Julia López López, *Inscribing Solidarity in Labor Law, Promise and Limitations,* in *Inscribing Solidarity, Debates in Labor Law and Beyond* (Julia López López ed., Cambridge University Press 2022).
69. Karine Abderemane refers to Alain Supiot, *Homo Juridicus, Essai sur la fonction anthropologique du droit* (Le seuil 2005) who also discusses the role of dignity (an integral part of Kantian philosophy) in abstracting from social realities by relying on ethics.
70. Regulation (EU, Euratom) 2020/2092 of the European Parliament and of the Council of 16 December 2020 on a general regime of conditionality for the protection of the Union budget, OJ L 433I, 22.12.2020.
71. *See* Cases C-156/21, *Hungary v. Parliament and Council*; C-157/21, *Poland v. Parliament and Council*, ECLI:EU:C:2022:98., para. 129.

goes beyond a 'dignity model' (which in fact constitutes a reflection of the liberal model)?

Alain Supiot's edited collection of interdisciplinary enquiries into the legal nature of the principle of solidarity makes it difficult to deny that solidarity is a legal principle.[72] His book traces the legal roots of the principle from Roman to French law in the context of collective creditors' responsibility and then describes the strong impact of Durkheimian sociology on the public-law theory of *État social,* which has marked French jurisprudence for generations.[73] In a similar vein, we also consider that solidarity in EU law is not only an elusive principle but also a legal and federative principle that EU law judges can rely on to develop the protection of social rights through the EU Charter of Fundamental Rights.[74] In practice, this could be done, for instance, by either referring more often to the principle of solidarity enshrined in Article 2 TEU or interpreting a situation falling within the scope of EU law and involving the application of the EU Charter in the light of Article 3(3) TEU. This provision, which concerns the objectives set up by EU law, clearly embodies a 'solidarity narrative' that could be used in adjudication related to the EU Charter – as the CJEU should have been done in the infamous *Mark-Alemo Herron* case.[75] The EU Charter and the CJEU case law do not need to reflect the fall of EU labour law and the degeneration of standards of social protection.[76] This is why it is important for the CJEU to apply the narrative of solidarity more extensively in its case law regarding the application of fundamental social rights enshrined in the EU Charter.

4 EPILOGUE: THE LAST WORD(S) FOR THE CRISIS

In evaluating the potential evolution of fundamental social rights, two options are possible: To look at the glass as half-empty or half-full. In the half-empty glass, it is impossible to deny that post-*Laval* CJEU case law such as *Mark-Alemo Herron* or the *TSN* doctrine has damaged the application of social rights. Chapter IV of the EU Charter of Fundamental Rights on solidarity remains an area of legal unclarity due to the presence of second-generation principles or rights that may never acquire a 'direct effect' status. As seen in the work of Jensen and Walton, the qualification of social rights as second-generation rights is also problematic. Moreover, the Charter has always been a contested document and has been so since the first discussions of the

72. Supiot, *supra* n. 65.
73. *See* Pierre Musso, *La Solidarité: Généalogie d'un Concept Sociologique*, in *La Solidarité: Enquête Sur Un Principe Juridique* 10 (Alain Supiot ed, Odile Jacob 2015) who traces the development of the concept of solidarity from its origins with August Comte in 1842; *see* Émile Durkheim, *De la division du travail social* 96–100 (Presses Universitaires de France 2013). *See* Musso, where he describes the theory of Durkheim as a reaction to liberalism.
74. *See* Eleni Karageorgiou, *Rethinking Solidarity in European Asylum Law: A Critical Reading of the Key Concept in Contemporary Refugee Policy* (Lund University 2018).
75. *See* Opinion of Advocate General Cruz Villalón in Case C-426/11, *Alemo-Herron and others,* 19.2.2013, ECLI:EU:C:2013:82 and the use of Art. 3(3) TEU.
76. *See* Stefano Giubonni, *The Rise and Fall of EU Labour Law,* European Law Journal (2018) https://doi.org/10.1111/eulj.12239.

Convention shaping the EU Charter at the end of the 1990s, when the UK representative refused to admit the existence of the concept of solidarity.[77]

In the half-full glass, we have seen that the European Pillar of Social Rights and the NextGenerationEU could push forward the application of social rights. New secondary legislation now on its way will stimulate the application of fundamental social rights. The case law of the CJEU has extended the scope of application of certain social rights and strengthened the application of the doctrine of horizontal direct effect. The Budget Conditionality cases issued last year considered the principle of solidarity to be a 'fundamental principle' of EU law. Solidarity is not only an elusive principle but also a legal and federal principle that may be used to counterbalance liberal claims and effect a shift of priorities in EU integration towards a more social values-based approach. Perhaps even more importantly, solidarity as a concept is now on the academic agenda in EU law and international law. New studies show the 'foundational nature' of this principle and consider that, from a historical perspective, social rights are perhaps not second-generation rights.

Nevertheless, the final words here would depend on the crisis. Specifically, it is impossible to ignore the poly-crisis context. The financial or economic crisis was the most damaging crisis for fundamental social rights. Many studies have shown its venomous impact on the application of social rights in EU law. At the same time, researchers have been pointing to the regenerated potential of social rights in the context of the Covid crisis. A new crisis of the first type (economic) will surely be disastrous for the blooming of fundamental social rights in Europe – and unfortunately, we are not far from it.[78] The crisis will have the last word.

77. Supiot, *supra* n. 65, at 9. Interestingly, he refers to an anecdote of Guy Braibant – the French member of the Convention drafting the EU Charter – who reported that the English delegate considered that the notion of solidarity, in its continental sense, was in fact unknown in the UK.
78. Klaus Tuori & Fernando Losada, *The Emergence of the New Over-Riding Objective of Financial Stability*, in *Social Rights and the European Monetary Union: Challenges Ahead* (Maribel González Pascual & Aida Torres Pérez eds, Edward Elgar Publishing 2022); Klaus Tuori & Fernando Losada, *Integrating Macroeconomics into the EU Single Legal Order: The Role of Financial Stability in Post-Crisis Europe*, 6 European Papers 1367.

Part III Dynamics in Non-discrimination and Employment Protection

CHAPTER 5

Strategic Litigation, Discrimination Law, and Older Workers

Jenny Julén Votinius[*]

1 INTRODUCTION

Strategic litigation is a method to push legal development within a field by bringing cases to court with the aim of achieving far-reaching legal, policy, and societal changes that extend beyond the specifics of the case at hand. In the past few years, increasing interest in and promotion of strategic litigation in the field of discrimination law has been noted among EU-level institutions and organisations, and to a varying degree, the same development is visible at the national level – though many EU Member States can be described as typically non-litigious and lacking a strong tradition of political lawyering.

The chapter explores this increased turn to strategic litigation in discrimination law in the EU and the Member States, with Sweden as the main national example. In relation to discrimination law in general and with a particular focus on the outcomes for older workers, the chapter analyses and discusses the implications of an increasing use of courts by EU equality bodies and interest groups to enforce political demands for social change based on supranational rules on fundamental and human rights.

The apparent success stories in court, the chapter argues, call for a deeper analysis of effects primarily relating to the transference of powers from national level to supranational level and to the growing emphasis on interest groups. These effects are important for the legitimacy of discrimination law in general, and they are particularly relevant in terms of protection against discrimination of older workers.

* This research is carried out within the research project 'Prolonged Working Lives, Older Workers, and Dismissals', funded by the Swedish Research Council for Health, Working Life, and Welfare (*Forte*). The research project has received ethical approval by the Swedish Ethical Review Authority (dnr 2021-05026).

2 STRATEGIC LITIGATION IN THE FIELD OF NON-DISCRIMINATION IN THE EU

2.1 Introduction

Because litigation is a strategic activity, 'strategic litigation' might seem like a tautological concept. However, the term does not refer to clever lawyering in general but to litigation that is pursued as part of a *broader strategy* to bring about substantive changes for a particular group in society or in a particular area. The changes may stem from the actual judgment in the case or from subsequent legislation or policy, but they can also take the form of increased public attention to the issue and modifications of public attitudes. Strategic litigation has been described as the 'continuation of politics by other means' to obtain legal change that legislative and executive organs of democratic governance are unable or unwilling to realise.[1]

Since the early 1900s, strategic litigation has been applied mainly in the US and later in the UK to push societal transformation by challenging legal boundaries.[2] Early and well-known cases brought by the US civil-rights movement include *Brown v. Board of Education* (1954), which led the US Supreme Court to rule out the racial segregation of students under the separate-but-equal doctrine, and the recently overturned *Roe v. Wade* (1973), which recognises the right to abortion.[3] Another landmark case resulting from strategic litigation is *Grant v. South-West Trains Ltd* (1996), litigated by the British Stonewall Lobby Group (today Stonewall Equality) to achieve equal rights for same-sex couples.[4] Although the plaintiff did not win the case, it was considered a success because it eventually led to the adoption of new and improved legislation.[5] Over the years, a number of cases have proved that strategic litigation has the potential to be very successful in inciting development towards broad legal and policy changes. Interest groups and advocates in many countries have applied strategic litigation to pursue a variety of matters, including basic health care for citizens, equal rights for minorities, and the theme of this chapter: non-discrimination.

In pursuing strategic litigation, supranational rules safeguarding and promoting fundamental and human rights provide powerful resources. In the European context, these resources consist primarily of EU law and the accompanying exclusive jurisdiction of the European Court of Justice on the one hand and the conventions and bodies under the Council of Europe on the other hand, including the exclusive jurisdiction of the European Court of Human Rights.[6] In the following, EU law is the focus. Nevertheless, it should be stressed that many examples of successful strategic litigation

1. Aidan O'Neill, *Strategic Litigation Before the European Courts*, ERA Forum 16, 495–509 (2015).
2. Emily Zackin, *Popular Constitutionalism's Hard When You're Not Very Popular: Why the ACLU Turned to Courts*, 42 Law & Society Review 2 (2008) https://doi.org/10.18574/nyu/9780814789339.003.0011.
3. *Brown v. Board of Education*, 347 U.S. 483 (1954), *Roe v. Wade*, 410 U.S. 113 (1973).
4. Case C-249/96 *Grant v. South-West Trains Ltd* ECLI:EU:C:1998:63.
5. Lisa Vanhala, *Anti-discrimination Policy Actors and Their Use of Litigation Strategies: The Influence of Identity Politics*, 16(5) Journal of European Public Policy 738–754, 751 (2009) https://doi.org/10.1080/13501760902983473.
6. *See* Birgitta Nyström's chapter in this book.

from the 1980s and onwards can be found in discrimination cases before the European Court of Human Rights, including cases brought by the disability movement, the gay movement and, more recently, organisations pushing for Roma rights.[7]

As for litigation before the European Court of Justice, there is a possibility under Article 263 TFEU for individuals to bring action directly before the Court in matters relating to the legality of EU law. Because this provision has proved to be very limited in scope, it does not normally provide a useful route for strategic litigation for organisations, although it is possible in some cases. An organisation can also join an action in these matters brought by a Member State. It is far more common to see cases concerning the conformity of national law with EU law.[8] Here, the procedural rules do not allow individuals to bring action directly before the European Court of Justice. Instead, action must be brought before a national court, claiming that national law or its application contravenes EU law and requesting the national court to refer the case to the European Court of Justice for a preliminary ruling under Article 267 TFEU.

In the development of EU discrimination law, the role of strategically litigated cases cannot be overstated. Some of the earliest examples are the preliminary rulings in the well-known *Defrenne* cases on equal pay between men and women, designed and initiated by the lawyer, academic, and feminist activist Eliane Vogel-Polsky and brought against Belgium for failure to implement Article 157 (former Article 119) of the TEFU.[9] These cases were the first in a long line of cases that have contributed to the development and expansion of EU gender equality policy since the 1970s.[10] Some years later, numerous strategically litigated cases concerning other grounds of discrimination emerged, including *Coleman*[11] on the ground of disability, *Bougnaoui*[12] on the ground of ethnicity, and *Asociaţia Accept*[13] on discrimination on the ground of sexual orientation.

With regard to older workers, one case stands out in terms of strategic litigation. This is the controversial 2005 *Mangold*[14] case, which was the first to address the matter of age discrimination. The litigant was a lawyer who had previously sought to resist the introduction of a particular national law on fixed-term employment for people over the

7. Oliver Lewis, *Advancing Legal Capacity Jurisprudence*, 6 European Human Rights Law Review 700–714 (2011); Marion Guerrero, *Lawyering for LGBT Rights in Europe. The Emancipatory Potential of Strategic Litigation at the CJEU and the ECtHR* (EUI 2018).
8. Takis Tridimas, *Knocking on Heaven's Door: Fragmentation, Efficiency and Defiance in the Preliminary Reference Procedure*, 40 Common Market Law Review, 1, 9-50 (2003) https://doi.org/10.54648/5115417.
9. Cases C-80/70 *(Defrenne I)* ECLI:EU:C:1971:55, C-43/75 *(Defrenne II)* ECLI:EU:C:1976:56 and C-149/77 *(Defrenne III)* ECLI:EU:C:1978:130.
10. Elise Muir, *Anti-discrimination Law as a Laboratory for EU Governance of Fundamental Rights at the Domestic Level: Collective Actors as Bridging Devices*, in Elise Muir, Claire Kilpatrick, Jeffrey Miller & Bruno De Witte (eds), *How EU Law Shapes Opportunities for Preliminary References on Fundamental Rights: Discrimination, Data Protection and Asylum* (EUI 2017); Konstantinos Alexandris Polomarkakis, *Gendered Capital and Litigants in EU Equality Case-Law*, 85 Modern Law Review 1387–1418, 1396 (2022) https://doi.org/10.1111/1468-2230.12745.
11. Case C-303/06, *Coleman*, ECLI:EU:C:2008:415. Cf., Jeffrey A. Miller, *Peering Inside the Preliminary Reference Box: Coleman v. Attridge Law*, 6(3) European Papers 1553–1574 (2021).
12. Case C-188/15, *Bougnaoui*, ECLI:EU:C:2017:204.
13. Case C-81/12, *Asociaţia Accept* ECLI:EU:C:2013:275. Cf., Guerrero (2018), *supra* n. 7, 235.
14. Case C-144/04, *Mangold* ECLI:EU:C:2005:709, para. 78.

age of 52 on the grounds that it was discriminatory on grounds of age. After the law went into effect, the litigant decided to challenge it in court. Under the new national rules, he hired another lawyer, Mr Mangold, whom he then represented in a case to overturn the national rules for being age discriminatory and therefore contrary to EU law. A prohibition against age discrimination in statutory EU law had been introduced through the Framework Directive 2000/278/EC. At the time of the *Mangold* case, the Directive had not been transposed into national legislation and the transposition period had not expired. It was thus not possible for the CJEU to base its judgment directly on this Directive, which was the only apparent legal basis for rejecting the national legislation in this case. However, quite surprisingly and partly in line with what the national judge had argued, the CJEU referred to a general principle of equality in EU law that included a right to non-discrimination on grounds of age, and to which the Framework Directive 2000/78/EC merely gave specific expression. In practice, the judgment gave a direct horizontal effect to the prohibition against age discrimination in the Directive. The *Mangold* case has been further developed by the CJEU in subsequent cases, most importantly *Kücükdeveci* and later *Dansk Industri*, both emphasising the direct horizontal effect of the prohibition against age discrimination.[15]

2.2 The Ideas and Practices of Strategic Litigation

The detailed definition of strategic litigation and its key components varies slightly depending on the contexts addressing and promoting this practice. Nevertheless, the overall architecture and the logic of the working process are the same. Starting from the matter that the actor wants to address, the first step is to frame the matter as a problem within the legal order in which one intends to litigate. For European lawyers who find national law insufficient, the legal order would be EU law or the conventions of the Council of Europe. Next, the task is to search and select a suitable case. A suitable case must present the legal problem in a convincing way. The facts of the case should be undisputed to avoid excessive focus on the facts instead of the legal matter to be pursued.[16] Ideally, the case should also possess traits that will invoke sympathy. As put in a handbook on strategic litigation produced a few years ago by the European Network of Equality Bodies, Equinet, the case should have a strong moral dimension where a court or the media is likely to find it reasonable to condemn the perpetrator of discrimination, in support of the victim.[17] In parallel with the legal work, and to achieve maximum output of the case, strategic litigation normally also involves a considerable amount of media contacts and public relations directed to the wider community and aimed to gain public support for the cause.

The search for a suitable case is key for the outcome of any strategic litigation activities. The case can arise from an applicant asking for legal advice on the specific

15. Cases C-555/07 *Kücükdeveci* ECR I-365 and C-441/14, *Dansk Industri* ECLI:EU:C:2016:278.
16. Helsinki Foundation for Human Rights, *Strategic Litigation in the Area of Human Rights Proceedings Before the Court of Justice of the European Union. A Guidebook for Non-governmental Organisations and Human Rights Defenders* 10 (2019).
17. Equinet, *The Equinet Handbook on Strategic Litigation* 18 (2017).

matter that the litigating actor has chosen to pursue. However, many times, it is the attentive lawyer who finds a particular case well suited to pursuing the target matter, though the applicant has sought redress for a very different problem. Apart from cases stemming from individual complaints, the search for cases can be directed towards external sources such as the media, independent lawyers, and public entities.[18] Ultimately, as in the *Mangold* case described above, it could also be that the lawyer actively construes a case by detecting a potential claimant and asking for permission to bring a case on their behalf.[19]

Once a suitable case has been identified, the detailed litigation must be planned in a persuasive way; the litigation must 'sell' the particular outcome as attractive to the court.[20] It is considered crucial for the litigator to demonstrate, clearly and convincingly, how the legal arguments can be applied to justify the desired outcome, and the legal argument should be supported as far as possible with reference to expertise.[21] If the aim is to reach for a reference to the European Court of Justice for a preliminary ruling, this selling approach includes the drafting of the questions to be submitted by the national court.[22] In convincing the national court to make such a referral, substantial and detailed knowledge of EU and European law is crucial. As been highlighted in scholarship, strategic litigation aiming towards the European Court of Justice is and has long been pursued by lawyers who are often more knowledgeable and specialised in EU law than the national judges themselves.[23]

2.3 Strategic Litigation in Today's EU and Recent Policy Developments

Although strategic litigation represents a long-standing and strong tradition in the European supranational legal context in terms of non-discrimination, this practice has been highlighted and advocated in recent years at EU level in a systematically supportive manner. A 2020 report from the European Commission's Network of Experts on Gender Equality maps the preconditions for strategic litigation in the EU Member States in the area of sex discrimination. Providing several policy proposals to support the emergence of strategic litigation, the report presents numerous ways in which stakeholders can participate in these activities, in the capacity of funders or initiators, or in terms of advocacy and training, and by bringing actual processes to court.[24] The report shows that, in many Member States, the national equality body has become an important agent in promoting and implementing strategic litigation in discrimination cases. Equinet, the European Network of Equality Bodies, provides a

18. *Ibid.*, 36.
19. Tommaso Pavone, *The Ghostwriters: Lawyers and the Politics Behind the Judicial Construction of Europe* (Cambridge University Press 2022).
20. Equinet (2017), *supra* n. 17, 20.
21. A list of indicators to provide anchor points for activist interventions can be found in Guerrero (2018), *supra* n. 7, 440. Equinet (2017), *supra* n. 17, 20 underlines that the desired outcome should be one that the court can easily reach.
22. Helsinki Foundation (2019), *supra* n. 16, 10. Drafting of submissions and even rulings have been important in landmark strategic litigation cases before the CJEU, Pavone (2022), *supra* n. 19.
23. Pavone (2022), *supra* n. 19.
24. Guerrero (2018), *supra* n. 7, 440.

platform for support and exchange of best practices and resources; in recent years, this organisation has carried out substantive internal work to increase the strategic litigation competence of its network members – i.e., national equality bodies. One output of these activities is the abovementioned handbook for strategic litigation, co-funded by the European Commission. The handbook, which defines strategic litigation as aiming to have a wider impact on law and society beyond those involved in an individual case, deals with the underpinning principles of this method, the selection of cases, possible risks and, not least, the importance of public relations and media communication in helping the litigation case to realise full dividends.[25]

Equinet's work and handbook for strategic litigation are in line with recent policy and legislative documents, which stress the role of national equality bodies in this development. For instance, in the EU anti-racism action plan 2020–2025, the European Commission encourages enabling of strategic litigation activities at national level and defines such activities as key for the protection of human rights.[26] The pending proposed directives on standards for equality bodies specifically mention the pursuit of strategic litigation before national courts in order to contribute to the proper interpretation and application of equal-treatment legislation.[27]

Other than equality bodies, which are independent public institutions and thus state actors, important agents of strategic litigation are those who were the first to promote this method: independent advocacy organisations and interest groups – non-state actors. While such organisations or groups have successfully used strategic litigation for a long time in relation to some grounds of discrimination, primarily disability and sexual orientation, stakeholders in a variety of fields are now working to increase and improve more systematic use of strategic litigation way.[28] This trend, which can be seen in many parts of the world and is not specific to Europe and the EU, has been described as a remarkable transnational movement anchored in a globalised legal order, where activists can seek to pursue legal and social change in various ways through courts at the domestic, regional, or international level.[29] At the European level, in recent years, numerous organisations, interest groups, networks, and law clinics have organised activities and published documents on strategic litigation to promote fundamental rights and have done so not only in relation to the specific area of discrimination but also in other areas of law.[30] Many of these initiatives have been funded or partly funded by the European Commission.

---

25. Equinet (2017), *supra* n. 17, 18.
26. COM (2020) 565 final, 4.
27. COM (2022) 688 final and COM (2022) 689 final.
28. Lisa Vanhala, *Fighting Discrimination Through Litigation in the UK: The Social Model of Disability and the EU Anti-discrimination Directive*, 21(5) Disability & Society 551–565 (2006) https://doi.org/10.1080/09687590600786801. Guerrero (2018), *supra* n. 7. European Roma Rights Centre, Interights and Migration Policy Group, *Strategic Litigation of Race Discrimination in Europe from Principles to Practice* (2004); Children's Rights Information Network, *Children's Rights: A Guide to Strategic Litigation* (2009).
29. Paul Lappalainen, *The Transformation of EU Equality Law: From a Common Market Issue to a Fundamental Right*, 1 Europarättslig Tidskrift 89–112 (2021); Michael Ramsden & Kris Gledhill, *Defining Strategic Litigation*, Civil Justice Quarterly 38, 31 (2019).
30. For instance, ETUC Resolution on ETUC human rights, legal and strategic litigation network: ETUCLEX, October 2020; Helsinki Foundation (2019), *supra* n. 16. Cf., the International

In the terminology of the European Commission, the previously used term 'interest groups' has been gradually replaced by 'civil society organisations' or CSOs.[31] The terminological difference is linked to two different conceptual framing processes, where the term 'civil society organisations', on the one hand, emphasises democracy, participation, citizens, the connection between citizens and governmental institutions, and working 'with the state', often in participatory and deliberative democratic frameworks, whereas the term 'interest groups', on the other hand, belongs to a set of ideas emphasising influence, aggregation of interests, and political advocacy.[32] In the following, the term 'interest groups' is used because this term appears to be most suitable given the theme of the chapter. However, the term 'civil society organisations' is applied when referring to content in documents from the European Commission.

Since the late 1990s and increasingly, the European Commission has included interest groups in various stages of the governance process and at the same time has directed substantial financial support to them.[33] One theme for funding measures has been the exploration and promotion of strategic litigation. For instance, in 2021, the European Commission launched a call for projects on the EU Charter and strategic litigation for civil society organisations, National Human Rights Institutions, Equality Bodies and Ombuds Institutions, identifying strategic litigators as key to fostering the promotion and protection of Charter rights. One of the two key aims of the call is to promote activities on strategic litigation by strengthening the knowledge and ability of practitioners, legal professionals, civil society organisations, and independent human rights bodies to engage effectively in litigation practices at national and European levels.[34] Along the same lines, the Commission launched an action grant in 2023 directed to support the development by organisations and equality bodies of strategic litigation involving rights enshrined in the Charter.[35] These calls do not define strategic litigation but do specify expected project impacts to include increased awareness, improved knowledge, and better use of the Charter by both rights holders and actors at all levels in and across the Member States; improved cooperation between actors; and increased litigation capabilities of actors, including the ability to bring strategic litigation cases before national courts and the European Court of Justice.

Commission of Jurists ICJ project Rule of Law for Lawyers on recommendations on strategic litigation for practitioners in the EU.

31. Beate Kohler-Koch & Barbara Finke, *The Institutional Shaping of EU–Society Relations: A Contribution to Democracy via Participation?*, 3(3) Journal of Civil Society 205–221 (2007) https://doi.org/10.1080/17448680701775630.
32. Jonas Schoenefeld, *Interest Groups, NGOs or Civil Society Organisations? The Framing of Non-state Actors in the EU*, 32 International Journal of Voluntary and Nonprofit Organizations 3 (2020) https://doi.org/10.1007/s11266-020-00283-w.
33. European Commission, *European Governance: A White Paper* COM (2001) 428; Sabine Saurugger, *The Social Construction of the Participatory Turn: The Emergence of a Norm in the European Union*, 49 European Journal of Political Research 471–495 (2010) https://doi.org/10.1111/j.1475-6765.2009.01905.x.
34. *Promote capacity-building and awareness on the EU Charter of Fundamental Rights and activities on strategic litigation relating to democracy, the rule of law and fundamental rights breaches* (CERV-2022-CHAR-LITI), CERV-2022, CERV-PJG CERV Project Grants.
35. *Promote civil society organisations' awareness of capacity building and implementation of the EU Charter of Fundamental Rights* (CERV-2023-CHAR-LITI).

The increased focus in the EU on promoting strategic litigation for the development and enforcement of non-discrimination law has the potential to play out very differently in different Member States, depending on aspects such as the previous occurrence of strategic litigation, the structure of the procedural system, and the commitment to this development among equality bodies, interest groups, and other stakeholders.[36] In the following, some of these nationally specific aspects will be discussed from the Swedish perspective.

3 STRATEGIC LITIGATION IN THE FIELD OF NON-DISCRIMINATION IN SWEDEN

3.1 Introduction

In 2021, a speaker at a conference of the European equality bodies and national human rights institutions presented a conceptual guiding model for successful strategic litigation, in which the core approach was to consider the case a vehicle for bringing the right questions to the court and the desired outcome as something to be sold to the judges. Consequently, the speaker stressed, the case must be chosen wisely and of reasonable scope, and the outcome should be 'chewable, digestible, and preferably palatable'.[37] The person behind these colourful metaphors was the former head of litigation at the Swedish Equality Ombudsman. The wording represents an approach to litigation that is atypical in the Swedish legal setting and particularly unusual for a representative of a public administrative authority. After all, though, the field of non-discrimination does stand out as slightly different. Strategic litigation has been present in this arena to some extent and during the last decade, albeit still on a very limited scale, in gradually more pronounced and elaborated forms. This development will be discussed below.

In Sweden, litigious activity is not usually seen as a route to social change. Traditionally, the division of governance functions means that the role of the courts is to interpret and apply the laws enacted by the legislator.[38] This is an embodiment of the principle of government by the people and the democratic principle that underpins the entire system of government.[39] Sweden has no constitutional court; instead, every court has a responsibility to assess whether a provision may be applied.[40] Compliance with international-law obligations has traditionally been considered to be primarily the responsibility of the legislator, through the drafting of legislation in accordance with

36. Cf., Marion Guerrero, *Strategic Litigation in EU Gender Equality Law, European Network of Legal Experts in Gender Equality and Non-discrimination* (Publications Office of the European Union 2020).
37. European Union Agency for Fundamental Rights FRA, European Network of Equality Bodies EQUINET, European Network of National Human Rights Institutions ENNHR, *Your Key Take-aways, Virtual Seminar on the Role of the Charter of Fundamental Rights of the European Union in the Work of Equality Bodies and National Human Rights Institutions 20–22 October 2021*, 13.
38. Marlene Wind & Andreas Føllesdal, *Nordic Reluctance Towards Judicial Review under Siege*, 2 Nordic J Hum Rights 131–141 (2009).
39. Chapter 1, section 1 of the Instrument of Government (1974:152).
40. Chapter 11, section 14 of the Instrument of Government (1974:152).

international standards. The role of the courts has gradually changed, most significantly since the mid-1990s following the Europeanisation process, but in fact, the substantive changes are still limited to situations where Swedish law must be interpreted in line with European law.[41] This development has been accompanied by debates about the democratic consequences of the shift in power from the legislator to the courts, which are not elected by the people.[42]

In similarity with that which applies in the other Nordic countries, the Swedish justice system is characterised by the search for pragmatic solutions and many out-of-court dispute-resolution mechanisms.[43] The procedural-law system encourages settlements, and there is a legal obligation for the courts to strive for such settlements.[44] In labour law disputes, where the trade union normally represents the employee, the completion of grievance negotiations is a requirement for the case to be brought before the Swedish Labour Court. The Swedish industrial-relations model is characterised by autonomous social partners, a high degree of unionisation, and virtually no state intervention. The mechanisms for preventing and resolving labour disputes are an important component of this model. The Swedish Labour Court is a joint body where the majority of the members are representatives of the social partners. However, the overwhelming majority of all labour disputes are resolved in grievance negotiations and thus never reach the Swedish Labour Court.[45]

Work and employment constitute an important area for discrimination law. The early laws prohibiting discrimination on various separate grounds first exclusively – and later mainly – covered working life.[46] The Equality Ombudsman has a mandate to represent individuals in cases concerning discrimination, but in labour disputes, this

41. Jaakko Husa, *Constitutional Mentality*, in Ditlev Tamm, Pia Letto-Vanamo & Bent Ole Gram Mortensen (eds), *Nordic Law in European Context* 41–60 (Springer 2019); Laura Ervo, *Culture and Mentality in East-Nordic Courts*, in Laura Ervo, Pia Letto-Vanamo & Anna Nylund (eds), *Rethinking Nordic Courts* 101 (Springer 2021). In the same book, *see also* Anna Nylund, *Europeanisation of Nordic Civil Procedure: Does the Map Match the Terrain?.*

42. Thomas Bull, *Institutions and Divisions of* Power, in Helle Krunke & Björg Thorarensen (eds), *The Nordic Constitutions. A Comparative and Contextual Study* (Hart Publishing 2018); Martin Sunnqvist, *The Changing Role of Nordic Courts*, in Ervo, Letto-Vanamo & Nylund (2021), *supra* n. 41, 101.

43. Anna Nylund, *Institutional Aspects of the Nordic Justice Systems: Striving for Consolidation and* Settlements, in Ervo, Letto-Vanamo & Nylund (2021), *supra* n. 41, 188.

44. Chapter 42, section 7 of the Swedish Code of Judicial Procedure (1942:740). Cf., for instance, Government Bill prop. 2010/11:128, p. 23; Jenny Julén Votinius, *Sweden*, in Minawa Ebisui, Sean Cooney & Colin Fenwick (eds), *Resolving Individual Labour Disputes: A Comparative Overview* 249 (ILO 2016).

45. Chapter 4, section 7 of the Labour Disputes Act (1974:371). Around 70 % of the entire workforce are trade union members, although rate varies between sectors. For these employees, disputes are handled by the trade union. An estimated 90 %–98 % of all legal disputes subject to collective bargaining are resolved in grievance negotiations. Government Report SOU 2012:62 *Uppsägningstvister*, 74.

46. The first statute prohibiting discrimination applied in working life only, Act (1979:1118) on Equal Treatment Between Men and Women in Working Life, Government Bill prop. 1979/80:175. Later, non-discrimination acts were adopted on the grounds of sexual orientation and disability, in working life only, and ethnicity, in all areas of society with a particular emphasis on employment.

applies only when the trade union refrains from doing so.[47] In 1979, the then-titled Sex Equality Ombudsman was introduced; the social partners objected to this ombudsman being given legal standing in the Swedish Labor Court. The reform meant that a state actor was allowed into the labour-dispute resolution arena, which until then had been reserved for the social partners.[48] This situation also led to a further change, as the lawsuits brought by the Sex Equality Ombudsman also sparked a debate on the impartiality of the Swedish Labour Court in discrimination cases, which resulted in a change in the composition of the court: members of the social partners were no longer the majority in discrimination cases.[49]

3.2 Strategic Litigation Influencing the Work of the Swedish Equality Ombudsman

The debate on the Swedish Labour Court's impartiality in discrimination cases was fuelled not least by the so-called midwife cases, brought by the Sex Equality Ombudsman in 1996 and 2001.[50] These cases, transferred from the midwives' trade union to be used as pilot cases, contested collectively bargained pay differences between the female-dominated category of midwives and various male-dominated categories of workers; they are an early example of strategic litigation in the field of discrimination in the Swedish context. By bringing action, the authority aimed to eliminate the wage discrimination that it considered to be present and at the same clarify how work of equal value should be assessed - two objectives that clearly corresponded to the authority's role and mandate. However, it is clear from statements of the Sex Equality Ombudsman that the authority also had a more general strategic purpose with these cases: to draw attention to and come to terms with the lower wages in female-dominated sectors as a whole.[51] Although the plaintiff lost in these cases, the success in achieving a preliminary ruling from the European Court of Justice was an important output of the litigating activity.[52] So, also, were the national court rulings in two of these cases, in which compared work types were determined to be of equal value. The then-head of the Swedish Association of Health Professionals noted that the publicity surrounding the complaints increased public awareness of pay discrimination and

47. Chapter 3, sections 1-3 of the Labour Disputes Act (1974:371). The members are 8 neutral legal experts; 3 neutral persons with specialised knowledge of the labour market; and 14 representatives of the social partners. In the less common case, where the employee is not represented by a trade union, the case is brought before a local District Court under the Swedish Code of Judicial Procedure (1942:740).
48. Laura Carlson, *The Metamorphosis of Swedish Discrimination Law*, in Kerstin Ahlberg, Kent Källström, Jonas Malmberg & Michaël Koch (eds), *Vänbok till Ronnie Eklund* 94 (Iustus 2010).
49. *Legal Procedure in Discrimination Cases*, Debate in Lag & Avtal 2001-2002 (2002).
50. Swedish Labour Court cases AD 1996 No. 4; AD 2001 No. 13 (C-236/98) and AD 2001 No. 76.
51. Göteborgsposten 18 May 1994*'Gör lönediskrimineringen synlig' Nya JämO vill sätta jämställdhetslagen på prov i arbetsdomstolen*; Göteborgsposten 27 January 1997, *Jämo vill ha fler AD-domar*; Västerbottenskuriren 31 August 1998, *Nya processer mot lönediskriminering*.
52. Göteborgsposten 11 April 1996 *AD:s dom stoppar inte Jämo*.

influenced people's attitudes.[53] In retrospect, the former Sex Equality Ombudsman has noted that while the cases were pending in the Labour Court, Swedish midwives received pay increases that were higher than they had ever received previously.[54]

The replacement of the separate non-discrimination acts with the current Discrimination Act in 2008 meant that all grounds for discrimination were included in one law. Two new grounds for discrimination were also introduced, one of them being age. Supervision was assigned to a single authority, the Equality Ombudsman. In 2011, after an initial period of turbulence and criticism for lack of efficiency, a new Director was appointed for the authority. Shortly thereafter, the authority recruited an EU law specialist as head of litigation; many years later, this very same person would provide the abovementioned colourful metaphor about the mindset for successful strategic litigation. The change in management marked the start of a transformation process towards what the authority itself described as a more strategic approach to its work, aiming for a major impact on the development of society. From 2013 and with respect to litigation, this approach included a strategic selection procedure which focused on cases that had the potential to drive change.[55] The ambition was not to bring fewer cases – although that eventually became a result of the new approach – but to prioritise cases that could have a major impact and that could advance legal development.

In developing its working methods and increasing its competence, the Equality Ombudsman participates in various international networks. The most important of these is the Network of Equality Bodies in the EU, Equinet, which in recent years has engaged in developing and promoting strategic litigation, a project to which the Equality Ombudsman has contributed.[56] From 2015, and in parallel with its own internal reform process, the Equality Ombudsman was engaged in a thematic cluster within the Equinet that focused on strategic litigation in discrimination cases and contributed to training on strategic litigation and the authoring of a chapter in Equinet's 2018 handbook on strategic litigation.[57] At this point, the internal work to change the direction of the Equality Ombudsman's activities and methods had begun to pay off. In its annual report of 2019, the authority concluded that the process to develop strategic litigation had been fruitful: the Ombudsman had carried out increasingly sophisticated litigation activities and, generally, its work in litigation had indeed evolved strategically.[58]

In parallel, however, the Equality Ombudsman met with growing criticism from experts and interest groups. Later, under new management, the authority reconsidered

53. Eva Fernvall, *DN debatt: Vårdfacket tar avstånd från JämO: 'Jämställdhetslagen och Jämställdhetsombudsmannen är hinder i kampen mot lönediskriminering,* Dagens Nyheter 29 October 1997.
54. Ann Norrby, *Det behövs en särskild DO för arbetslivet,* Lag & Avtal 4 (2017).
55. Equality Ombudsman, *Annual Report 2012*. Cf., Government Report SOU 2016:87, 162, 168 and 183.
56. Equality Ombudsman, *Annual Report 2017*, 34 and *Annual Report 2018*, 36 which states that Equinet is prioritised in networking activities.
57. Equality Ombudsman, *Annual Reports 2016*, 25, *Annual Report 2017*, 34 and *Annual Report 2018*, 36. Equinet (2017), *supra* n. 17, 7.
58. Equality Ombudsman, *Annual Report 2019*, 57.

its approach, and in 2021, it largely abandoned this way of working.[59] The core of the criticism related to the profound shift in focus from supporting individuals by investigating individual complaints towards promotion and preventive work in the form of information and awareness-building, along with the issuing of decisions that are not legally binding; the result was that discriminated persons had almost no possibilities for redress.[60] A very visible effect was that the number of cases brought before a court by the Equality Ombudsman significantly decreased. The limited collection of cases concerned a few discrimination grounds, and age was not one of these. The Equality Ombudsman has not brought action in a case on age discrimination in employment since 2014.[61]

Given the criteria by which the cases were selected during this period, all cases brought by the Equality Ombudsman could be labelled to some extent as strategic cases. However, the strategic element related mainly to the selection of cases, in the sense that selection was made to match the strategy guiding the work of the authority – including a requirement that the case should be of relevance for a large group of persons and that it should relate to a matter that the authority had identified as relevant.[62] In contrast, there is one case that stands out more than any other as a more clear-cut instance of strategic litigation (although it was not related to working life and thus was not tried before the Swedish Labour Court): the *Braathens* case, involving a passenger who considered himself the subject of ethnic profiling when asked to leave an aircraft for an additional check before travelling on a domestic flight.

The case did not concern the incident as such; instead, it pinpointed a rule in Swedish procedural law which precludes the court from hearing private-law cases where the defendant has already agreed to pay the requested amount. The Equality Ombudsman had requested that the airline pay a very low compensation amount, which the airline accepted, and to admit discrimination on the grounds of ethnicity, which the airline refused to do. When bringing the case before the court for a declaratory judgment that discrimination had taken place, the Equality Ombudsman invoked EU law and asked for a referral to the European Court of Justice for a preliminary ruling; this request was accepted. The question was whether, in the light of Article 47 of the EU Charter of Fundamental Rights, the Racial Equality Directive 2000/43 should be interpreted as obliging national courts to examine whether discrimination has occurred if an alleged victim of discrimination requests this examination.

59. Equality Ombudsman, *Annual Report 2021*.
60. Lena Svenaeus, *Tio år med Diskrimineringsombudsmannen: En rapport om nedmontering av diskrimineringsskyddet* (Arena Idé 2020). Already in 2016, a governmental enquiry concluded that the authority should investigate, and settle, a greater number of complaints. This did not happen; indeed, the number decreased. Government Report SOU 2016:87 *Bättre skydd mot diskriminering*.
61. Swedish Labour Court AD 2015 No. 51.
62. Paul Lappalainen, *Country Report Non-discrimination Transposition and Implementation at National Level of Council Directives 2000/43 and 2000/78 Sweden, Reporting Period 1 January 2021–31 December 2021*, 81 (2022).

The European Court of Justice answered in the affirmative and stated that the Swedish procedural rules in question must be set aside.[63]

Recourse to supranational law is an important tool for strategic litigation in the field of discrimination. The most powerful outcome is a successful petition for a preliminary ruling from the European Court of Justice on the correct application of EU law. This path had already been applied in connection with the midwife cases brought by the Swedish Sex Equality Ombudsman in the mid-1990s.[64] In recent years, the Equality Ombudsman has requested a preliminary ruling in about half of the cases brought before national courts, but it was not granted until the *Braathens* case. In a pending disability discrimination case, the Equality Ombudsman refers to this case in reminding the District Court that it has to set national procedural law aside and rule on the case should the defendant agree to pay compensation but refuse to admit discrimination. This pending case was transferred to the Equality Ombudsman from an anti-discrimination agency, one of the non-state actors that litigate in parallel with the Equality Ombudsman (and trade unions) in the area of non-discrimination.[65]

3.3 Strategic Litigation in the Work of Non-state Actors in Sweden

Generally, strategic litigation is not primarily associated with public authorities but with the activities of interest groups seeking to advance their positions; this is how the method was launched and used in its early stages in the US and the UK. Comparative legal scholarship has described the Nordic legal tradition, to which Swedish law belongs, as based in a collectivist culture where the state has traditionally been seen positively, as in the service of the individuals and not as an enemy.[66] Excluding a few instances, there is no tradition in Sweden of interest groups that provide legal support to their members. Furthermore, as mentioned above, Sweden is not usually considered a litigious society. In line with this, Swedish non-state actors have normally not been litigation-based and have pursued their interests by other means, primarily directed towards influencing the legislative process and policy developments. As a rule, Swedish procedural law does not allow organisations to take the place of the actual party in a case. There are a few exceptions – mainly the abovementioned one concerning the standing of employee and employer organisations in labour disputes.

Another exception is the right of non-profit organisations to represent a claimant before courts in cases of discrimination, provided that the organisation can be considered 'suitable to represent the individual in the case, taking account of its

63. Case C-30/19 *Braathens* ECLI:EU:C:2021:269. In the final trial before the Swedish Supreme Court, the airline recognised discrimination to the extent required for the passenger's right to have the existence of the alleged discrimination examined and upheld by a court, according to the judgment of the Court of Justice of the European Union, Swedish Supreme Court judgment NJA 2021, p. 1093.
64. C-236/98 *Jämställdhetsombudsmannen* ECLI:EU:C:2000:173.
65. Equality Ombudsman, *Annual Report 2022*, 34.
66. Pia Letto-Vanamo & Ditlev Tamm, *Nordic Legal Mind*, in Ditlev Tamm, Pia Letto-Vanamo & Bent Ole Gram Mortensen (eds), *Nordic Law in European Context* 8 (Springer 2019); Helle Krunke & Björg Thorarensen, *Introduction*, in Krunke & Thorarensen (2018), *supra* n. 42, 7.

activities and its interest in the matter, its financial ability to bring an action and other circumstances'.[67] This right, which is subsidiary to that of a trade union, was introduced in 2008 partly with reference to the Europeanisation process and partly for pragmatic reasons. The preparatory works explain that the legal standing is meant for associations with genuine potential to assist individuals to the same extent as the Equality Ombudsman or an employee organisation. The preparatory works specifically emphasise that this right was not introduced to enable many small associations to join forces in bringing cases to court. For this reason, an individual can be represented by only one organisation in the same case, and an organisation cannot act as a party alongside the Equality Ombudsman or a trade union.[68]

Among the few non-profit organisations that provide legal counselling and support in matters regarding discrimination, the local anti-discrimination agencies are of special importance. Established and operated by local interest groups and non-governmental organisations, they are funded mainly through state subsidies along with contributions from municipalities and the involved organisations.[69] They offer advice and assistance to victims of discrimination and collaborate with each other as well as with the Equality Ombudsman. Only a few of these agencies engage in litigation themselves, owing to a combination of the financial risks involved and a lack of legal resources. Nevertheless, the number of cases brought by anti-discrimination agencies is slowly increasing.[70]

In terms of strategic litigation, there are even fewer independent actors. Non-state actors can influence and initiate strategic litigation cases brought by the Equality Ombudsman, thus without necessarily having to litigate the cases themselves. This has happened on some occasions, although the Equality Ombudsman has also been criticised for failing to make sufficient use of this opportunity to identify strategic complaints.[71] A pioneer in strategic litigation in Sweden is the Centrum för Rättvisa (Center for Justice), a public-interest law firm formed in the early 2000s to follow the American example of strengthening the protection of constitutional rights and freedoms through litigation in order to establish precedents. It has assisted, negotiated, and litigated in numerous cases on fundamental rights, including freedom of association and protection of property rights, but also in cases on equal treatment, where the latter mainly has concerned the use of unlawful application of quotas in education and working life.[72]

67. Chapter 6, section 2 of the Discrimination Act (2008:567).
68. Government Bill prop 2007:568 *Ett starkare skydd mot diskriminering*, 441.
69. Ordinance (2002:989) on State subsidies for organisations preventing and counteracting discrimination.
70. Paul Lappalainen, *The Role of Civil Society Advocacy in Equality Law: Lessons for the Nordics*, Scandinavian Studies in Law 451, 487 (2022).
71. Emma Lantschner, *Strategic Litigation: Equality Bodies' Strategic Use of Powers to Enforce Discrimination Law*, European Quality Law Review 1, 8 (2020). Cf., Aude Lejeune, *Litigating with or Against Other Groups? The Influence of Inter-organisational Relations on Legal Mobilisation in Europe*, 18 Comparative European Politics 840–857 (2020) https://doi.org/10.1057/s41295-020-00212-7.
72. Swedish Supreme Court Judgment NJA 2006, p. 683.

In 2012, RFSL – Sweden's largest sexual-identity and -orientation organisation – litigated successfully against the previous requirement of sterilisation for those who want to change their legal gender.[73] The requirement was abolished by the introduction of new legislation, following a ruling of the Administrative Court of Appeal that the requirement contravened both the Swedish Constitution and Articles 8 and 14 of the European Convention on Human Rights.[74] This case belongs to the field of non-discrimination but was outside the scope of the Discrimination Act. More recently, strategic litigation has been pushed within the Swedish disability movement, where the majority of the organisations are not engaged in litigation; the Disability Rights Defenders Association is an exception. Among other cases, this group assisted in the submission of an individual communication in 2018 to the UN Committee on the Rights of Persons with Disabilities. The case concerned reasonable accommodation and had previously been brought, and lost, by the Equality Ombudsman before the Swedish Labour Court. The Committee found a violation of the UN Convention on the Rights of Persons with Disabilities (CRPD) not only in terms of denial of the accommodation but also in the sense that the Equality Ombudsman should have considered other possible accommodation measures than the one requested, thus allowing the Labour Court to rule on those as well.[75] In 2022, the organisation brought three other cases before the Committee on reasonable accommodation of students with a disability in school exams.[76] These cases are still pending.

There are thus examples of strategic litigation activities from non-state actors in Sweden. Though still only a few, these cases have increased awareness of strategic litigation internationally, and in Europe they have also influenced organisations in Sweden, and it has been suggested that the role of interest groups and other non-state actors is slowly changing.[77]

4 RISKS, STRATEGIC LITIGATION, DISCRIMINATION LAW, AND OLDER WORKERS

4.1 Introduction

If used in a systematic way in the EU Member States, strategic litigation could make a difference in relation to key matters and thus induce advancements of certain positions in the field of non-discrimination. At the same time, as is the case with any powerful tool, strategic litigation activities entail certain risks. Educational and awareness-raising literature on strategic litigation emphasises that it must be used with discernment. The risks mentioned here relate both to the emotional and financial well-being of the client and, perhaps most significantly, to the strategic interest that the case is

73. Swedish Federation for Lesbian, Gay, Bisexual, Transgender, Queer and Intersex Rights, RFSL.
74. Stockholm Administrative Court of Appeal, Judgment 20 December 2012, Case 1968-12. Act (2013:405) amending Act (1972:119) concerning recognition of gender in certain cases.
75. *Sahlin v. Sweden* CRPD/C/23/D/45/2018 (2020). Swedish Labour Court judgment AD 2017 No. 51.
76. Pending cases 98/2022 *Sweden* CRPD-4, CRPD-5, CRPD-24.
77. Lappalainen, *The Role* (2022); Lappalainen, *Country Report* 81 (2022).

intended to serve. In the latter case, risks include negative publicity along with the incitement of undesired changes of the law, either because of the outcome in the court or ensuing legislative changes.[78]

In relation to the recent developments, where EU-level institutions and organisations push for strategic litigation in discrimination cases, it is not enough to consider the possible downsides of strategic litigation from the individual and grassroots perspectives. The policies and measures to promote an increased use of strategic litigation in the EU context also raise concerns of a different and more transversal character related to discrimination law on a broader scale. The following section takes this broader perspective when viewing the turn to strategic litigation. It first discusses legitimacy aspects in relation to discrimination law in general and then explores some concrete considerations regarding the increased weight attributed to activist lawyering, particularly when it comes to the protection of older workers.

4.2 The Legitimacy of Non-discrimination Law at Risk

The abovementioned risk of decreasing support following negative publicity in relation to strategic litigation is commonly framed as a risk for the movement in question. However, at least in the long run, strategic litigation activities may result as well in decreased support for or trust in the law in that field. Recourse to law for socio-political or other reasons beyond simply seeking justice in an individual case always runs the risk of being considered a misuse of the legal system. Should this risk materialise, the case may not only spark a broader political and social backlash against the movement pursuing the lawsuit; in the end, it can also undermine the legitimacy of the very law that allows itself to be used for wider purposes, for instance, in the case of discrimination law.

The great majority of the European Court of Justice milestone cases in the area of non-discrimination were initiated, designed, and litigated in the national courts by organisations advocating in the interests of particular groups.[79] What makes the recent development different is that it is driven not only by the interest groups themselves but also, to a large extent, by the EU institutions. Here, notably, strategic litigation has historically played a prominent role in the development and expansion of EU law through the law-making of the European Court of Justice. In a substantial number of court cases, including some of the most famous ones, litigators have brought action with the specific aim of increasing the scope of EU law.[80] Many of these consciously designed cases were built on provisions protecting fundamental rights, including the right to non-discrimination.

With strategic litigation now gaining ground as an important component of a more comprehensive governing approach to the enforcement of EU discrimination policy, considerations arise relating to the division of powers between the EU and the Member States. Every strategically litigated case that ends up in the European Court of

78. Equinet (2017), *supra* n. 17; Helsinki Foundation (2019), *supra* n. 16.
79. Rachel Cichowski, *The European Court and Civil Society* (Cambridge University Press 2007).
80. Pavone (2022), *supra* n. 19.

Justice for a preliminary ruling has the potential to impact heavily on national law, but at the same time, the matter has an equally important function for EU law. These cases provide a platform for the European Court of Justice to interpret, develop, clarify, and sometimes expand on the detailed content of EU law and thus also to establish its superiority.

The recent *Braathens* case illustrates how strategic litigation can incite a transfer of legal competence from the Member States to the EU level. In this case, the European Court of Justice deviated from its established case law, which emphasised the procedural autonomy of the Member States in cases where secondary EU legislation does not exhaustively address a question of remedies.[81] It has been noted that while the *Braathens* ruling is based on Article 47 of the EU Charter of Fundamental Rights, this provision was invoked by the Court itself; it was mentioned only in passing in the national court's request for a preliminary ruling. This has been seen as an indication that the European Court of Justice is actively seeking to increase the relevance of Article 47 of the Charter in equality law.[82] The ruling strengthened the bargaining power for persons alleging discrimination (because recognition of discrimination now can be requested at the risk of judicial review), but just as importantly, it also reduced the procedural autonomy of Member States to the benefit of the EU.

The current push from EU-level institutions and organisations for increased use of strategic litigation to enforce EU discrimination law should be considered in this context, so should also the risks associated with this development. To the extent that national and EU provisions to counteract discrimination appear to serve as a platform for a broader strategy to promote the interests of the European Union by generating legal proceedings before the European Court of Justice, this effort threatens to undermine the legitimacy of anti-discrimination legislation in Member States in the longer term.

More immediately, there is a concern related to the fact that the dispute-resolution systems in many EU Member States have a distinctly non-litigious character; in addition, virtually all the Member States lack a tradition of strategic litigation as a means to effect social change.[83] When the European Commission encourages the Member States to enable strategic litigation activities at national level and defines such activities as key for the protection of human rights, this is in practice a call for the promotion of an element that is not inherent in legal tradition and practice in these countries.[84] It is one thing to find examples of strategic litigation activities in all Member States, as we have seen in Sweden, and that these activities have at times been instrumental in strengthening protection against discrimination as well as other fundamental rights; it is quite another if Member States were required to specifically

81. Case C-33/76 *Rewe* ECLI:EU:C:1979:42, p. 5; case C-45/76 *Comet* BV ECLI:EU:C:1976:191.
82. Anna Wallerman Ghavanini, *Remedies for Non-material Damages: Striking Out in a New Direction? Braathens*, 59 Common Market Law Review 151–170 (2022) https://doi.org/10.54648/cola2022007. This conclusion is drawn in the light of two other recent rulings pointing in the same direction: case C-414/16 *Egenberger* ECLI:EU:C:2018:257 and case C-396/17 *Leitner* ECLI:EU:C:2019:375.
83. Guerrero (2020), *supra* n. 36.
84. COM (2020) 565 final, p. 4.

cultivate strategic litigation activities. This by extension would imply a state-driven expansion of the powers of the judiciary at the expense of the legislature and the executive. The court is neither elected by nor a representative of the people and cannot be removed by the people in the case of discontent; in countries with a different constitutional tradition, such a shift in power is likely to be perceived as undemocratic and could erode the legitimacy of discrimination law.

The fact that national equality bodies have a key role in the expansion of strategic litigation activities in the EU non-discrimination arena adds further to the complexity of the matter.[85] While interest-group activities in the courtrooms are distinctly and unmistakably rooted in a pursuit to defend the causes of their members, public administrative authorities are obliged to act objectively and impartially. An increased emphasis on strategic litigation by national equality bodies may well raise concerns in relation to these requirements. Strategic litigation involves a series of judicial and non-judicial decisions, for instance, in the search for and selection of cases that can generate good publicity and in the framing of the crucial matter in order to yield the desired results. These decisions – aimed at achieving the strategic objective – create the impression, right or wrong, that the litigant has already chosen a side long before the case reaches the court. This may pose a potential risk with respect to the legitimacy of discrimination law.

4.3 The Flip Side of Emphasising Group Interest and the Influence of Identity Politics

Activist and interest groups have historically played an important role in the development of EU equality policies and anti-discrimination legislation.[86] The function and importance of these groups in policy development within the European Union have long been formally recognised in governance documents, and the European Commission recently launched a proposal for a directive designed to strengthen civil society organisations and harmonise their regulation.[87] The involvement of interest groups has been repeatedly identified as key in developing a stable system of influence to boost the European integration process and provide expertise and information in certain fields. However, it has also been noted that these governance practices have bolstered the supranational stature of the European Commission.[88]

85. COM (2022) 688 final and COM (2022/689) final, and COM (2020) 565 final, p. 4.
86. *See*, for instance, Pieter Bouwen & Margaret McCown, *Lobbying Versus Litigation: Political and Legal Strategies of Interest Representation in the European Union*, 14 Journal of European Public Policy 3, 422–443 (2007) https://doi.org/10.1080/13501760701243798; Isabelle Chopin, *The Starting Line Group: A Harmonised Approach to Fight Racism and to Promote Equal Treatment*, 1 European Journal of Migration and Law, 111–129, 113 (1999).
87. European Commission, *Proposal for a Directive of the European Parliament and of the Council on European cross-border associations*, COM (2023) 516 final 2023/0315 (COD). Cf., European Commission, *'Europe 2020: A Strategy for Smart, Sustainable and Inclusive Growth'*, COM (2010) 2020 final.
88. Sophie Jacquot & Tommaso Vitale, *Law as a Weapon of the Weak? A Comparative Analysis of Legal Mobilization by Roma and Women's Groups at the European Level*, 21 Journal of European Public Policy 587 (2014) https://doi.org/10.1080/13501763.2014.887138.

While issues raised in the previous section – relating to subsidiarity and the ability of EU law to set aside national systems – are of a more general nature and apply to all areas of law, other concerns are of specific relevance in relation to political efforts to increase the use of strategic litigation to realise non-discrimination protection under EU law. One line of criticism from within the interest groups themselves has been that Commission-funded projects and partnerships in fact primarily target the interests and aims of the EU rather than those of the interest group or the ideas that they represent and that this tends to silence or limit the voices of the groups.[89] This is problematic: if certain EU interests outcompete the particular concerns of interest groups, this may ultimately weaken the protection for the individuals that these interest groups represent.

Another important point of criticism has been that while incentives and inclusionary measures for interest groups developed by the Commission have promoted and facilitated the activities of these groups, the measures have involved an element of external control with the effect of limiting whom the groups can and should represent, and thus creating divisions within communities.[90] This argument not only serves as a warning that political measures to cultivate grassroots movements can produce negative side effects but also highlights the fact that the construction of a collective identity forms the basis for every interest group. It is true that legal and economic structures must be in place for interest groups to be able to pursue court cases, strategic or not. However, this is not enough. In order for interest groups to even exist and be active, identity concerns are crucial. In scholarship on interest groups' driving forces in pursuing strategic litigation, based on studies of disability and LGBTQ movements, it has been suggested that identity politics frameworks can make a difference: groups are more likely to adopt a litigation strategy when their framing processes define the membership primarily as rights holders and the courts as an appropriate venue to pursue policy.[91]

These findings raise concerns regarding the value and effects of strategic litigation in counteracting age discrimination of older persons in working life. This is because the group referred to as older workers is very heterogeneous.[92] A significant share of persons who occupy integral positions in society – be it in politics, management, or working life, including trade unions where older workers display a higher unionisation rate and are represented in leading functions, and where the interests of the established and experienced workforce tend to enjoy strong support – would be

89. Jacquot & Vitale (2014), *supra* n. 88; Kristin Edquist, *EU Social-Policy Governance: Advocating Activism or Servicing States?* 13(4) Journal of European Public Policy 500–518 (June 2006) https://doi.org/10.1080/13501760600693879.
90. Jacquot & Vitale (2014), *supra* n. 88.
91. Lisa Vanhala, *Anti-discrimination Policy Actors and Their Use of Litigation Strategies: The Influence of Identity Politics*, 16(5) Journal of European Public Policy 738–754, 744 (2009) https://doi.org/10.1080/13501760902983473.
92. Sonia McKay, Steve Jefferys, Anna Paraskevopoulou & Janoj Keles, *Study on Precarious Work and Social Rights. Carried Out for the European Commission (VT/2010/084)*, Working Lives Research Institute, London Metropolitan University 2012; Jenny Julén Votinius, *Intersectionality as a Tool for Analysing Age and Gender in Labour Law*, in Simonetta Manfredi & Lucy Vickers (eds), *Challenges for Active Ageing: Equality Law and the Workplace* (Palgrave Macmillan 2016).

defined as older workers. However, it is in this group that we also find the largest number of persons with outdated competencies, age-related health problems, and disabilities caused by a long and hard working life, along with the unemployed persons who have the most difficulty in finding employment. Older workers form a precarious group in the labour market; in fact, older female workers are among those at the highest risk for precarious work within the EU, ahead of groups such as interns, apprentices, women in general, older workers in general, and pregnant women. Thus, the diversity of the 'older workers' group is vast and could almost be described in terms of polarisation. In this respect, the older workers diverge from all other groups in the labour market.

Although older workers are at a higher risk of exposure to ageism and age discrimination than younger workers, in most cases, this does not appear to be a sufficient basis for a collective, transgressive identity upon which interest groups can be established to pursue matters of common concern. It is not possible to estimate with any certainty the number of interest groups with expertise in non-discrimination in the EU Member States, but it can be noted that while the number of interest groups is quite substantial, very few of these target older workers in their specific capacity of being older.[93] Because the prevalence and activities of interest groups are decisive factors for how the potential of strategic litigation will play out in the development of non-discrimination law and how the developments can benefit particular groups, this aspect is crucial for understanding what a stronger focus on strategic litigation could mean for older workers.

5 A POWERFUL TOOL WITH POTENTIAL KNOCK-ON EFFECTS

This chapter has explored the increasing emphasis on strategic litigation as a key component of a more comprehensive approach to the enforcement of EU discrimination policies and legislation and some of the implications of the strategic litigation approach. The analysis and discussion have particularly highlighted outcomes for older workers while also emphasising crucial aspects of this development in relation to discrimination law in general.

One important effect of the increased turn to strategic litigation is the more prominent role attributed to interest groups in the development of discrimination law, and the chapter has discussed what this may mean for older workers. In terms of counteracting discrimination, the prohibition against age discrimination works in the same way as for the other protected grounds, with the important difference that it allows greater scope for exceptions. However, as a node for catalysing legal development driven by a group defined by identity politics, the prohibition against age discrimination in working life appears to be considerably less effective than the other grounds for discrimination covered by EU law. Against this background, there is reason

93. Rare exceptions are 50plus Hellas in Greece and 2young2 Retire/Cercle des Seniors Actifs, C'Sa in France. That established interest groups exist primarily within the LGBTQ and disability movements is reflected in the allocation of EU funding in the abovementioned projects on strategic litigation.

to ask: to what extent will older workers be truly able to benefit from the potential advantages of strategic litigation, as envisaged by the current promotion of this method in the field of discrimination law?

It is quite possible that older workers could gain ground through increased use of strategic litigation pursued by interest groups outside the labour market context. Interest groups for older persons mainly represent pensioners and therefore are usually found in other areas of society than working life. Although there is no protection in EU law against age discrimination outside the labour market, the national legislation in almost all Member States also prohibits age discrimination to a varying extent outside working life.[94] The Swedish Discrimination Act prohibits age discrimination in all fields of society, including the provision of goods and services, housing, health and medical care, social services, and the social-security system. In these areas, unlike working life, interest groups for older people are more common; one such example is the pensioners' organisation. An increased focus on strategic litigation could activate the willingness and ability of interest groups for older persons to influence social development through litigation. In so far as such strategically litigated cases outside working life would raise matters of general importance for the ban on age discrimination, they could also prove valuable to older persons in their capacity as employees or job seekers.

In the specific context of working life, many times – and in countries like Sweden, almost always – the trade union is the most likely initiator of a court case. Within the trade union movement, older workers, as a group, have a comparatively strong position; they have a high level of unionisation, many persons holding senior positions in the trade unions are older, and in trade union work, issues related to the established and experienced workforce tend to be high on the agenda. Hypothetically, should trade unions become more active in pursuing strategically litigated cases, emphasis in court cases on matters of relevance for older workers could increase. The question, however, is whether the trade unions would be willing to adopt a more litigious approach. The risks that come with costly court proceedings, where the consequences of a negative outcome could be far-reaching, provide a strong incentive for labour market parties on both sides to choose alternative means for pursuing their issues – and this would translate into a very low propensity to engage in strategic litigation. This applies not only in Sweden, where the national industrial-relations model is characterised by cooperation between the parties and where the regulatory framework promotes consultations and negotiations, but also elsewhere, for instance, in the UK.[95]

In the working-life context, older workers tend to be most likely to benefit from interest groups' strategic litigation based on other discrimination grounds than age –

94. Elaine Dewhurst, *Age Discrimination Law Outside the Employment Field* (Publications Office of the European Union 2020).
95. For instance, a similarly hesitant or sceptical approach to strategic litigation as a tool in other industrial, political, or social activities to promote the interests of a group's members has been observed among many trade unions in the UK, both with reference to the balancing of cost and benefits and from the perspective that litigation tends to depoliticise industrial disputes; Ruth Dukes & Eleanor Kirk, *Legal Change and Legal Mobilisation: What Does Strategic Litigation Mean for Workers and Trade Unions?*, 33(4) Social and Legal Studies 479–500 (2023) https://doi.org/10.1177/09646639231204942.

for example, when these groups pursue cases on general matters relevant to all persons covered by discrimination law, irrespective of ground. Should interest groups intensify their strategic litigation activities as a response to EU policies, we can expect to see an increase in such generally applicable cases. This would also reinforce the protection against age discrimination. However, strategic cases brought by other interest groups can just as easily result in an advancement for those groups in their particular areas, without these gains offering benefits to older workers. Indeed, such advancements may even be at the expense of older workers. This is because strategic litigation to achieve broader political and social change is based on group interests rather than those of the individual. With the aim of strengthening the rights and positions of the group in question, this approach involves challenging established social structures and hierarchical orders – and in working life, older workers make up a large proportion of those holding strong positions in these structures and orders. However, as discussed above, the older workers' group is characterised by duality; even while occupying strong positions, older workers also represent one of the weakest groups in the labour market. There is a risk that pushing emancipatory interests for a group other than older workers may entail not only an adjustment of positions at the cost of older workers who are in a strong position but also a deterioration of the position for older workers who are in a weak position and whose main asset lies in the very structures being challenged.

The current development also gives reason for concern on a general level as regards the future of discrimination law. The evolution of EU law and the law-making of the European Court of Justice have a strong tradition of strategic litigation; strategically litigated cases, brought primarily by interest groups and activists, have contributed to crucial breakthroughs in EU non-discrimination law and have been decisive for the advancements of equality rights in the Member States. This method to achieve social change has proven efficient in the development of discrimination law. Nevertheless, now, as the EU designates strategic litigation to ensure compliance of Member States' national law with supranational EU law, there are reasons for concern. For several important reasons – three of which have been discussed in this chapter – this development puts the legitimacy of discrimination law at risk. The first is that the turn to strategic litigation may reveal itself primarily (or at least to an important extent) as a means to pursue the interests of the EU. Second, most Member States do not have a tradition of social transformation through the courts, so the strategic litigation development also raises fundamental questions relating to democracy, governance, and the rule of law. The third reason discussed in the chapter is the role attributed to the national equality bodies in carrying out strategic litigation; these bodies are supervisory authorities for discrimination law in the Member States.

The force of strategic litigation in pushing for implementing and protecting fundamental rights, including the right to non-discrimination, has been evidenced for a long time, not least in the successes of civil-rights movements in various parts of the world. However, traditionally, strategic litigation has gained public support because it has been the voice of social movements that act to guarantee the rights of disadvantaged groups, often in relation to the government. When strategic litigation activities are included by EU-level decision-makers in the governance toolbox for enforcement of EU law in the Member States, the character of these activities changes. The boundary between the grassroots and the supranational dimensions blurs, and the same applies to the role of the activist in relation to the role of the legislator and the government. These boundaries are central to the idea of the rule of law, and in any legal field, they are an essential part of the integrity of the law. In the long term, therefore, the current developments threaten to seriously undermine the legitimacy of the entire legal field of non-discrimination.

CHAPTER 6

Modernizing EU Anti-discrimination Law to Better Combat Discrimination Against Older Workers in the Context of 'Just Transition'

Sophie Robin-Olivier

1 INTRODUCTION

Although Directive 2000/78[1] aims at combatting age discrimination in the European Union, the very text of this Directive makes clear that age is a specific discriminatory ground that is not strictly prohibited by EU law.[2] From the abundant case law of the Court of Justice of the European Union (CJEU)[3] – which is not so easy to synthesize – at least two conclusions can be drawn: first, age-based distinctions remain rampant in many national legislations and practices,[4] and second, there is a high degree of

1. Council Directive 2000/78/EC of 27 November 2000 establishing a general framework for equal treatment in employment and occupation, OJ L 303, 2.12.2000, pp. 16–22.
2. As indicated by Art. 6 of the Directive, laying down extensive possibilities to justify discrimination on age.
3. A majority of decisions of the Court of Justice of the EU regarding the Employment Equality Directive concern age-related differences of treatment (Report from the Commission to the European Parliament and the Council on the application of Council Directive 2000/43/EC and of Council Directive 2000/78/EC establishing a general framework for equal treatment in employment and occupation, 19.3.2021, COM (2021) 139 final, p. 24).
4. This may explain why, despite recent increases, the employment rate among older workers in the EU remains lower than the average (for what groups?), according to the EU Commission Green Paper on Ageing (27.1.2021, COM (2021) 50 final, p. 7). The Green paper adds that in 2019, only 59.1 % of those aged 55–64 were employed versus 73.1 % of all those aged 20–64, and after the age of 50, the risk of long-term unemployment increases. It also reminds us that many older workers face difficulties when it comes to recruitment, access to training opportunities, job transitions and age-adapted tasks.

uncertainty regarding the outcome of actions brought before courts on the basis of age discrimination. This situation results namely from more open possibilities to justify discrimination on age than on other grounds[5] and a variable (and often not very strict) control of proportionality by the CJEU. All in all, age discrimination does not seem to be considered as seriously as other grounds of discrimination,[6] although it is not only at variance with social policy and human rights objectives pursued by the EU but also stands in the way of EU economic targets for increasing employment of senior workers.[7]

Against this backdrop, it is uncertain whether the prohibition of discrimination on age has efficiently helped older workers – as it should have done[8] – to remain active and benefit from good working conditions. Rather, there are good reasons to think that the existing legal framework is unable to achieve the aim of inclusion and protection of older workers in the workplace. But anti-discrimination law is not static. Law and legal reasoning can change. New concepts are emerging, and existing ones can become more active and effective. In addition, although climate-change impact on older workers can be another factor fostering their exclusion from the workplace, the European Green Deal,[9] the European Commission's vast programme to combat climate change, is an opportunity to revisit discrimination on age. Indeed, the Green Deal includes a commitment to a 'just transition' – a concept that may be a resource for anti-discrimination law.

The objective of this chapter is to explore possible evolutions in anti-discrimination law that could help better address discrimination against older workers, at a time when the Green Deal has become the global framework for law development at EU level. The chapter starts with a look back, considering the enduring problems resulting from the CJEU conception of the proportionality test. Looking forward, the chapter moves on to assess the perspectives offered by intersectionality and then turns to the factors that could help an enriched version of the central 'reasonable accommodation' concept to emerge in the context of a 'just transition'.

5. Cf., Art. 6, Directive 2000/78.
6. On this idea, *see* namely Equinet (European Network of Equality Bodies), 'Fighting Discrimination on the Ground of Age', 2018, p. 5, https://equineteurope.org/wp-content/uploads/2019/03/Age-Discrimination_updated-electronic-1.pdf.
7. The economic convergence achieved through the European semester refers to the European Pillar of Social Rights, which is to be implemented through an 'action plan' mentioning three 'EU headline targets on jobs, skills and poverty reduction', one of them being that 'at least 78 % of the population aged 20 to 64 should be in employment by 2030'.
8. As recommended by Claudia Mahler, the UN Independent Expert on the enjoyment of all human rights by older persons, in a report which mentions the need for 'a paradigm shift from a welfare model to a rights bearers' model, that would guarantee dignity, equality, autonomy and participation during the entire life course' (Report on Ageism and Age Discrimination, UN Human Rights Council, 4.8.2021, p. 17).
9. Communication from the Commission to the European Parliament, the European Council, the Council, the European Economic and Social Committee and the Committee of the Regions, 'The European Green Deal', 11.12.2019, COM (2019) 640 final.

2 THE LONG-LASTING PROBLEM OF PROPORTIONALITY

One of the most challenging legal questions concerning discrimination against older workers concerns maximum age limits and dismissals or refusals to hire when an employee or jobseeker reaches a certain age.[10] To be sure, such rules or practices need to be justified by a legitimate aim, but both the CJEU and national courts tend to accept rather easily aims that are sufficiently linked to social-policy objectives (a specificity for age discrimination)[11] or safety and security concerns (which also apply for all other grounds).[12]

Whether the measure will be accepted depends mostly on the proportionality test;[13] the method for assessing proportionality (in other words, as the CJEU puts it, whether the means deployed to achieve the aims are 'appropriate and necessary') remains a source of uncertainty and dissatisfaction. In balancing the individual right not to be discriminated against public-policy objectives, the courts have often accepted the use of generalization abstract conceptions concerning both the capacities of older workers and the needs of the labour market or corporations,[14] and statistical data concerning a certain age cohort.[15] This has not helped senior workers in their quest for a better and longer career.

However, even if an age-discrimination matter eventually comes down to the national courts to decide, the Court of Justice sometimes works out a framework for assessing proportionality that can contribute to tilting the balance in favour of older workers' participation in the labour market. To do so, the Court, in *CO*,[16] has referred to the right to work enshrined in Article 15(1) of the EU Charter of Fundamental Rights. It required that attention be paid to the participation of older workers in the labour force and, more extensively, their participation in economic, cultural, and social life. It added that retaining these persons in work promotes diversity – an objective that has recently played an important role in limiting justification of discriminatory measures based on grounds other than age.[17] In addition, the CJEU expressed doubt regarding the argument concerning opportunities created for younger people if retired persons (as in this case) were prevented from participating in calls for expressions of interest for the award of analysis and consultancy roles. Looking concretely at the assignments

10. Equinet, Fighting Discrimination on the Ground of Age, *supra* n. 6, pp. 29–30.
11. *See, e.g.*, Case C-143/16, *Abercrombie*, 19.7.2017, ECLI:EU:C:2017:566: 'Member States enjoy a broad discretion in their choice, not only to pursue a particular aim in the field of social and employment policy, but also in the definition of measures capable of achieving it'. *See also* Case C-670/18, *CO*, 2.4.2020, ECLI:EU:C:2020:272, which considers as legitimate aims: 'rejuvenation of current personnel', 'encouragement of recruitment', establishment of 'an age structure that balances young and older civil servants in order to facilitate the recruitment and promotion of young people', and also insists on 'the broad discretion' granted to Member States.
12. *See, e.g.*, Case C-190/16, *Fries*, 5.7.2017, ECLI:EU:C:2017:513.
13. On early developments of the CJEU case law, *see* namely Claire Kilpatrick, *Age, Retirement and the Employment Contract*, 36(1) Industrial Law Journal 119–135 (2007) https://doi.org/10.1093/indlaw/dwl044.
14. For an illustration, *see* namely Case C-670/18, *CO*, *supra* n. 11.
15. *See* Equinet Discussion paper, n. 6.
16. *Supra* n. 11.
17. *See* in particular Case C-344/20, *S.C.R.L.*, 13/10/2022, ECLI:EU:C:2022:774, §41.

concerned, it does not seem so evident that younger people would be in a better position to gain access to the labour market if older workers were set aside: further evidence was needed, and general ideas were not sufficient to convince the Court in the case. Lastly, in assessing the effect of the measure on older workers, the Court required that their legitimate claims, which stated that the level of the retirement pension was sufficient, would be taken into account. Overall, strict scrutiny applied in a case of direct age discrimination could become a model for future cases, especially when a discriminatory measure is justified by the abstract idea that younger workers' access to the labour market would be facilitated by seniors' exclusion.

Strict scrutiny should also apply when 'genuine and determining occupational requirements' are invoked to justify another important limit to older workers' access to work and possibilities of retraining: maximum recruitment ages or age limits for certain activities. Such was the situation, for instance, in a case in which the Court had to decide on legislation requiring that police-officer candidates must be under 35 years of age.[18] Before considering that national law was appropriate to the objective of ensuring the operational capacity and proper functioning of the police service concerned, and necessary for the attainment of that objective, the Court of Justice took into account data and information provided by the employer and required the national court to test their accuracy. However, the Court did not go so far as to oppose the very principle of an age limit and admitted that an individual physical test would not constitute a less restrictive alternative because 'the possession of particular physical capacities should be envisaged not statically, at the time of recruitment competition tests, but dynamically, taking into consideration the years of service that can be accomplished by a police officer after he or she has been recruited'.[19]

All in all, despite the uncertainties and limits of the proportionality test, the prohibition of discrimination on age has contributed to improvements in the situation of older workers.[20] In its most recent case law, the Court of Justice seems to take age discrimination more seriously. By referring to the objectives of EU anti-discrimination legislation,[21] and insisting on the importance of promoting diversity in the workforce,[22] the Court now tends to do a stricter review of age discrimination. This reasoning, which aligns recent case law on age with the case law concerning discrimination on other grounds, is likely to strengthen the fight against the exclusion of older people from work and other occupations.

18. Case C-258/15, *Salaberria Sorondo*, 15.11.2016, ECLI:EU:C:2016:873.
19. *Ibid.*, §47.
20. *See, e.g.*, Case C-144/04, *Mangold*, 22.11.2005, EU:C:2005:709 (on fixed-term employment) or Case C-499/08, *Ingeniørforeningen i Danmark*, 12.10.2010, EU:C:2010:600 (exclusion of workers from entitlement to a severance allowance, when they are eligible for an old-age pension from their employer). *See also*, more recently, the extensive interpretation of the personal scope of application of the prohibition of discrimination on age, to include the position of a politically elected sector convenor of a Union: Case C-587/20, *HK/Danmark and HK/Privat*, 2.9.2022, ECLI:EU:C:2022:419.
21. *See* Case *HK/Danmark and HK/Privat*, *supra* n. 20, §32. For a similar reference to the objectives of anti-discrimination law, in a case of discrimination on sexual orientation, *see* Case C-356/21, *J.K.*, 12.1.2023, ECLI:EU:C:2023:9.
22. *See* Case *C.O.*, *supra* n. 11, §43.

3 INTERSECTIONAL DISCRIMINATION AS A WAY FORWARD?

As ageism intertwines with other forms of 'isms', including sexism, racism and ableism, and age combines with other grounds of discrimination, an intersectional approach could help redress ageism and complex forms of discrimination in the context of older age.[23] According to the Commission Green Paper on Ageing,[24] age discrimination at work can affect certain groups more – especially people with a minority racial or ethnic background. Taking into account the intersection of age, race, and sex is particularly crucial. It has been observed that the intersection of ageism and sexism, patriarchal norms, and a preoccupation with youth result in faster deterioration of older women's status compared with that of men, thereby creating specific and aggravated disadvantages for older women.[25] For instance, older women are often expected to continue in their caregiving roles while neglecting their own well-being, physical and mental health, and economic independence.[26] In addition, whereas older men can be seen as wise and experienced, women tend to face greater pressure to hide physical signs of ageing that others consider unattractive.[27] Menopause in particular is considered to have historically framed women's experiences of ageing through negative associations with the loss of fertility, productivity, youth, and importance.[28]

Despite all the data and research on the specific disadvantages suffered by sub-groups of older workers, especially older women, EU law has still not taken on the concept of intersectional discrimination.[29] To be sure, in 2016, the CJEU acknowledged that 'discrimination may indeed be based on several of the grounds' protected under EU law.[30] However, the Court refused to consider the existence of a 'new category of discrimination resulting from the combination of more than one of those grounds' where discrimination on the basis of those grounds taken in isolation has not been established.[31] As a result, 'intersectional discrimination', defined as discrimination based on an inseparable combination of protected grounds, and not on a combination of (multiple) grounds operating separately ('additive discrimination'), was not considered a form of discrimination prohibited by Directive 2000/78. That age and sexual orientation combined, in the case, resulted in a person being deprived of a survivor's

23. Report on Ageism and Age Discrimination, *supra* n. 8, p. 16.
24. Cited *supra* n. 6, p. 6.
25. *Ibid.* On the intersection of sex and age, *see* 'Human Rights and Older Women: The Intersection Between Ageing and Gender', Report of the Independent Expert on the enjoyment of all human rights by older persons Claudia Mahler, UN Human Rights Council, 17.7.2021. *See also* the Global Report on Ageism of the World Health Organization (WHO), Geneva, 2021, pp. 10–11 mentioning that ageist attitudes disadvantage older women more than men.
26. Report on Ageism and Age Discrimination, *supra* n. 8, p. 12.
27. 'Human Rights and Older Women: The Intersection Between Ageing and Gender', *supra* n. 25, p. 5.
28. *Ibid.*
29. For a recent study on intersectional discrimination in EU law: Raphaële Xenidis, 'Beyond the "Master's Tools": Putting Intersectionality to Work in European Non-discrimination Law, a Study of the European Union and the Council of Europe Non-discrimination Law Regimes', Florence, European University Institute, 2020, EUI PhD theses, Department of Law, https://hdl.handle.net/1814/68050.
30. Case C-443/15, *Parris*, 24.11.2016, ECLI:EU:C:2016:897.
31. *Ibid.*

pension did not lead to any questioning of the conditions under which the contested pension scheme operated.[32]

However, the CJEU is not the only one to blame for ignoring intersectionality: there is no reference to the notion of intersectional discrimination in the provisions of Directive 2000/78, especially in Article 2, where the concept of discrimination is defined. The Directive is not completely silent, but reference to intersectionality appears only in the preamble, where Recital 3 mentions that 'in implementing the principle of equal treatment, the Community should, in accordance with Article 3(2) of the EC Treaty, aim to eliminate inequalities, and to promote equality between men and women, especially since women are often the victims of multiple discrimination'. When the Directive envisages the relationship between age and sex in its Article 6(2), concerning occupational social-security schemes, it is only to prevent the risk of sex discrimination:[33] sex discrimination is given more importance than discrimination on age, and the very idea of intersectionality is not embraced by this hierarchy between discriminatory grounds. Hence, to include intersectionality, especially discrimination on age and sex, the Directive needs to be updated, or the CJEU case law must evolve. Such an evolution could be fostered by the inclusion and definition of the notion of intersectional discrimination in the new Directive, 'to strengthen the application of the principle of equal pay for equal work or work of equal value between men and women through pay transparency and enforcement mechanisms'.[34] There is no doubt that significant changes would take place if intersections between age and sex were taken into account, both in the case law of the Court of Justice[35] and in Member States' or companies' policies.[36]

In addition to sex and age, other intersections should be considered in order to improve older workers' situation at work. The most important of these is the combination of age and disability[37] because disability creates a much greater disadvantage for older workers. This was acknowledged (but not conceptualized as a consequence of

32. *Ibid.*
33. According to Art. 6(2): 'Member States may provide that the fixing for occupational social security schemes of ages for admission or entitlement to retirement or invalidity benefits, including the fixing under those schemes of different ages for employees or groups or categories of employees, and the use, in the context of such schemes, of age criteria in actuarial calculations, does not constitute discrimination on the grounds of age, provided this does not result in discrimination on the grounds of sex.'
34. Directive (EU) 2023/970 of the European Parliament and of the Council of 10 May 2023, OJ L 132, 17.5.2023, pp. 21–44.
35. For instance, in *Rosenbladt* (Case C-45/09, 12.10.2010, ECLI:EU:C:2010:601), the CJEU accepted the clause of a collective agreement on automatic termination of the employment contracts of employees who have reached the age of 65, which led to rejecting Ms Rosenbladt's claim that this clause was violating a right to non-discrimination on the ground of age. Taking into consideration the sex and age of the claimant might have led to a different solution: it could have been shown that the possibility of finding another job – which at least partly determined the solution – was extremely limited for a woman of the claimant's age.
36. The prohibition of intersectional discrimination on sex and age could justify, for instance, the introduction of specific leave intervals for menopause that are separate from other sickness absence.
37. On the relation between age and disability, *see* namely UN Department of Economic and Social Affairs, 'Ageing and Disability', https://www.un.org/development/desa/disabilities/disability-and-ageing.html.

intersectional discrimination) in the *Odar* case.[38] It would also be an important step forward to consider the situation of older migrant workers: age and nationality, combined, can contribute to exclusion from opportunities - especially, one might think, in the context of mobility within the EU - not only for EU citizens but also for third-country nationals. Indeed, it might be the case that mobility of older workers is hindered by a series of barriers that younger workers do not face. An example of the type of instruments that can be imagined to facilitate mobility of EU citizens, by taking into account the specific situation of discriminated groups, is the project to create a European Disability Card recognized in all Member States.[39] The aim of this new instrument is to help people with disabilities travel more easily between EU countries by developing a system of mutual recognition of disability status to ensure equal access to a range of benefits across borders.[40] This project could also contribute to facilitating the mobility of older workers, who form a substantial proportion of disabled persons. Another interesting aspect is that it sheds light on discriminations taking place in the context of intra-EU mobility, which are not based on nationality, but on other grounds. In the same vein, considering nationality and age as combined barriers to mobility could foster the emergence of solutions to improve the mobility of older workers across the EU.

If there is hardly any doubt that intersectionality stands out as a particularly important notion for improving the situation of older workers at the workplace, the various consequences that the concept would produce in case law, legislation, and firms' policies still need to be explored further. One of these consequences is a stronger and more central conception of (reasonable) accommodation.

4 THE CENTRAL ROLE OF 'REASONABLE ACCOMMODATION'

As the Commission 'Green Paper on Ageing' suggests, increasing employment among older people, while taking into account the fact that disability tends to increase with age, requires reasonable accommodation and an accessible work environment.[41] According to the Commission, 'physical aspects - whether ergonomic or to do with accessibility - and flexible working conditions would allow older workers to postpone their retirement should they choose to do so'. Because accidents at work and occupational diseases are more dangerous as people get older, good working conditions - including sound occupational safety and health - can contribute to reducing early retirement rates.[42] According to the Green Paper, 'digital technologies can

38. Case C-152/11, *Odar*, 6.12.2012, ECLI:EU:C:2012:772.
39. The European Commission announced its intention to propose legislation to create a European Disability Card in the European Union Strategy for the Rights of Persons with Disabilities 2021–2030, published in March 2021, https://ec.europa.eu/social/main.jsp?catId = 738&langId = en&pubId = 8376&furtherPubs = yes.
40. *See* namely Antoine Fobe, 'Equal Citizenship for Persons with Disabilities', ETUI, https://www.socialeurope.eu/equal-citizenship-for-persons-with-disabilities, 27 March 2023.
41. *Supra* n. 6, p. 7.
42. *Ibid.*

support workers and offer better adapted working environments, with ICT-based personalized systems, wearables and mobile health applications'.

The genuine, but still limited, efficiency of the employer's duty to accommodate (older) workers' needs was illustrated in the recent *HR Rail* case,[43] in which a worker employed as a technician for railway tracks was diagnosed with a heart condition that required the fitting of a pacemaker, a device which is sensitive to the electromagnetic fields present, *inter alia*, near railway tracks. According to the Court of Justice, the concept of 'reasonable accommodation' for disabled persons requires that a worker who, owing to his or her disability, has been declared incapable of performing the essential functions of the post that he or she occupies be assigned to another position. However, the requirement to accommodate and (in this case) reassign the worker to another position is strictly limited in the CJEU conception: not only must the worker have the necessary competence, capability and availability to occupy another position; in accordance with the Directive, the measure must not impose a disproportionate burden on the employer.

As far as the first condition is concerned, it is derived, as the Advocate General mentioned,[44] from Recital 17 of the Directive, which indicates that the Directive 'does not require the recruitment, promotion, maintenance in employment or training of an individual who is not competent, capable and available to perform the essential functions of the post concerned or to undergo the relevant training, without prejudice to the obligation to provide reasonable accommodation for people with disabilities'. However, inferring necessary competence and capability for the new post from the language of Recital 17 constitutes a 'broad' interpretation, as the Advocate General himself admitted: not to compel employers to recruit disabled workers who are not competent, and not capable of performing the tasks that the job implies, is indeed different from making it necessary to provide training (within the limits of reasonableness) for another position, if that is necessary to avoid dismissing a worker. Workers who become disabled while they are in employment are not in the same situation in terms of their integration into the firm as those who have not yet been hired.

In addition, the issue of competence and capability can be included in the test of reasonableness (or avoidance of 'disproportionate burden'). The conception of what can be considered reasonable, which remains largely unclear, will determine the effectiveness of the requirement to accommodate disabled workers. So far, as the Court of Justice recalls, deciding whether required measures entail a disproportionate burden requires one to refer to Recital 21 of the Directive, which provides that 'account should be taken in particular of the financial costs entailed, the scale and financial resources of the organization or undertaking and the possibility of obtaining public funding or any other assistance'. This allows one to conclude only one thing: accommodation is not without financial cost, and reasonableness must be assessed concretely in respect of the organization's specific situation.

Although the scope of reasonable accommodation still needs clarification, an extensive conception of accommodation could be justified by references to the Charter

43. Case C-485/20, *HR Rail*, 10.2.2022, ECLI:EU:C:2022:85.
44. Opinion of 11.11.2021 in the *HR Rail* Case, ECLI:EU:C:2021:916, §74.

of Fundamental Rights: as stated in *HR Rail*,[45] the Charter not only includes a general prohibition of discrimination (Article 21) but also requires that the European Union recognizes and respects the right of persons with disabilities to benefit from measures designed to ensure their independence, social and occupational integration, and participation in the life of the community (Article 26). However, EU law contains another important limit to reasonable accommodation: it concerns only disabled workers under Directive 2000/78. Accommodation for older workers is not formally covered by the duty to accommodate. In this regard, things may be changing, although rather discreetly: the case law of the Court of Justice suggests that the concept of accommodation could spread beyond disability and become an element to be considered in assessing the proportionality of a discriminatory rule.[46] If so, accommodation could be required in order to retain older persons in work.

5 THE 'JUST TRANSITION' PARADIGM: A NEW FRAMEWORK FOR EXTENDING THE CONCEPT OF ACCOMMODATION

The extension of the domain of (reasonable) accommodation seems particularly important in the context of climate change and climate-change reforms. Indeed, it has now been amply documented that some climate-change consequences influence the lives and health of older people more than others. Studies have indicated that adults aged 65 and older are the most likely to die from heat exposure during heatwaves and extreme cold weather or winter storms and in hurricanes and other natural hazards.[47] The case of older women is even worse: they experience higher rates of poverty than older men and face other economic hardships that are made worse by climate change; they also face more health risks, including a greater likelihood of experiencing chronic diseases and harm from air pollution, and have higher rates of death and other health complications from extreme heat than any other population group.[48] So far, policies have failed to account for this.

In addition to the more severe impact of climate change on seniors, policies to address climate change can also affect older workers more than others if no adjustment is made. Cycling to work, limiting the use of air conditioning, or adjusting room temperature, to take trivial examples, can impact the ability of older workers to continue working if their particular situation is not considered. The study on the promotion and protection of the rights of older persons in the context of climate change, published by the Office of the High Commissioner for Human Rights,[49] recommended that a series of measures be taken, including making sure that measures to reduce climate change consider age and gender, and take into account the needs and

45. §42.
46. *See* Case C-157/15, *Achbita*, 14.3.2017, ECLI:EU:C:2017:203 §43 and Case C-795/19, *Tartu Vangla*, 15.7.2021, ECLI:EU:C:2021:606, §52.
47. Analytical study on the promotion and protection of the rights of older persons in the context of climate change, Report of the Office of the High Commissioner for Human Rights, A/HRC/47/46, 20 April 2021, p. 4.
48. *Ibid.*
49. *Ibid.*

rights of older women and men. To achieve this objective, older people and organizations working to ensure older persons' rights should be consulted, and these groups should take part in defining transformations that are necessary for sustainable livelihoods.[50]

This concern for older people's needs in the context of climate-change reforms is part of what 'fair transition' requires. The notion of 'fair transition' relies on the idea that 'the effects of climate change are not the same for everyone' and that 'existing inequalities affect the impact of climate change and the ability to respond to it'.[51] The concern is also based on the consideration that not only climate change itself but also measures introduced to reduce climate change or to adapt to it have different effects on people 'according to their gender, class, wealth, ethnicity, physical ability and other structural inequalities'.[52] The ILO Guidelines on just transition[53] highlight the need to secure the livelihoods of those who might be negatively affected by the green transformation and also stress that the emerging low-carbon economy should be inclusive and based on decent work and lower inequality. In order to achieve such an outcome, the transition should be guided by principles of distributional justice,[54] which requires taking into account the most affected persons and groups and compensating for the adverse effects of both climate change and measures to address it.

In the EU, the programme of the Green Deal[55] includes a commitment to a 'just transition' and 'leaving no one behind'. It was also described by the Commission as an opportunity to address existing inequalities. The vast cross-cutting transformation of EU law envisaged by the Green Deal to combat climate change stands out as an unprecedented opportunity to promote actions aimed at accommodating older workers' needs. The context is favourable to a more thorough conception of the duty to accommodate older workers' needs in upcoming policies aiming at sustainable development. At EU level, resources for measures specifically tailored for dealing with climate-change impact on older workers could be obtained through EU funds, including in particular the Recovery and Resilience Facility,[56] which is the key recovery instrument at the heart of Next Generation EU. The objective of the Facility is to provide Member States with financial support, with a view to achieving reforms and investments set out in national plans that target EU-defined objectives, including green transition and its social dimension.[57] The resources provided by the EU should help

50. *Ibid.*
51. *See* namely Gill Allwood, *Mainstreaming Gender and Climate Change to Achieve a Just Transition to a Climate-Neutral Europe*, 58(1) Journal of Common Market Studies 182 (September 2020) https://doi.org/10.1111/jcms.13082.
52. *Ibid.*
53. 'Guidelines for a just transition towards environmentally sustainable economies and societies for all', 2015.
54. *Cf.*, Daren McCauley & Raphael Heffron, *Just Transition: Integrating Climate, Energy and Environmental Justice*, 119 Energy Policy 1-7 (2018) https://doi.org/10.1016/j.enpol.2018.04.014; Peter Newell & Dustin Mulvaney, *The Political Economy of the 'Just Transition'*, 179(2) The Geographical Journal 132-140 (2013) https://doi.org/10.1111/geoj.12008.
55. *Supra* n. 9.
56. Regulation (EU) 2021/241 of the European Parliament and of the Council of 12 February 2021 establishing the Recovery and Resilience Facility, OJ L 57 of 18.2.2021, p. 17.
57. On the objectives of the Recovery and Resilience Facility, *see* Art. 4 of Regulation 2021/241.

eradicate one of the most significant barriers to efficient accommodation (as mentioned above): the action must not entail a disproportionate burden for the employer. As Directive 2000/78 mentions,[58] and the Court of Justice insists on,[59] the possibility of obtaining public funding or any other assistance must be taken into account to determine whether the burden on the employer is disproportionate.

6 CONCLUSION

In this chapter, we have considered the evolutions in anti-discrimination law that would help better address discrimination against older workers, taking into account the challenges and the opportunities brought about by climate change and climate-change reforms, especially the objective of a 'just transition'. An extensive conception of accommodation is sorely needed to take into account various types of discrimination that affect older workers. Taking 'just transition' seriously could foster the emergence of an enriched version of 'reasonable accommodation'. The Green Deal programme, together with new funding facilities, represents fertile ground for the evolution of EU anti-discrimination law and can serve to better ensure that older workers can retain access to work and remain employed.

58. Article 5.
59. *See* namely *HR Rail, supra* n. 44, §45.

CHAPTER 7

Dismissed Older Workers at Conceptual and Legal Crossroads: An Interplay Between Employment Protection, Non-discrimination, and Collective Bargaining

Mia Rönnmar[*]

1 INTRODUCTION

An ageing population is a major trend in the EU as well as in many developed economies due to declining birth rates and rising life expectancy. This has important implications for economic performance, intergenerational solidarity, social cohesion, and the sustainability of pension, healthcare, and eldercare systems.

The ageing of the workforce poses specific possibilities and challenges for labour law, industrial relations, and collective bargaining. From a societal perspective, there is a need to promote active ageing, counteract ageism, advance the inclusion of older workers in the labour market, and adapt work and the working environment. Not least from the perspective of the sustainability of welfare systems, there is also a need to make older persons work until 'normal' retirement age and to prolong working life beyond this point. At the same time, it is important to address potential intergenerational tension between older and younger workers, varying possibilities for active ageing and prolonged working lives in different labour market sectors and professions, and the possible conflict between the societal need of prolonged working lives and the

* This research is carried out within the research project 'Prolonged Working Lives, Older Workers, and Dismissals', funded by the Swedish Research Council for Health, Working Life, and Welfare (*Forte*). The research project has received ethical approval by the Swedish Ethical Review Authority (dnr 2021-05026).

autonomy and right of an individual to choose when to retire.[1] In comparative European terms, the employment rate among older workers in Sweden is high, and the average retirement age is about 66 years. In recent years, the age limits within the pension system and the statutory compulsory retirement age have been increased (in the latter case, from 67 to 69 years).[2]

This chapter focuses on dismissed older workers and aims to explore the legal protection offered to older workers in dismissal situations and the conceptual and legal interplay of employment protection, non-discrimination, and collective bargaining in this context. The discussion is focused on Swedish labour law and industrial relations within an EU law context. Recent major statutory and collective bargaining reforms of employment protection in Sweden are of importance for this interplay, as is case law from the Swedish Labour Court (*Arbetsdomstolen*) and the Court of Justice of the European Union (CJEU).[3]

The outline of the chapter is as follows. Section 2 introduces the legal frameworks of employment protection, non-discrimination, and collective bargaining. Section 3 focuses on dismissed older workers and explores some key legal concepts as well as the conceptual and legal crossroads of employment protection, non-discrimination, and collective bargaining when it comes to dismissals of older workers for personal reasons and for reasons of redundancy, respectively. Section 4 contains some concluding remarks.

1. *See, e.g.*, the 2012 EU Year of Active Ageing (Decision No. 940/2011/EU, 14 September 2011 on the European Year for Active Ageing and Solidarity between Generations (2012), OJ 23.9.2011, No. L 246/5), European Commission, *Green Paper on Ageing. Fostering Solidarity and Responsibility Between Generations*, COM(2021) 50 final, UN Independent Expert on the enjoyment of all human rights by older persons/Claudia Mahler, *Report on Ageism and Age Discrimination*, Report to the UN Human Rights Council, 2021, A/HRC/48/53, and OECD, *Promoting Better Career Choices for Longer Working Lives. Stepping Up Not Stepping Out* (OECD 2024).
2. In 2022, the average retirement age for the entire Swedish labour market was 64.8 years. In 2023, following an increase in the statutory pension-related age limits, that entered into force at the turn of 2022/2023, the general average retirement age rose sharply to 66 years. This sharp increase is likely to moderate in 2024, as the marginal effect of the legislative change fades. *See* Pensionsmyndigheten, *Pensionsåldrar och arbetslivets längd: svar på regeringsuppdrag 2024* (Pensionsmyndigheten 2024) and Pensionsmyndigheten, *Statistics* (accessed at 25 April 2023): https://www.pensionsmyndigheten.se/nyheter-och-press/pressrum/da-gar-olika-yrkesgrupper-i-pension.
3. This chapter focuses on older workers and *dismissals* for personal reasons and reasons of redundancy. Aspects related to older workers and termination of employment through compulsory retirement are, for example, discussed in Numhauser-Henning's chapter in this book. Furthermore, aspects related to older workers and the relation between employment protection and social security (including pensions, sickness insurance, and unemployment insurance) are omitted here, *see, e.g.*, Ann Numhauser-Henning (ed.), *Elder Law. Evolving European Perspectives* (Edward Elgar, Cheltenham 2017).

2 LEGAL FRAMEWORKS

2.1 Employment Protection

At EU level, employment protection is only partly regulated and harmonised. Article 30 of the EU Charter of Fundamental Rights contains protection against unjustified dismissal.[4] Article 30 states that 'every worker has the right to protection against unjustified dismissal, in accordance with Union law and national laws and practices'. So far, the Court of Justice has interpreted Article 30 of the EU Charter restrictively and, for example, denied its application in cases challenging national austerity measures and deregulatory employment protection reforms in the wake of the economic crisis. The reference in Article 30 to 'national laws and practices' also limits its application.[5] The rights to non-discrimination and gender equality in Articles 21 and 23 of the EU Charter of Fundamental Rights are also relevant in the context of employment protection. Bans on discriminatory dismissals constitute a 'core element' of protection against unjustified dismissal.[6] In addition, the Directives on fixed-term work (99/70/EC), transfers of undertakings (2001/23/EC), and collective dismissals (98/59/EC) regulate some aspects of employment protection.

At Swedish level, comprehensive statutory employment protection was first put in place in the beginning of the seventies and is now regulated by the (1982:80) Employment Protection Act, from which deviations can be made through the means of collective bargaining. Permanent employment contracts are the main rule and can only be terminated if the requirement for just cause in section 7 of the (1982:80) Employment Protection Act (*lagen om anställningsskydd, LAS*) is met. Partly separate rules apply in relation to dismissal for personal reasons and dismissal for reasons of redundancy, respectively. Whereas all dismissals require just cause, impose an obligation on the employer to try to find alternative work for the employee facing the risk of dismissal, and include processes of trade union influence and information and consultation, dismissals for personal reasons also impose a number of obligations on employers and involve a close scrutiny of their actions in the individual situation in order to avoid arbitrariness. The regulation of redundancy dismissals entails a great

4. The EU Charter interplays with fundamental rights regulation in the Council of Europe and the ILO. The right to protection against unjustified dismissals is found in Art. 4 of the ILO Termination of Employment Convention 1982 No. 158 and in Art. 24 of the Council of Europe revised European Social Charter. Furthermore, on an evolving right to protection against unjustified dismissal in the framework of the European Convention on Human Rights, related to case law of the European Court of Human Rights on the right to respect for private and family life in Art. 8, *see* Hugh Collins, 'An Emerging Human Right to Protection Against Unjustified Dismissal' (2021) *Industrial Law Journal*, Vol. 50(1), pp. 36–69 https://doi.org/10.1093/indlaw/dwaa003.
5. *See, e.g.*, Catherine Barnard, 'The Charter in Time of Crisis: A Case Study of Dismissal', in Mark Freedland & Nicola Countouris, *Resocialising Europe in a Time of Crisis* (Cambridge University Press, Cambridge 2013), pp. 250–277 and Jeff Kenner, 'Article 30', in Steve Peers et al. (eds), *The EU Charter of Fundamental Rights: A Commentary* (2nd edn, Hart, Oxford, 2021).
6. *See*, for example, the non-discrimination Directives 2000/43/EC, 2000/78/EC, and 2006/54/EC. – *See* further Mia Rönnmar, 'Fixed-Term and Zero-Hours Contracts', in Guy Davidov, Brian Langille & Gillian Lester (eds), *The Oxford Handbook of the Law of Work* (Oxford University Press 2024), pp. 293–306.

respect for managerial prerogative, and employee protection mainly relies upon seniority rules, trade union involvement, and support through collectively bargained transition agreements.[7]

Employment protection and the balance between employee protection, on the one hand, and managerial prerogative and business management, on the other hand, are often debated. In recent years, important statutory and collective bargaining reforms and developments have resulted in a partly reshaped Swedish employment protection.

The major reform of Swedish employment protection in 2022 was a response to a political agreement on the need for deregulatory employment protection reform (the so-called January Agreement, *Januariavtalet*) and the outcome of a parallel process and interplay of legislation and collective bargaining. The final content of the reform was based on a cross-sectoral social-partner agreement, which formed the basis for both legislative reform and the conclusion of a new cross-sectoral collective agreement on security, transition, and employment protection.[8]

In autumn 2020, a new cross-sectoral social-partner agreement on security, transition, and employment protection was concluded.[9] This agreement contained a draft for a new national, cross-sectoral collective agreement, a so-called main agreement (*huvudavtal*), which according to the social partners would be concluded if certain conditions were met, including a requirement that the government proposed and the parliament adopted new legislation on employment protection, transition support, and transition study aid. The legislation was subsequently adopted, and the main agreement was signed in June 2022 by the employers' organisation, the Confederation of Swedish Enterprise; the white-collar trade union confederation, PTK; and the

7. *See* Government Bill prop. 1973:129 and Lars Lunning & Gudmund Toijer, *Anställningsskydd. Kommentar till anställningsskyddslagen* (Norstedts juridik/JUNO, Stockholm). For an analysis of Swedish employment protection regulation from the perspective of flexicurity and case law developments from the Swedish Labour Court, *see* Mia Rönnmar & Ann Numhauser-Henning, 'Swedish Employment Protection in Times of Flexicurity Policies and Economic Crisis' (2012) *International Journal of Comparative Labour Law and Industrial Relations*, Vol. 28(4) https://doi.org/10.54648/ijcl2012024.
8. *See* Government Inquiry Report SOU 2020:30, Government Inquiry Report Ds 2021:17, Government Bill prop. 2021/22: 176 and Svenskt Näringsliv samt PTK, *Huvudavtal om trygghet, omställning och anställningsskydd*, and Svenskt Näringsliv samt LO, *Huvudavtal om trygghet, omställning och anställningsskydd*. The political parties that formed a government coalition after the 2018 general election signed the 'January Agreement'. The agreement listed areas in which the government should intervene. One such area was employment protection reform, which was addressed in a parallel process of a government inquiry and negotiations among the social partners. In spring 2020, the government inquiry presented a proposal to revise the (1982:80) Employment Protection Act, and in autumn 2020, the cross-sectoral social-partner agreement was concluded. The government chose to base the legislative reform on the social-partner agreement instead of on the proposal by the government inquiry, *see* Government Bill prop. 2021/22:176.
9. The contracting parties were the Confederation of Swedish Enterprise and PTK. At this point, and after having participated in the negotiations, LO chose not to join the agreement. Later, two trade unions affiliated with LO, IF Metall and the Swedish Municipal Workers' Union, and then LO as such joined the agreement. *See* Svenskt Näringsliv samt PTK, *Partsöverenskommelse om trygghet, omställning och anställningsskydd* (4 December 2020) and Svenskt Näringsliv samt LO, *Partsöverenskommelse om trygghet, omställning och anställningsskydd* (10 November 2021).

blue-collar trade union confederation, LO. Later, a number of employers' organisations and trade unions in various labour market sectors joined and approved the agreement.

These collective bargaining and statutory developments have entailed a substantial reform of the (1982:80) Employment Protection Act and strengthened support for transition and lifelong learning of importance for both individual employees' competence development and the competence provision of companies and the overall Swedish labour market.[10]

The partly deregulatory reform of the (1982:80) Employment Protection Act entails, in response to employer interests and as regards employment protection for permanent employees, some deregulatory reorientation as regards the notion of just cause for dismissal for personal reasons, including an emphasis on transparency, foreseeability and breach of the employment contract, revised rules for selection of employees in redundancy dismissals with increased scope for unilateral employer exemptions for 'key employees', and new procedures for dismissal disputes, aimed at reducing costs for employers. In response to worker and trade union interests and as regards, *inter alia*, fixed-term contracts, the reform includes quicker conversion from fixed-term to permanent employment, quicker qualification for a priority right to re-employment in redundancy situations for fixed-term employees, and a new main rule on full-time employment. General fixed-term employment is replaced by specific fixed-term employment (*särskild visstidsanställning*, section 5a LAS), and a specific fixed-term employment contract is converted into a permanent employment contract after a total period of employment of 12 months within a 5-year period.[11] Furthermore, the cross-sectoral collective agreement entails important proactive support for transition and lifelong learning for both permanent and fixed-term employees and for sick employees, of importance for individual employees' competence development and the talent management of Swedish companies and the overall labour market. Collectively bargained transition support is extended through legislation to companies and employees not covered by collective bargaining. In addition, a new form of study aid, so-called transition study aid, is introduced to enable and support employees' lifelong learning and general competence provision. A new semi-compelling element is introduced in section 2c LAS, which allows only the top social-partner organisations at the cross-sectoral level to deviate from some of the key elements of the statutory employment protection regulation by way of collective bargaining, including interpretation of the notion of just cause for dismissal.

These developments reflect the dynamics and interrelation between employment protection and fixed-term contracts, as well as elements of flexicurity, such as a more equal treatment of permanent and fixed-term employees through a progressive build-up of rights of fixed-term employees and a weakened employment protection for permanent employees. At the same time, the cross-sectoral collective agreement

10. *See* Government Bill prop. 2021/22:176.
11. A new rule on the calculation of the total period of employment, adapted to the current realities of fixed-term contracts, zero-hours contracts, and on-call work, has been introduced according to which an employee who has had three or more (short) specific fixed-term employments during one month may include also the time spent in between employments during that month in the calculation of the total period of employment, section 3(2) LAS.

emphasises employability and provides strong support for transitions and training. This cross-sectoral collective agreement can be seen as a strengthening of the autonomous collective bargaining system and social partnership. However, this process has also been criticised as the cross-sectoral social-partner agreement had a decisive influence on the legislative process and the substantive content of the legislative reform. Not all social partners, for example, social partners in the public sector, were part of the negotiations, and the agreement and the ordinary legislative referral procedure and thorough legislative preparation process were curtailed.[12]

The reform has resulted in a more 'fragmented' employment protection regulation. Key elements of Swedish employment protection are now found in both the legislation and the cross-sectoral collective agreement. The coverage of the cross-sectoral collective agreement varies between the public and private sector and within sectors of the private sector.

At the same time, the substantive content of the (1982:80) Employment Protection Act and of the cross-sectoral collective agreement is aligned to a great extent, for example, as regards the content and interpretation of the notion of just cause. This alignment is achieved by writings in the preparatory works and the cross-sectoral collective agreement.

A bilateral social-partner Committee on the interpretation of the cross-sectoral collective agreement has been set up (*Huvudavtalsnämnden*), tasked with the interpretation of the collective agreement. This Committee is to be referred to in employment protection disputes in the Swedish Labour Court when the cross-sectoral collective agreement applies. At present, before case law has developed, the impact of the reorientation of the just-cause requirement, the interrelation between statutory and collective bargaining interpretation, and a number of issues related to the interplay, mandate and authority of the Court and the Committee, respectively, remain unclear.[13]

2.2 Non-discrimination

Non-discrimination law plays an increasingly important role in the protection of workers and has expanded in scope and strength in recent decades.

At EU level, there is fundamental rights protection and extensive primary and secondary legislation on non-discrimination. According to Articles 8 and 10 TFEU, the

12. *See* further Mia Rönnmar, 'Fixed-Term and Zero-Hours Contracts', in Guy Davidov, Brian Langille & Gillian Lester (eds), *The Oxford Handbook of the Law of Work* (Oxford University Press 2024), pp. 293–306. For an analysis and debate of this development and the employment protection reform, *see*, for example, Niklas Selberg & Erik Sjödin (eds), *Anställningsskydd i utveckling* (Iustus, Uppsala 2022), Petra Herzfeld Olsson, 'Den svenska modellen i en ny era' (2021-2022) *Juridisk Tidskrift*, No. 3, pp. 783–798, and Niklas Selberg & Erik Sjödin, '2020-talets modernisering av anställningstrygghet. Gränserna mellan politik och kollektiva förhandlingar förskjuts och partsöverenskommelser blir lag' (2022) *Arbetsmarknad & Arbetsliv*, Vol. 28, pp. 69–83.
13. *See* Niklas Selberg & Erik Sjödin (eds), *Anställningsskydd i utveckling* (Iustus, Uppsala 2022). *See* Labour Court judgment AD 2024:49 on the interpretation of a collective bargaining provision on employment protection in relation to the 2022 employment protection reform.

EU must adopt a mainstreaming approach in relation to equality and non-discrimination. A number of Articles in the EU Charter of Fundamental Rights, including Article 21 on non-discrimination and Article 23 on equality between women and men, contain protection against discrimination on various discrimination grounds, including, age, disability, and gender, as do a number of non-discrimination directives, including the (2006/54/EC) Recast Directive, the (2000/43/EC) Race Directive, and the (2000/78/EC) Employment Equality Directive. Furthermore, the Court of Justice has contributed greatly to the development of EU non-discrimination law, and principles and rules developed by the Court in case law have often later been codified in secondary law.[14]

At Swedish level, non-discrimination is regulated by the (2008:567) Non-discrimination Act, which implements EU law. The Act covers the discrimination grounds of gender, transgender identity or expression, sexual orientation, ethnic origin, religion or belief, disability, and age and applies in working life as well as in other areas of society. The (2008:567) Non-discrimination Act contains bans on direct and indirect discrimination, inadequate accessibility for persons with disabilities (previously legally framed as a requirement for reasonable accommodation), sexual harassment and harassment, and instruction to discriminate. The Act also contains provisions on a reversed burden of proof, positive action, active measures and a systematic and proactive approach.[15]

2.3 Collective Bargaining

At EU level, there is fundamental rights protection and some primary and secondary regulation on collective bargaining. Article 28 of the EU Charter of Fundamental Rights and Article 11 of the European Convention of Human Rights provide for freedom of association and the right to collective bargaining and collective action. Furthermore, the European social dialogue, as regulated in the Treaty of the Functioning of the European Union, forms an important part of EU labour law, and the EU (2022/2041/EU) Directive on adequate minimum wages also entails regulation on the promotion of collective bargaining.[16] The Swedish social partners jointly and strongly opposed the proposal for a Directive on adequate minimum wages in the EU with

14. On the development and characteristics of EU non-discrimination law, including its interaction with regulation within the ILO and the Council of Europe, *see* Mark Bell, 'EU Anti-discrimination Law: Navigating Sameness and Difference', in Paul Craig & Grainne de Búrca (eds), *The Evolution of EU Law* (3rd edn, Oxford University Press, Oxford 2021), Mark Bell & Ann Numhauser-Henning, 'Equal Treatment', in Teun Jaspers, Frans Pennings & Saskia Peters (eds), *European Labour Law* (2nd edn, Intersentia), Claire Kilpatrick & Hanna Eklund, 'Article 21', in Steve Peers et al. (eds), *The EU Charter of Fundamental Rights: A Commentary* (2nd edn, Hart Publishing, Oxford 2021), and Dagmar Schiek & Biljana Kotevska, 'Article 23', in Steve Peers et al. (eds), *The EU Charter of Fundamental Rights: A Commentary* (2nd edn, Hart Publishing, Oxford 2021).
15. *See* Susanne Fransson & Eberhard Stüber, *Diskrimineringslagen. En kommentar* (3rd edn, Norstedts Juridik, Stockholm 2021).
16. *See, e.g.*, Beryl ter Haar & Attila Kun (eds), *EU Collective Labour Law* (Edward Elgar 2021).

reference to collective autonomy and key principles of collective bargaining and wage formation in Sweden.[17]

At Swedish level, self-regulation through autonomous collective bargaining is central to the labour law and industrial-relations system and to the development and functioning of the labour market and the welfare state. Collective agreements are regulated in the (1976:580) Co-determination Act and constitute an important legal source. Wages and employment conditions are generally set by collective agreements, and there is no minimum wage legislation or system for extending collective agreements.

Collective bargaining in Sweden is influenced and supported by a tradition of social partnership, high trade union and employer organisation rates, extensive collective bargaining coverage, and strong legal rights and industrial-relations practices of freedom of association, collective action, and employee representation and information, consultation, and co-determination. The content of Swedish collective labour law and material scope for collective bargaining are set through an interplay between labour law legislation and collective bargaining at international, EU/European, and national/constitutional levels.

Collective agreements are entered into at different levels. There are three main categories of collective agreements in Sweden: national cross-sectoral collective agreements (i.e., long-term so-called main agreements), such as the new cross-sectoral collective agreement on security, transition, and employment protection (and its precursors, so-called transition agreements); national sectoral collective agreements, forming the core of the collective bargaining system and regulating wages and terms and conditions of employment; and local collective agreements. Collective bargaining is characterised by 'organised decentralisation' and an emphasis on local and individual bargaining within a framework of national sectoral and multi-employer collective bargaining. The so-called industry mark links wage increases in the Swedish labour market to wage increases set by national, sectoral collective agreements in the industrial export sector and functions as a cross-sectoral mechanism for collective bargaining coordination. However, the 'industry mark' is frequently criticised, by both scholars and trade union representatives, from the perspective of gender equality. They argue that the 'industry mark' makes it difficult to effectively address gender pay gaps and improve wages in female-dominated low-wage sectors.[18]

Most Swedish labour law legislation – including the (1982:80) Employment Protection Act – is semi-compelling (*semidispositiv*) and allows for deviations by way of collective bargaining, to both the advantage and detriment of individual employees. Collective agreements are legally binding, both for the contracting parties and for their members, and have normative and mandatory effects. Furthermore, an employer bound by a collective agreement is obliged to apply the agreement to all employees, irrespective of trade union membership.

17. Cf., COM(2020) 682 final.
18. *See* Mia Rönnmar & Andrea Iossa, *CODEBAR. Comparisons on Decentralised Bargaining: Towards New Relations Between Trade Unions and Works Councils? Swedish Country Report* (open access, 2022).

At present, there is perceived tension between a number of new EU Directives and the Swedish autonomous collective bargaining and wage formation system, including opposition by the social partners, despite the aims of the Directives to promote adequate minimum wages, collective bargaining, and gender equality and equal pay.

3 CONCEPTUAL AND LEGAL CROSSROADS

3.1 Concepts

This section explores and discusses some key legal concepts of relevance for the scope and strength of the legal protection of dismissed older workers.

The concept of *older workers* must be defined in a contextual way. In the political discourse on the ageing workforce, as well as in policies and actions directed towards older workers in the EU context, older workers are primarily understood as workers aged 55 years or older. Similarly, the case law of Court of Justice on age discrimination reflects the idea that the critical age with regard to employment is the period starting in the early end of a person's working life, and the case law mainly concerns employees from the age of just above 50 years of age and older. *Ageism* refers to beliefs, attitudes, norms and values to justify age-based prejudice, discrimination and subordination. Older workers is one group on the labour market that typically may be vulnerable in cases of dismissals. This is partly because older workers more often than younger workers have, are presumed to have, or are expected to get, reduced working ability, sometimes because of an age-related disability.[19]

Age, *disability*, and *gender* are three protected discrimination grounds of particular importance for the legal protection of dismissed older workers. In general, the concept of *age* can refer to chronological age, biological age, social age, and functional age. The protection against age discrimination in EU and Swedish law covers all chronological ages, but due to, for example, the problem of an ageing population, there is a clear emphasis on old age in the design and development of age discrimination law. The EU Member States, including Sweden, and the EU as such have signed the United Nations Convention on the Rights of Persons with Disabilities. The Court of Justice has aligned its interpretation of the concept of *disability* with that of the UN Convention and emphasised that 'the concept of disability must be understood dynamically and that the understanding of disability is constantly evolving'.[20] Article 1 of the UN Convention states that 'persons with disabilities include those who have long-term physical, mental, intellectual or sensory impairments which in interaction with various barriers may hinder their full and effective participation in society on an equal basis with others'. Furthermore, the relation between *age*, *disability*, and *illness* has important implications for older workers and the protection offered in dismissal situations by

19. *See, e.g.*, Ann Numhauser-Henning (ed.), *Elder Law. Evolving European Perspectives* (Edward Elgar, Cheltenham 2017).
20. *See* Joined Cases C-335/11 and C-337/11 *HK Danmark*, ECLI:EU:C:2013:222, cf., also Case C-152/11 *Odar*, ECLI:EU:C:2012:772.

way of the interplay of employment protection, non-discrimination, and collective bargaining.[21] The risk of illness and disability increases with old age. At the same time, and in the context of ageism and human rights of older persons, it can be problematic to relate, or even worse equate, old age with illness and disability.

Multiple and *intersectional discrimination*, and especially the interrelation between age, disability, and gender, also comes to the fore in discussions on the legal protection of dismissed older workers.[22] In 2023, a new Directive (2023/970) on Pay Transparency was adopted. The Directive lays down minimum requirements to strengthen the application of the principle of equal pay for equal work or work of equal value between men and women, in particular through pay transparency and reinforced enforcement mechanisms. Furthermore, and interesting in this context, the Directive contains the first EU law provision on intersectional discrimination. Article 3(2)(e) states that, in the context of the Directive, discrimination includes 'intersectional discrimination, which is discrimination based on a combination of sex and any other ground or grounds of discrimination protected under Directive 2000/43/EC or 2000/78/EC' (i.e., a combination of sex and religion or belief, disability, age, sexual orientation and racial and ethnic origin).[23]

Furthermore, in the employment protection context, the dismissal grounds *personal reasons* and *redundancy*, and the distinction between these two concepts, are crucial. The Swedish Labour Court has developed principles in case law (on so-called *fingerad arbetsbrist* and *splittrad motivbild*) on how to make this distinction and prevent attempts to 'misclassify' personal reasons as redundancy in order to circumvent the employment protection provided in case of dismissal for personal reasons by way of a strict just-cause requirement and scrutiny of employer actions.[24] In the collective bargaining context, *collective autonomy* is a key notion discussed in both classical and current labour law scholarship.[25]

21. On the relation between disability and illness, the Court of Justice in *HK Danmark* stated that 'if a curable or incurable illness entails a limitation which results in particular from physical, mental or physiological impairments which in interaction with various barriers may hinder the full and effective participation of the person concerned in professional life on an equal basis with other workers, and the limitation is a long-term one, such an illness can be covered by the concept of "notions of disability" within the meaning of Directive 2000/78'. The Court also held that '[i]llness as such cannot be regarded as a ground in addition to those in relation to which Directive 2000/78 prohibits discrimination'.
22. *See, e.g.*, Dagmar Schiek, 'On Uses, Mis-uses and Non-uses of Intersectionality Before the Court of Justice (EU)' (2018) *International Journal of Discrimination and the Law*, Vol. 18(2–3), pp. 82–103 https://doi.org/10.1177/1358229118799232 and Judy Fudge & Ania Zbyszewska, 'An Intersectional Approach to Age Discrimination in the European Union. Bridging Dignity and Distribution', in *Age Discrimination and Labour Law: Comparative and Conceptual Perspectives in the EU and Beyond*, Ann Numhauser-Henning & Mia Rönnmar (eds) (Alphen aan den Rijn, Kluwer Law International 2015).
23. *See, e.g.*, Laura Carlson, 'Unravelling Equal Pay: The EC's Pay Transparency Proposal in a Swedish Context' (2021/2022) *Juridisk Tidskrift* No. 2, p. 320.
24. *See, e.g.*, Labour Court judgment AD 2018:76.
25. For an analysis of discourses on collective autonomy and collective laissez faire, *see, e.g.*, Andrea Iossa, *Collective Autonomy in the European Union: Theoretical, Comparative and Crossborder Perspectives on the Legal Regulation of Collective Bargaining* (Lund University, Lund 2017) and Ruth Dukes, *The Labour Constitution: The Enduring Idea of Labour Law* (Oxford University Press 2014).

3.2 Dismissal for Personal Reasons and Older Workers

This section explores and discusses the conceptual and legal interplay of employment protection, non-discrimination, and collective bargaining when it comes to dismissals of older workers for personal reasons.

The vulnerability of older workers, due to ageism, possibly out-of-date competence and training, and weakened performance, has influenced the content of employment protection in Sweden and many other EU Member States, and special protection for older workers has been afforded. Such protection, by way of employment protection and especially seniority rules, is seen by some as affording necessary protection for older workers, while others view them as barriers for the entry of younger workers into the labour market.

In Sweden, a concern for older workers, as well as sick employees, has formed a basis for the statutory employment protection regulation from the beginning. As a rule, sickness or old age does not constitute just cause for dismissal. The employer is obliged to conduct a thorough investigation into the possibilities for adaptation and rehabilitation and find alternative work for the employee.[26] In this context, the employer's obligations are extensive and relate, for example, to the adjustment of the work environment, work organisation, working time, and work tasks. These obligations follow not only from regulation in the (1982:80) Employment Protection Act but also from related regulation on individual work environment adaption in the (1977:160) Work Environment Act and regulation on rehabilitation in the (2010:110) Social Insurance Code. An employee can be dismissed only after such measures have been taken, the possibility of finding alternative work has been tried and ruled out, and the employee can no longer perform work of any importance for the employer. Furthermore, the Swedish Labour Court has clarified, for example, in judgment AD 2022:34, that the requirement for adequate accessibility and reasonable accommodation in the context of disability discrimination and the (2008:567) Non-discrimination Act and the requirement for rehabilitation and work adaptation in the context of dismissal for personal reasons and the (1982:80) Employment Protection Act are basically the same.[27]

26. Cf., Government Bill prop. 1973:129, p. 18, and e.g., Labour Court judgments AD 2013:78 and AD 2014:26.
27. *See also* Labour Court judgment AD 2024:12 and AD 2020:58. On the issue of reasonable accommodation (regulated in Art. 5 of the (2000/78/EC) Employment Equality Directive), the Court of Justice has, for example, clarified that a reduction in working hours and a reassignment to another post may constitute reasonable accommodation measures, cf., Joined Cases C-335/11 and C-337/11 *HK Danmark*, ECLI:EU:C:2013:222 and Case C-485/20 *XXXX v. HR Rail SA*, ECLI:EU:C:2022:85. In the Swedish context, *see also* Labour Court judgment AD 2010:3 and the following complaint and critique from the Committee on the UN Convention on the Rights of Persons with Disability. According to Swedish law, there is only a legal requirement for reasonable accommodation and adequate accessibility in the context of disability discrimination; for a broader discussion, *see* Robin-Olivier's chapter in this book and Frank Hendrickx (ed.), *Reasonable Accommodation in the Modern Workplace. Potential and Limits of the Integrative Logics of Labour Law*, Bulletin of Comparative Labour Relations, Vol. 93 (Wolters Kluwer, Alphen aan den Rijn 2016).

Dismissals of older workers for personal reasons with links to aspects of old age, disability, sickness, and lack of performance may also raise questions of potential discrimination on grounds of age or disability or of potential multiple or intersectional discrimination, where also in particular gender but also other discrimination grounds may play a role.

Direct or indirect age-related dismissals – both for personal reasons and for reasons of redundancy – related, e.g., to ageism, age stereotypes or seniority may constitute age discrimination. At the same time, both direct and indirect age-related differential treatment can be objectively justified according to Article 6 of the (2000/78/EC) Employment Equality Directive, for example, with reference to legitimate employment policy, labour market, and vocational training objectives.

The recent statutory and collective bargaining developments in employment protection have important implications for the legal protection of dismissed older workers – both for personal reasons and for reasons of redundancy – and for older workers' possibilities for transition, retraining, and employability.

3.3 Dismissal for Reasons of Redundancy and Older Workers

This section explores and discusses the conceptual and legal interplay of employment protection, non-discrimination, and collective bargaining when it comes to dismissals of older workers for reasons of redundancy.

In Sweden, seniority is the main rule when it comes to redundancy selection. The employer has a unilateral right to decide when and if a redundancy situation exists, and in principle redundancy amounts to just cause.[28] The statutory seniority rules in section 22 of the (1982:80) Employment Protection Act imply that the priority and selection of employees are to be made according to the last-in-first-out principle, i.e., according to each employee's total period of employment with the employer (and in the event of equal periods of employment, giving priority to senior age). The employee must have sufficient qualifications for the tasks which remain after the redundancy. In principle, the order of dismissals encompasses all employees in the same production unit and who are covered by the same collective agreement (redundancy unit).

The seniority rules are semi-compelling, and deviations by way of collective bargaining can be made through the conclusion of a local collective agreement between the employer and the local trade union (a so-called *avtalsturlista*), whereby another order of dismissals can be decided. According to case law from the Swedish Labour Court, such a local collective agreement may not contravene good labour market practice or be discriminatory or arbitrary.[29] Furthermore, general principles and rules on redundancy dismissals, the content, adjustment, and application of the seniority rules, and various transition measures can also be regulated by way of sectoral and

28. *See*, for example, Labour Court judgments AD 1993:61 and AD 1993:101. On the principle of seniority in employment protection and labour law, *see* Birgitta Nyström, Bernard Johann Mulder & Monika Schlachter, 'Seniority in a Comparative Perspective' (2020) *Arbeidsrett*, Vol. 17(2), pp. 114–151 https://doi.org/10.18261/issn.1504-3088-2020-02-02.
29. *See*, for example, Labour Court judgment AD 1983:107.

cross-sectoral collective agreements (as the new cross-sectoral collective agreement on security, transition, and employment protection and existing transition agreements).

The (1982:80) Employment Protection Act also provides a scope for unilateral employer exemptions for 'key employees' who are of particular importance for the continuance of the business. The recent statutory and collective bargaining reform has widened the scope for such exemptions.

In redundancy dismissals, seniority rules as such, local collective agreements on order of dismissals, and unilateral employer decisions to exempt 'key employees' from the application of seniority rules can be legally challenged through non-discrimination law, importantly on grounds of age, disability, and gender, and with possible reference to multiple or intersectional discrimination.

The statutory seniority rules and the last-in-first-out principle are potentially indirectly age discriminatory (with a directly age-discriminatory element, in the way in which the employee's age is decisive in situations when the period of employment of two or more employees is the same) and favour older employees. Legitimate aims for justifying age-related treatment in the context of seniority, age and length of service are, for example, the value of experience on the job and of rewarding loyalty as well as the need for extra protection of older workers.

As regards collective agreements on order of dismissals, the case law of the Court of Justice and EU age discrimination law clarify that the social partners enjoy a broad margin of appreciation (perhaps even broader than the Member States) when it comes to justifying differential treatment on grounds of age. The Court has pointed to the fact that collective agreements differ from measures adopted unilaterally by Member States.[30]

In Labour Court judgment AD 2005:32, the redundancy dismissal of a disabled employee, resulting from the employer's decision to exempt two 'key employees' from the application of the statutory seniority rules, was found to be discriminatory on grounds of disability.

4 CONCLUDING REMARKS

This chapter focuses on dismissed older workers and aims to explore the legal protection offered to older workers in dismissal situations and the conceptual and legal interplay of three, basically protective, regulatory frameworks, namely, employment protection, non-discrimination, and collective bargaining. The discussion concerns Swedish labour law and industrial relations within an EU law perspective.

In this context, employment protection is the primary protective regulation to which non-discrimination protection and collective bargaining relate. The influence of EU law is stronger in the area of non-discrimination than in the area of employment

30. *See*, for example, Case C-45/09 *Rosenbladt v. Oellerking Gebaudereinigungsges. mbH* ECLI: EU:C:2010:601, where the Court of Justice, *inter alia*, discusses the fundamental right to bargaining collectively and the characteristics of collective bargaining. However, see the Swedish Labour Court judgment AD 2011:37, where redundancy dismissals resulting from such a local collective agreement on order of dismissals were found to be age discriminatory.

protection, and the importance of fundamental rights protection is also more significant here.

Employment protection – depending on its substantive regulation and strength – offers protection to older workers. In the Swedish setting, the distinction between personal reasons and redundancy when it comes to dismissals is important and not always clear-cut. The scope for managerial prerogative varies and is more extensive in redundancy situations. Thus, the conceptual framework and the operational handling of dismissals, in general, and in relation to dismissals of older workers, entail a risk of 'blurred boundaries', conscious 'misclassification' and risks of circumvention of individual employment protection. This is partly addressed by case law principles of the Swedish Labour Court (on so-called *fingerad arbetsbrist* and *splittrad motivbild*).

Employment protection in dismissal situations can both be strengthened and weakened by non-discrimination law and collective bargaining, which in turn interact with each other.

Non-discrimination law can reinforce existing protection of older workers, for example, in dismissals for personal reasons. It can also provide new and extended protection, for example, by way of reference to discrimination on grounds of disability and/or age in the context of dismissals for reasons of redundancy and rules for selection of employees, application of seniority rules, and scope for unilateral employer exceptions as regards 'key employees'. At the same time, however, non-discrimination law can challenge, from the perspective of age discrimination and younger workers, existing age-related statutory employment protection afforded to older workers through seniority rules and the principle of 'last-in-first-out'.

In turn, collective bargaining can reinforce the protection of older workers, for example, through the so-called transition agreements, which provide various transition support measures and severance pay. However, as a result of the semi-compelling character of important rules in Swedish employment protection legislation and most Swedish labour law legislation, there is also scope for collective bargaining to derogate from statutory individual rights and weaken the protection of older workers. Experiences in the field of gender equality and persisting gender pay gaps reflect the risk that collective bargaining might reinforce, or unsuccessfully address, existing discriminatory structures. Similarly, the case law of the European Court of Justice on age discrimination permits a wide 'margin of appreciation' for Member States and social partners and respect for collective autonomy and collective bargaining.

There are a number of interesting and important questions related to future employment protection developments and implications of the Swedish major statutory and collective bargaining reforms, such as: Will there be a shift towards more individual agreements on termination of the employment relationship and a weakening of the statutory employment protection, in general and/or for older workers?; Will the main Swedish rule on strong employment protection for old and sick employees prevail?; Will the new and strengthened rights to transition, retraining, and employability be effective against ageism, increase protection of older workers, and promote active ageing?; Will fundamental rights protection, non-discrimination law and case law developments from EU/European and international courts and supervisory bodies further influence Swedish courts and social partners, and in what ways?; and Will there be new collective bargaining initiatives in this area?

Given the overlapping regulatory frameworks and complex interplay of employment protection, non-discrimination, and collective bargaining, these and other questions are awaiting adjudication and legal interpretation and clarification. In the meantime, there is a continued need for critical discussion, socio-legal scholarly analysis, and comparative and interdisciplinary research approaches.

CHAPTER 8

Older Workers, Unfair Dismissal, and Age Discrimination Law: Strengthening Employment Protection? Comparative Perspectives from Australia and the UK

Alysia Blackham[*]

1 INTRODUCTION

Dismissal, retirement and redundancy are critical points in the employment relationship where older workers might be subject to unfair treatment. In the Australian Human Rights Commission's (AHRC) National Prevalence Survey, of those who had experienced age discrimination at work in the last two years (n = 309), 11% reported that they had experienced poor treatment that resulted in them leaving the job or had been made redundant or dismissed, and 12% reported being threatened with redundancy or dismissal, or being asked to retire.[1] While this is less frequent than other reported experiences of age discrimination (such as having limited employment, promotion, or training opportunities, at 52% of affected respondents), the consequences of experiencing discrimination at the point of dismissal, retirement or redundancy are personally and financially significant for older workers. Older workers

* This research was funded by the Australian Government through the Australian Research Council's *Discovery Projects* funding scheme (project DE170100228) and a Visiting Researcher position funded by the Swedish Research Council for Health, Working Life and Welfare (Forte) within the research project *Prolonged Working Lives, Older Workers and Dismissals: A Study of the Dynamics Between Employment Protection, Non-discrimination and Collective Bargaining*. The views expressed herein are those of the author and are not necessarily those of the Australian Government or Australian Research Council.

1. Australian Human Rights Commission, *National Prevalence Survey of Age Discrimination in the Workplace: The Prevalence, Nature and Impact of Workplace Age Discrimination Amongst the Australian Population Aged 50 Years and Older*, 34 (2015).

(particularly older women) may struggle to gain new employment after leaving their role, in part due to age discrimination in recruitment.[2] Thus, experiencing discrimination or unfair treatment in dismissal, retirement and redundancy may consign older workers to early or earlier retirement; this runs directly counter to government attempts to extend working lives for older workers.[3]

The question, then, is what can law do about this? Do existing legal frameworks – structured around discrimination law and unfair dismissal law – strengthen employment protection for older workers who experience unfair treatment in dismissal, retirement and redundancy? And how, if at all, can discrimination law and unfair dismissal law interact to strengthen employment protection? It is possible, for example, that discrimination law and unfair dismissal law could operate in separate spheres, rarely interacting; be overlapping and mutually supportive, with different legal rights complementing each other; or be overlapping, yet detracting, with different forms of legal protection undermining or limiting each other.

Drawing on a mixed-method, multi-year comparative study of the enforcement of age discrimination law in the UK and Australia, this chapter interrogates the relationship between age discrimination law and unfair dismissal, particularly as it affects older workers. Integrating statistical analysis of claims and cases, including 1,208 reported UK Employment Tribunal decisions and 108 Australian cases; qualitative expert interviews with 101 expert respondents; and a survey of 76 legal practitioners and advocates who work in this area,[4] I consider the ways in which age discrimination and unfair dismissal are linked in practice, and whether these linkages work to strengthen or undermine employment protection.

This mixed-methods research design offers new insights into how employment protection is framed 'on the books' and how that law is translated and implemented in practice. By considering comparative perspectives from the UK and Australia – which, despite their common legal roots and traditions, have adopted different approaches to the interaction of employment and discrimination law – we can better examine how different legal frameworks interact to strengthen or undermine employment protection. In an area of law where few cases progress to the courts and the public arena, and

2. Marc Bendick Jr, Lauren E Brown & Kennington Wall, *No Foot in the Door*, 10 J. Age'g & Soc. Pol'y 5 (1999) https://doi.org/10.1300/j031v10n04_02; David Neumark, Ian Burn & Patrick Button, *Is It Harder for Older Workers to Find Jobs? New and Improved Evidence from a Field Experiment*, 127 J. Pol. Eco'y 922 (2018) https://doi.org/10.3386/w21669.
3. *See, e.g.*, Alysia Blackham, *Addressing the Ageing Workforce: A Critical Examination of Legal Policy Objectives and Values*, 37 Age'g & Soc'y 1362 (2017) https://doi.org/10.1017/s0144686x16000313.
4. These methods, their limits and broader findings have been described in detail elsewhere: Alysia Blackham, *Reforming Age Discrimination Law: Beyond Individual Enforcement* (Oxford University Press 2022). This research had ethics approval from the Human Research Ethics Committee of the University of Melbourne (ID number 1748973.4). To maintain source anonymity, each interview respondent is identified with A or UK and a number (e.g., A1). I return to this question of methods in the conclusion below.

most claims are settled or abandoned,[5] it is critical to look to empirical methods to understand the practical operation of the legal framework and barriers to realising employment rights in practice. In drawing on the perspectives of legal practitioners, unions, and statutory equality agencies, and comparing this with data on claims and cases, this project offers a nuanced picture of the limits of law and legal protection for older workers and new insights into the interplay of different legal rights. Drawing on these multiple forms of data, I identify gaps in enforcement and in the legal framework, flagging the need for new approaches to advance employment protection.

2 THE LEGAL FRAMEWORK

Both age discrimination law and unfair dismissal law may provide older workers with employment protection in dismissal, retirement and redundancy. Age discrimination law has been in place in Australia progressively since the 1990s. It is now unlawful in every state and territory, and federally, to discriminate on the basis of age in employment. Unusually, age discrimination in employment is regulated in Australia under both industrial law (the *Fair Work Act 2009* (Cth) (FWA) adverse action provisions) and discrimination law (the federal *Age Discrimination Act 2004* (Cth) (ADA) and state and territory equality statutes). It is not possible to bring a claim under both industrial law and discrimination law or under both state/territory and federal law; claimants must choose the jurisdiction in which they will pursue their claim.[6] This means, then, that unfair dismissal claims – under the FWA – preclude a claim under discrimination law, and vice versa. It is likely, then, that discrimination law and unfair dismissal law operate in largely separate spheres, with limited interaction. Problematically, too, the FWA has the strictest time limits in the country for claims relating to dismissal, which must be brought within 21 days of the dismissal taking effect.[7] The Fair Work Commission (FWC), which receives such claims, may allow a further period only in 'exceptional circumstances'.[8]

These provisions have resulted in only limited case law. In my examination of cases decided until 31 December 2017, I found only 108 Australian age discrimination cases; 12 were substantively successful.[9] The first successful case under the federal ADA was finally handed down in 2021,[10] a gap of nearly 17 years between the passage of federal age discrimination law and the first successful substantive claim in the

5. Alysia Blackham & Dominique Allen, *Resolving Discrimination Claims Outside the Courts: Alternative Dispute Resolution in Australia and the United Kingdom*, 31 Austl. J. Lab. L. 253 (2019) https://doi.org/10.2139/ssrn.3362157; Blackham, *Reforming Age Discrimination Law*, *supra* n. 4.
6. ADA, §12 (2004); FWA, §§725, 727, 729, 732, 734 (2009).
7. FWA, §366(1)(a) (2009).
8. *Ibid.*, §366(2).
9. Alysia Blackham, *Why Do Employment Age Discrimination Cases Fail? An Analysis of Australian Case Law*, 42 Sydney L. Rev. 1 (2020).
10. *Gutierrez v. MUR Shipping Australia Pty Limited*, FedCFamC2G 56 (2021); successfully appealed to increase the remedy in *Gutierrez v. MUR Shipping Australia Pty Limited*, FCA 399 (2023).

courts. I have argued elsewhere, then, that age discrimination law, and its individual enforcement model, represents a limited way of advancing age equality at work.[11]

The UK legal framework is more straightforward. The *Equality Act 2010* (UK) (EqA) prohibits age discrimination in employment in Great Britain (GB). The provisions are, for the most part, largely replicated in Northern Ireland (NI) in the Employment Equality (Age) Regulations (Northern Ireland) 2006 (NI). Unfair dismissal in the UK is regulated by the *Employment Rights Act 1996* (UK) (ERA) Part X. A claim can be brought to an Employment Tribunal (ET) under both the EqA and the ERA; there is no need to elect one jurisdiction over the other.

In GB, the processes for enforcing the EqA (in relation to work) and the ERA are essentially the same: claims are first filed with the statutory conciliation agency Acas, then proceed to an ET if not conciliated successfully. Pursuing a claim under the EqA might be preferable in some circumstances, as compensatory damages are not capped as under the ERA. Further, there is no need to fulfil the statutory qualifying period of two years of service before filing a claim of discrimination. Thus, a discrimination claim may offer advantages to unfair dismissal law in some contexts. That said, it is generally not necessary for claimants to make a firm decision as to which claim to pursue; both can be pursued in tandem. There is potential, then, for claims to overlap.

3 STRENGTHENING EMPLOYMENT PROTECTION?

In the expert interviews conducted in this project, there were widespread concerns regarding the capacity of age discrimination law to respond to age-based inequality at work, particularly in Australia. In Australia, age discrimination law was seen as overly technical, costly to enforce, and subject to slow conciliation processes at statutory equality agencies (as opposed to the more efficient conciliation conducted for unfair dismissal claims at the FWC). Some practitioners and unions, then, preferred to pursue claims via unfair dismissal law, seeing it as offering quicker and easier mechanisms to obtain a remedy:

> if someone's been dismissed, and they're not seeking a whole tonne of damages, unfair dismissal is just the easiest way to go. ... you're going to go with the easier, faster, quicker, more efficient route [of unfair dismissal], even though there is potentially a bigger issue at play [of discrimination].[12]

There was recognition, though, that this did not always address the underlying discrimination or structural inequality that prompted the claim in the first place.[13] Unfair dismissal law can also overcome some of the difficulties of proof that affect discrimination law.[14] In sum, then, as one respondent noted: 'if an unfair dismissal

11. Blackham, *Reforming Age Discrimination Law*, *supra* n. 4; Alysia Blackham, *Extending Working Life for Older Workers: Age Discrimination Law, Policy and Practice* (Hart Publishing 2016).
12. A107.
13. A108.
14. A157. Also A109.

[claim] were available to me, I would use that in preference to discrimination law. … it is faster; it is simpler; it is cheaper'.[15]

Thus, in jurisdictions where only one claim is possible, respondent practitioners tend to choose industrial law and unfair dismissal law where possible. In the advocate survey, for example, federal industrial law (the FWA) was the preferred route for bringing or defending a claim (*see* Figure 8.1). As two respondents noted, though, the appropriate jurisdiction generally depends on the individual claim or case and has to be determined on a case-by-case basis.

Figure 8.1 Responses to the Question 'If Presented with a Potential Age Discrimination Claim, in Which Jurisdiction Would You Be Most Likely to Advise Your Client to Pursue the Claim/Prefer to Defend the Claim?'; Advocate Survey (n = 26)

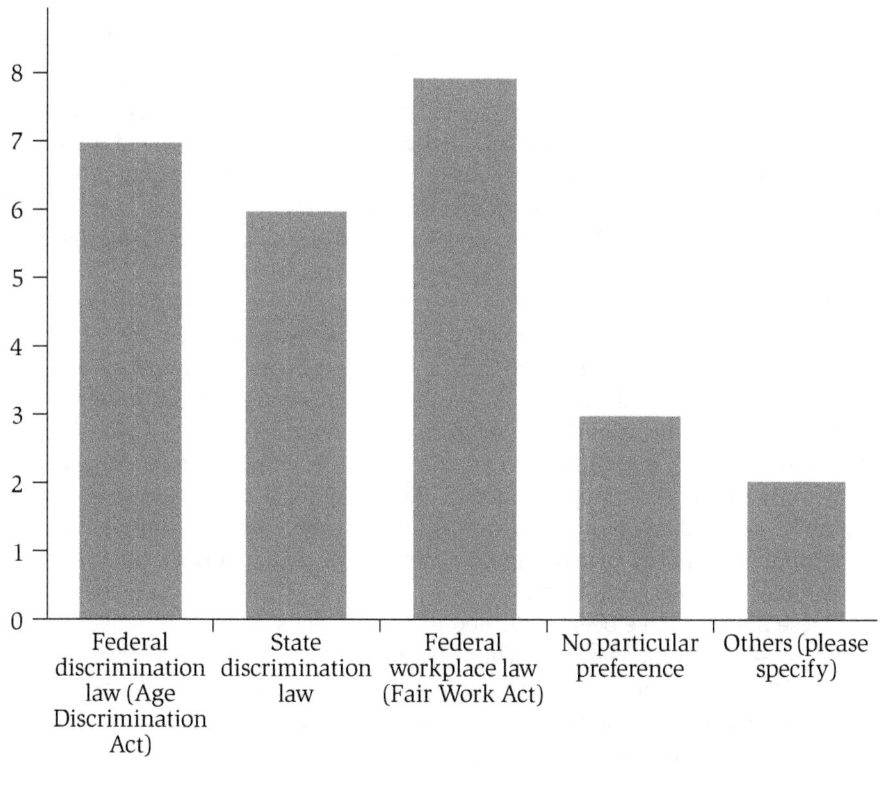

That said, there are distinct advantages to bringing an age discrimination claim in some circumstances. In both Australia and the UK, claims in the age discrimination jurisdiction offer four distinct advantages over those in unfair dismissal law: first, discrimination law applies to a broader group of workers than 'employees', meaning

15. A115.

employment status is slightly less problematic for bringing a discrimination claim. Second, compensation is not capped under discrimination law, and compensation for injury to feelings can be awarded. Third, discrimination law does not have a qualifying period of service, which may particularly assist those with disrupted work histories. Fourth, time limits under discrimination law may be more flexible than those under unfair dismissal law. That said, age discrimination law is beset by its own substantive challenges, being seen as overly technical and relying on restrictive legal tests (such as the comparator requirement). In the sections that follow, then, I consider whether allowing claims under both unfair dismissal law and age discrimination law (as in the UK) can strengthen employment protection for older workers or whether the interaction between the two jurisdictions simply reflects the need to strengthen employment protection more generally.

4 STRENGTHENED PROTECTION? CASE-BASED ANALYSIS

To what extent are these views and concerns reflected in age discrimination case law? Case law represents a key public artefact of how individuals use law to advance their individual rights. However, it is important to recognise that publicly reported judicial decisions may not fully represent the diversity of claims that are received by statutory equality agencies; most claims are resolved via confidential conciliation, often with a non-disclosure agreement, and few claims proceed to the public arena.[16] It is critical, then, to acknowledge the limits of case-based analysis in understanding individual employment protection in practice.

Of the 108 cases in the Australian case law sample (which included cases under both industrial and discrimination law), 63 related to dismissal (including 12 relating to retirement and 10 relating to redundancy). These areas are therefore overrepresented in the case sample compared to their reported prevalence in the AHRC's Prevalence Survey. This is perhaps unsurprising, given the potential costs of bringing a complaint of age discrimination and the focus on compensatory damages as a remedy; only the most serious, financially damaging instances of discrimination are likely to be pursued in court proceedings. Further, the case law sample includes a disproportionate number of older male claimants, flagging gaps in enforcement for older women and younger workers.[17]

These findings have been replicated in the UK, considering a broader sample of 1,208 ET cases.[18] In this sample, where possible to discern, many cases related to dismissal (127), retirement (5) and redundancy (33), that is, the end of the working relationship. Again, men were slightly more likely to bring an age discrimination claim to an ET than women: the sample included 664 male claimants and 573 female

16. Blackham & Allen, *supra* n. 5; Dominique Allen & Alysia Blackham, *Under Wraps: Secrecy, Confidentiality and the Enforcement of Equality Law in Australia and the UK*, 43 Melb. U. L. Rev. 384 (2019).
17. Blackham, *Why Do Employment Age Discrimination Cases Fail? An Analysis of Australian Case Law*, *supra* n. 9, 9.
18. Alysia Blackham, *Enforcing Rights in Employment Tribunals: Insights from Age Discrimination Claims in a New 'Dataset'*, 41 Legal Stud. 390 (2021) https://doi.org/10.1017/lst.2021.11.

claimants.[19] This difference became more pronounced when withdrawn claims were excluded from the analysis, with women representing only 44.2% of claimants in non-withdrawn claims.[20]

Unlike in Australia, in the UK, it is straightforward to bring claims on the basis of both age discrimination and unfair dismissal. Unfair dismissal was the most common additional jurisdiction in the ET case sample, being raised in 764 age discrimination cases. This was far more common, for example, than raising additional grounds of discrimination, including disability discrimination (284); sex discrimination (267); or race discrimination (245). Thus, it appears that unfair dismissal law is often invoked in addition to age discrimination law. This is consistent, too, with statistics from Acas, which show that in 2018–2019, 50% of age discrimination early conciliation notifications (ECAs) and 62% of age discrimination ET1 forms (for making a claim to the ET) raised unfair dismissal as an additional ground. Thus, in jurisdictions where this is possible, age discrimination and unfair dismissal claims have significant overlap in practice.

5 REALISING THE ADVANTAGES OF AGE DISCRIMINATION LAW?

As noted above, claims in the age discrimination jurisdiction offer four distinct advantages over those in unfair dismissal law. In the parts that follow, I explore these advantages in more detail and consider the degree to which they are evident in the case sample.

5.1 Employment Status

Discrimination law might be used to challenge redundancy, dismissal or retirement where claimants are not 'employees', and employment status precludes a claim of unfair dismissal. That said, the scope of equality law in the UK is fairly constrained and likely excludes independent contractors and those engaged under complex contractual arrangements from the scope of equality law. The prohibition of discrimination in section 39 of the EqA, as it relates to work, is limited to 'employers' in relation to 'employment'.[21] 'Employment' is defined in the EqA as 'employment under a contract of employment, a contract of apprenticeship or a contract personally to do work'.[22] This definition of employment, and prohibition of discrimination, typically excludes independent contractors who are not engaged 'personally to do work'.[23] However, it does include a third category, 'workers'. In *Halawi v. WDFG UK Ltd*,[24] the UK Court of

19. *Ibid.*, at 398.
20. *Ibid.*
21. *See* similarly Employment Equality (Age) Regulations (Northern Ireland) 2006 (NI) reg 7.
22. EqA §83 (2010); *see also* §212(1). A similar definition applies in NI: 'employment under a contract of service or of apprenticeship or a contract personally to do any work': reg 2(3).
23. *Jivraj v. Hashwani* [2011] UKSC 40.
24. [2014] EWCA Civ 1387, [2015] 1 CMLR 31.

Appeal held that 'employment' under EU law (and, therefore, the EqA) required the putative employee to:

(1) agree personally to perform services; and
(2) be subordinate to the employer (i.e., generally bound to act on the employer's instructions).[25]

As in *Halawi*, this might exclude those engaged under complex contractual arrangements from the scope of equality law.[26]

The limited definition of 'employment' in the EqA may be remedied in part by the protection of contractors in section 41 of the EqA,[27] which provides that a 'principal' must not discriminate against, harass or victimise a 'contract worker' in contractual terms, access to work, benefits, facilities or services, or any other detriment. A 'principal' is defined as:

> a person who makes work available for an individual who is –
>
> (a) employed by another person, and
> (b) supplied by that other person in furtherance of a contract to which the principal is a party (whether or not that other person is a party to it).[28]

This, then, covers those employed by third parties who are deployed to the 'principal' (e.g., in agency work). It does not cover the self-employed, nor does EU law relating to age discrimination.[29] It would not cover the complex contractual arrangements in *Halawi*. Thus, as employment becomes more fragmented and fissured,[30] equality law is struggling to catch up.

That said, in some cases in the ET case sample, the broader scope of equality law (at least, compared to unfair dismissal law) proved critical for claimants. Despite claimants benefiting from the broader scope of equality law, few substantive age discrimination claims succeeded. In *Mortimer v. Cavendish School of English Ltd*,[31] for example, the claimant (a teacher) was held to be a 'worker' who had been misrepresented as being self-employed.[32] However, the claimant's age discrimination claim was

25. *Ibid.*, ¶4.
26. Note, though, the decision of the CJEU in *JK v. TP SA* (Case C-356/21) CJEU 9 (2023), which may serve to broaden the scope of equality law in the EU.
27. And the similar provision in Employment Equality (Age) Regulations (Northern Ireland) 2006 (NI) reg 10.
28. EqA §41(5) (2010).
29. Catherine Barnard & Alysia Blackham, *Self-Employed: The Implementation of Directive 2010/41 on the Application of the Principle of Equal Treatment Between Men and Women Engaged in an Activity in a Self-Employed Capacity*, 5–6 (2015).
30. David Weil, *The Fissured Workplace: Why Work Became So Bad for So Many and What Can Be Done to Improve It* (Harvard University Press 2014), Chapter 1.
31. [2018] UKET 2420957/2017.
32. *Ibid.*, ¶¶3, 25. This was determined at a preliminary hearing; this decision was not uploaded to the ET website, despite being decided on 10 May 2018.

still unsuccessful, as age did not play any part in the respondent's decision-making.[33] The claimant's claims for victimisation and holiday pay succeeded.[34]

In *Warrilow v. Openwork Ltd*,[35] the claimant performed his duties first as an employee, then as a self-employed contractor, then as sole principal in a firm under a franchise agreement, and then as a director of a limited company. The relevant contract was between the respondent and the company of which the claimant was a director; the claimant gave a guarantee of the company's responsibilities. The claimant was held to not be an employee for the purposes of unfair dismissal, as there was no 'correct contractual relationship'.[36] However, the Tribunal assumed that section 41 could potentially apply to bring the claimant's work within the EqA.[37] It was ultimately not necessary to decide this point, as a lack of evidence meant the age discrimination claim had no reasonable prospect of success.[38]

In *Law v. Wirral Golf Club Ltd*,[39] the claimant – a resident PGA professional golfer – was held to not be an employee for the purposes of unfair dismissal law but was under 'a contract personally to do work' for the purposes of discrimination law. The claimant was appointed to the role personally,[40] and his power to appoint a substitute was not unfettered; rather, it was a more limited power to provide appropriate cover when the claimant was absent,[41] meaning it 'was not inconsistent with personal performance'.[42] The age discrimination claim was therefore allowed to proceed but was later withdrawn.

Agency work and triangular employment relationships were also recurring issues in the case sample. *Ahmed v. Autism Consulting Ltd*,[43] for example, concerned an agency-supplied science teacher bringing a claim against the proprietor of the school. While within the scope of the EqA, the claimant's discrimination claims failed as the Tribunal preferred the other party's evidence, and the allegations were contradicted by a contemporaneous log written by the claimant herself.[44]

In *Worboyes v. FDR Ltd*,[45] an agency work arrangement was found to fall within section 41. While the respondent was not the claimant's employer, it was a 'principal', as the claimant was employed under a contract personally to do work with an agency (via a second agency). The claimant's contract with the agency was described as a 'contract for services';[46] however, the claimant was required to personally perform work and to work under the direction of the respondent.[47] Section 41 therefore applied,

33. *Ibid.*, ¶32.
34. *Ibid.*, ¶¶46–47.
35. [2018] UKET 3329040/2017.
36. *Ibid.*, ¶35.
37. *Ibid.*, ¶14.
38. *Ibid.*, ¶¶36–37.
39. [2017] UKET 2405273/2016.
40. *Ibid.*, ¶36.
41. *Ibid.*, ¶41.
42. *Ibid.*, ¶50.
43. [2017] UKET 3322728/2016.
44. *Ibid.*, ¶¶26–28.
45. [2017] UKET 3200314/2017.
46. *Ibid.*, ¶20.
47. *Ibid.*, ¶¶21, 22.

even if the respondent did not contract directly with the claimant's employing agency.[48]

Florian v. Adecco UK Ltd[49] involved an Amazon warehouse agency worker's claim against the employment agency itself. It is possible, however, that the discrimination claim was better directed at Amazon as principal:

> The Claimant submitted that she had worked as quickly as she could at Amazon and that the statement that she had not met the quota was discriminatory towards her on the basis of her age.[50]

A generous reading of this brief description might interpret this as a claim of indirect discrimination on the basis that Amazon work targets and required levels of work intensity are a provision, criterion or practice (PCP) that particularly disadvantages older workers.[51] However, this would probably be a difficult claim to bring and prove, especially given other older workers could likely meet Amazon's work targets. The claimant (perhaps understandably) therefore withdrew her complaint of age discrimination.[52] The claimant's other claims – of unfair dismissal and for redundancy pay – were dismissed as she did not meet the statutory requirements relating to length of service, and her claims for holiday pay, notice pay and failure to get wage slips were dismissed as having no reasonable prospect of success.

Hughes v. Rolls Royce plc[53] involved an agency worker who was held not to be directly employed by Rolls Royce. The ET held that the claimant had no reasonable prospects of success in showing that his agency status had 'turned into one of an employee'.[54] Regardless, section 41 could apply,[55] but the age discrimination claim was out of time[56] and had not been clearly particularised (remained 'ethereal' according to the ET).[57] The claim was therefore struck out in its entirety.

Thus, while employment status is less problematic under discrimination law, and may enable claimants to pursue a claim that would otherwise be precluded under unfair dismissal law, these cases illustrate that the difficulty of proving a discrimination claim may offset these benefits.

The scope of Australian discrimination law is broader than that in the UK. Under the FWA, 'employee' and 'employer' are (unhelpfully) defined in section 335 as having 'their ordinary meanings'. While there is no third 'worker' category in Australia, independent contractors are covered by the adverse action provisions of the FWA section 342. 'Adverse action' in relation to independent contractors includes where a principal with a contract for services with an independent contractor:

48. *Ibid.*, ¶23.
49. [2018] UKET 3200082/2018.
50. *Ibid.*, ¶15.
51. The claimant's age was not specified in this decision; I am assuming (guessing) the claimant was an older worker.
52. *Florian v. Adecco UK Ltd* [2018] UKET 3200082/2018, ¶15.
53. [2019] UKET 2601847/2018.
54. *Ibid.*, ¶24.
55. *Ibid.*, ¶30.
56. *Ibid.*, ¶31.
57. *Ibid.*, ¶30.

- terminates a contract with an independent contractor;
- 'injures' the independent contractor in relation to the terms and conditions of the contract;
- alters the position of the independent contractor to their prejudice;
- refuses to make use of, or agree to make use of, services offered by the independent contractor; or
- refuses to supply, or agree to supply, goods or services to the independent contractor.[58]

Independent contractors also receive protection under the adverse action provisions if a principal who proposes to enter into a contract for services with them: refuses to engage them; discriminates against them in the terms or conditions offered; or refuses to make use of services or supply goods or services to the independent contractor.[59]

Discrimination against independent contractors might be further captured by section 340 of the FWA, which prohibits adverse action by a 'person' because 'another person': has a workplace right; has, or has not, exercised a workplace right; or proposes to exercise a workplace right. A 'workplace right' includes having a benefit under a 'workplace law, workplace instrument or order made by an industrial body' or being able to make a complaint to a person or body which has the capacity under a workplace law to seek compliance with that law or a workplace instrument.[60] A 'workplace law' includes the *Independent Contractors Act 2006* (Cth) and 'any other law of the Commonwealth, a State or a Territory that regulates the relationships between employers and employees'.[61] This is broad enough to include rights under equality and discrimination law: in *Bayford v. MAXXIA Pty Ltd*,[62] it was held that the *Equal Opportunity Act 1995* (Vic) was a 'workplace law'.[63]

Under the ADA, 'employment' is defined broadly to include work 'under a contract for services' (i.e., independent contractors or the self-employed).[64] In Victoria, the definition of 'employee' in the *Equal Opportunity Act 2010* (Vic) extends to those 'engaged under a contract for services', the definition of 'employer' includes 'a person who engages another person under a contract for services', and the definition of 'employment' includes 'engagement under a contract for services'.[65] Thus, discrimination law clearly protects independent contractors at state and federal level.

58. FWA, §342 (2009).
59. *Ibid.*
60. *Ibid.*, §341 (2009).
61. *Ibid.*, §12 (2009).
62. [2011] FMCA 202 (12 April 2011).
63. *Ibid.*, ¶¶140–141. Though *see* the discussion in *Wroughton v. Catholic Education Office Diocese of Parramatta* [2015] FCA 1236 (17 November 2015) ¶¶75–79 where it was argued (but unnecessary to decide) that the *Sex Discrimination Act 1984* (Cth) was not a 'workplace law'. *See* further *Stephens v. Australian Postal Corporation* [2011] FMCA 448 (8 July 2011) and *CFMEU v. Leighton Contractors Pty Ltd* [2012] FMCA 487 (25 July 2012), which both related to workers' compensation statutes.
64. ADA, §5 (2004).
65. Equal Opportunity Act (Vic), §4 (2010).

Understandably, then, employment status was less contentious in the Australian case law sample than in the UK. Employment status was only flagged in two cases, both in Queensland.

In *Lidis v. Top Dog Minders Pty Ltd*,[66] the claim related to the grant of a management agreement which would outsource the day-to-day running of the business in exchange for a percentage of the revenue as a management fee. The Queensland Civil and Administrative Tribunal (QCAT) held that:

> entry into a 'management agreement' of this nature does not fall within the parameters of the definition of 'work' contained in the Schedule to the Act. Rather, this offer was a commercial business opportunity, and could not be classed as 'work'.[67]

This is surprising, as 'work' is defined broadly in the *Anti-Discrimination Act 1991* (Qld) to include: employment, work under a contract for services, work on a commission basis, under a statutory appointment, and so on.[68] Further, the claimant had previously done the 'work' involved in the management agreement as an employee. It appears, however, that the Tribunal did not need to consider this question in detail, as there was no evidence of discrimination.[69]

In *Gladdish v. Queensland*,[70] a fire services officer was compulsorily retired at the age of 65. After his retirement, a new collective agreement was certified, which provided for a pay increase to be back paid to a date prior to the claimant's retirement. The claimant argued that the failure to pay him the back pay was indirect discrimination on the basis of age. QCAT held that the claimant's position as a retiree did not fall within the definition of 'work' under the *Anti-Discrimination Act 1991* (Qld): 'There is no scope within the definition of "work" contained in the Act to include someone who is retired.'[71] If the claimant was not a 'worker', then it followed that a 'term' could not be imposed on him for the purposes of indirect discrimination:

> As at the time of his retirement, the parties ceased to have a relationship whereby it was possible for the Respondent to impose any terms upon Mr Gladdish, as there no longer existed an employer-employee context within which such an imposition could take place.[72]

The claim of indirect discrimination was dismissed.

It is rare, then, for employment status to be contentious in Australian age discrimination claims; this may reflect the advantages for claimants of the broad and inclusive wording of the statutory provisions. Thus, age discrimination law may offer significant advantages over unfair dismissal law for those who have uncertain or borderline employment status.

66. *Lidis v. Top Dog Minders Pty Ltd* [2011] QCAT 232, ¶21.
67. *Ibid.*, ¶21.
68. Discrimination Act (Qld) Sch. 1 (1991).
69. Lidis, *supra* n. 66, ¶22.
70. *Gladdish v. Queensland* [2012] QCAT 721.
71. *Ibid.*, ¶27.
72. *Ibid.*, ¶30.

5.2 Unlimited Damages

Age discrimination law might also offer advantages to claimants over unfair dismissal law as compensation is uncapped. In GB, for example, compensation for a claim of unfair dismissal is composed of:

- a fixed-sum 'basic award', calculated using length of service, age and gross weekly pay (capped at GBP 571 for dismissal on or after 6 April 2022);
- a compensation award, capped at a year's gross pay and GBP 93,878 (for dismissal on or after 6 April 2022).

Injury to feelings awards are not available for unfair dismissal claims.

By contrast, damages for discrimination claims are not capped. Under section 124(2)(b) of the EqA, ETs may, following a contravention of the EqA, order the respondent to pay compensation to the complainant. An award of damages may include compensation for injured feelings, irrespective of whether there is any other form of compensation.[73] There is no upper bound to the amount of compensation that can be awarded.

That said, compensation in discrimination claims is rarely very high: according to barrister Dee Masters, compensation is generally limited to one to two years' pay.[74] Workers on higher incomes therefore have more incentive to bring a discrimination claim, as their ultimate compensation will be higher. In practice, it is difficult – and rare – for claimants to benefit from the more generous remedies available under age discrimination law. In the UK case sample, of the 43 successful claims, a remedy was discernible in 30 cases. The primary (and generally sole) remedy was compensation, awarded in all 30 cases. The median award for the age discrimination claim was GBP 8,800, with a minimum of GBP 1,000 and maximum of GBP 386,059.73.[75] In 19 cases, the claimant was successful in multiple jurisdictions (not just on the basis of age discrimination). In these cases, age discrimination compensation ranged from 10% to 97% of the total award, typically reflecting whether loss of earnings was awarded in the age discrimination jurisdiction or not. Where specified, most cases (22) included awards for injury to feelings,[76] though the highest awards were typically for loss of earnings (awarded in the age discrimination jurisdiction in 11 cases).[77]

Of the 43 successful age discrimination claims, 22 also alleged unfair dismissal. In 13 of these 22 cases, the claim for unfair dismissal was also successful. In 9 of the cases, a remedy had been determined, as detailed in Table 8.1.

73. EqA, §119(4) (2010).
74. House of Commons, *Oral Evidence: Older People and Employment* (2018) HC 359 Q94 (17 July 2018), https://www.parliament.uk/business/committees/committees-a-z/commons-select/women-and-equalities-committee/inquiries/parliament-2017/older-people-and-employment-17-19/.
75. These calculations use gross figures.
76. The exception was *Fogarty v. Colman Greaves Fabrications Ltd* [2019] UKET 2410534/2018, where the claimant did not seek an award for injury to feelings.
77. Cf., *Shirin v. Wilson Barca LLP* [2019] UKET 2208035/2016, where GBP 46,908.38 was awarded for injury to feelings and aggravated damages; the claimant sought over GBP 1 million.

Table 8.1 Remedies in Successful Unfair Dismissal and Age Discrimination Claims (GBP), UK Case Sample

Case	*Unfair Dismissal Award*	*Age Discrimination Award*	*Total Compensation*	*AD%*	*Feelings Quantum*
Jolly v. Royal Berkshire NHS Foundation Trust [2019] UKET 3324869/2017	84,429.18	20,000	200,000	10	20,000
McGrann v. Wynne [2019] UKET 2423662/2017	24,673.77	10,036.22	35,129.99	43	9,000
Hodgkiss v. Travis Perkins Trading Company Ltd [2019] UKET 2411659/2018	18,921.64	21,101.47	41,557.47	51	0
Roberts v. Logo Design Grp Ltd [2018] UKET 2404024/2017	35,873.09	172,070.06	210,212.19	82	15,000
Roberts v. Voodoo Doll Ltd [2018] UKET 2403330/2017	16,487.42	13,500	29,987.42	45	12,500
Morrison v. JSB Healthcare Ltd [2018] UKET 1600440/2017	28,253.85	6,560	34,813.85	19	6,560
Robinson v. Schivo NI Ltd (In Liquidation) [2018] NIFET 00013/16FET	8,238	8,800	17,038	52	7,500
Wright v. Schivo NI Ltd (In Liquidation) [2018] NIFET 00012/16FET, 00270/16IT	16,624	8,800	25,424	35	7,500
Browne v. Schivo NI Ltd (In Liquidation) [2018] NIFET 00010/16FET, 00268/16IT	4,483	8,800	13,283	66	7,500

In all bar one of these cases, the remedy for the age discrimination claim included damages for injury to feelings. The awards for injury to feelings, as a proportion of the total compensation awarded, ranged from 7% to 56% of the total award; in practice, too, the award of interest typically increased this figure even further. Thus, the availability of damages for injury to feelings is an important aspect of discrimination law remedies and offers a significant advantage over the unfair dismissal jurisdiction.

It is possible, too, to achieve higher compensation overall in the discrimination jurisdiction, as remedies are not capped, though this is rarely seen in practice. The noticeable exception in this study was *Roberts v. Logo Design Grp Ltd*,[78] where the claimant received GBP 172,070.06 in the age discrimination jurisdiction. As well as compensation for injury to feelings, this represented the claimant's loss of income from the date of judgment to his 67th birthday (a period of 11 years). The claimant had previously earned GBP 29,500 a year; following his dismissal, he was only able to obtain work being paid the national living wage. The compensation awarded therefore represented the difference between the two salaries. The ET awarded 10 years of lost earnings (at GBP 15,249.52 a year), plus pension contributions of 3% of salary.[79] This far exceeds the compensation for an unfair dismissal claim; that said, if the respondent had participated in the hearing, it is likely that such a large sum would not have been awarded.

Thus, there may be benefits to claimants to pursue an age discrimination claim as well as an unfair dismissal claim; where successful, the discrimination jurisdiction offers significant benefits in terms of remedies, though this is rarely seen in practice.[80]

5.3 Qualifying Service

In GB, the qualifying period to make an unfair dismissal claim is generally two years of continuous service.[81] By contrast, there is no qualifying period to bring a claim under age discrimination law. Age discrimination law may therefore be particularly important for strengthening employment security for those with short periods of job tenure and disrupted work histories; this may particularly assist younger workers and women. In this case sample, in *Wilkinson v. Arnold Brickwork Ltd*,[82] for example, the claimant's unfair dismissal claim was rejected as they had not completed the period of qualifying service. Their age discrimination claim was upheld. Similarly, in *Ramzan v. Shop On Time Ltd*,[83] the unfair dismissal claim was withdrawn, mostly likely on the basis that the qualifying period had not been met.[84] This is consistent with Lockwood and others'

78. [2018] UKET 2404024/2017.
79. *Ibid.*, ¶14.
80. The small number of successful cases in the Australian jurisdiction, and even fewer with a recorded remedy, makes a comparative study of compensation difficult.
81. ERA, §108 (1996). Note, though, that this would be amended by the proposed Employment Rights Bill (UK) (2024).
82. [2019] UKET 1401376/2018.
83. [2018] UKET 1304475/2017.
84. *Ibid.*, ¶¶2, 18.

findings in relation to sexual harassment cases: discrimination law is often used when claimants do not meet the service threshold for an unfair dismissal claim.[85]

5.4 Limitation Periods

To bring a claim of unfair dismissal in GB, a claim must be filed within three months of the dismissal.[86] A claim may only be brought outside of this period 'in a case where [the ET] is satisfied that it was not reasonably practicable for the complaint to be presented before the end of that period of three months'.[87] Complaints relating to work under the EqA are also subject to a three-month time limit.[88] However, that time limit may be extended 'as the employment tribunal thinks just and equitable'.[89] I have explored elsewhere how this is applied in practice in this case sample; many age discrimination claims are presented out of time, and it is rare for time limits to be extended.[90] That said, the time limits for equality claims - and, in particular, the extension of time limits - may be more generous than those under unfair dismissal law. In *Winschief v. SRS Realisations 2017 Ltd (in administration)*,[91] for example, the claimant filed for unfair dismissal three months late. The ET held that the claimant could not show that it was not 'reasonably practicable' for her to file her claim on time.[92] However, the ET held that it *was* just and equitable to extend time on the age discrimination claim. This claim was ultimately successful.

In Australia, the difference in limitation periods between discrimination law and unfair dismissal law is even more dramatic. The FWA has the strictest time limits in the country for claims relating to dismissal, which must be brought within 21 days of the dismissal taking effect.[93] This applies to both unfair dismissal claims and adverse action claims relating to dismissal. The FWC may allow a further period only in 'exceptional circumstances'.[94] By contrast, under equality law, time limits vary across the jurisdictions. In some states and territories, there is no fixed time limit on claiming; rather, the statutory equality agency may choose to decline to conciliate,[95] terminate a complaint,[96] close a complaint[97] or decline a complaint[98] if the claim is out of time. This

85. Graeme Lockwood, Patrice Rosenthal & Alexandra Budjnaovcanin, *A Quantitative and Qualitative Analysis of Sexual Harassment Claims 1995–2005*, 42 Indus. Rels. J. 86, 89 (2011) https://doi.org/10.1111/j.1468-2338.2010.00599.x.
86. ERA, §111(2) (1996).
87. *Ibid.*, §111(2)(b) (1996).
88. EqA, §123(1) (2010).
89. *Ibid.*
90. Blackham, *Enforcing Rights in Employment Tribunals: Insights from Age Discrimination Claims in a New 'Dataset'*, *supra* n. 18.
91. [2019] UKET 1402539/2018.
92. *Ibid.*, ¶43.
93. FWA, §366(1)(a) (2009).
94. *Ibid.*, §366(2) (2009).
95. Equal Opportunity Act (Vic), §116(a) (2010).
96. Australian Human Rights Commission Act (Cth), §46PH(1)(b) (1986).
97. Human Rights Commission Act (ACT), §78(1)(a) (2005).
98. Anti-Discrimination Act (NSW), §89B(2)(b) (1977).

time period is 12 months in New South Wales (NSW)[99] and Victoria[100] and two years in the Australian Capital Territory (ACT)[101] and the AHRC.[102] Other jurisdictions have more fixed time requirements: in Tasmania, South Australia (SA), the Northern Territory (NT), Western Australia (WA) and Queensland, for example, complaints must be filed within 12 months; a complaint may be accepted outside this window in Tasmania if the Commissioner is 'satisfied that it is reasonable to do so';[103] in Queensland if 'satisfied the complainant has shown good cause';[104] in NT if 'appropriate to do so';[105] in WA on 'good cause being shown';[106] and in SA if there is 'good reason' why the claim was out of time or it is just and equitable to do so.[107]

Time limits are therefore a particularly important consideration in the Australian context, which may prompt claimants to prefer discrimination law over industrial law. Indeed, in the Australian case sample of 108 cases, a key procedural failure point under the FWA was time limits: only one application for an extension of time was granted; seven were refused; and one claim was held to be within time.[108]

6 THE LIMITS OF AGE DISCRIMINATION AND UNFAIR DISMISSAL LAW

While there are distinct advantages to claimants in bringing a claim in age discrimination law, this does not mean that it will be straightforward to successfully establish a claim. Success is the exception, not the norm. Further, some problems are shared by both discrimination law and unfair dismissal law, and age discrimination law has its own difficulties relating to causation and dealing with 'unfairness'.

6.1 Mutual Problems: 'Detriment' and 'Dismissal'

While age discrimination law offers some benefits to claimants, it is beset by challenges that are similar to those under unfair dismissal law. For example, in the UK, age discrimination occurs where A treats B *less favourably* than A treats or would treat others.[109] Issues with establishing detriment were encountered by claimants in the UK case sample, where claimants failed to establish there was a dismissal, including

99. *Ibid.*, §89B(2)(b).
100. Equal Opportunity Act (Vic), §116(a) (2010).
101. Human Rights Commission Act, §78(1)(a) (2005).
102. Australian Human Rights Commission Act (Cth), §46PH(1)(b) (1986), as amended by the Anti-Discrimination and Human Rights Legislation Amendment (Respect at Work) Act (Cth), (2022) increasing the time limit from 6 months to 24 months.
103. Anti-Discrimination Act (Tas), §63 (1998).
104. Anti-Discrimination Act (Qld), §138 (1991). Note this has been extended to two years by the Respect at Work and Other Matters Amendment Act (Qld), §29 (2024).
105. Anti-Discrimination Act (NT), §65 (1992).
106. Equal Opportunity Act (WA), §§83(4)–(5) (1984).
107. Equal Opportunity Act (SA), §§93(2)–(2a) (1984).
108. Blackham, *Why Do Employment Age Discrimination Cases Fail? An Analysis of Australian Case Law, supra* n. 9.
109. EqA, §13 (2010); *Employment Equality (Age) Regulations (Northern Ireland) 2006* (NI) reg 3.

because the claimant resigned (and it was not a case of constructive dismissal),[110] there was a voluntary mutual termination,[111] or the employment came to an end at the end of a contractual term.[112] This often affected both discrimination and unfair dismissal claims. The exception was in *Kopec v. BDW Trading Ltd*,[113] where the tribunal held that the claimant was entitled to resign due to the repudiatory breach by the respondent in failing to follow its own equality policy and recognise and address abuse by a delivery driver.[114] Thus, establishing that there is a 'dismissal' or detriment is a challenge for claimants under both age discrimination law and unfair dismissal law.

6.2 Singular Problems: Causation

Age discrimination law also has its own difficulties and limits, which might make recourse to unfair dismissal law preferable. For example, discrimination law in Australia generally has no shifting burden of proof,[115] despite a lack of proof being a fundamental barrier to claiming and success.[116] The FWA, though, does have a shifting burden of proof.[117] Further, discrimination laws in Australia and the UK often rely on a 'comparator',[118] which can seriously inhibit successful claims, particularly for those who experience intersectional discrimination.[119] (Though, rather than requiring a comparator, Victoria, the ACT and SA define direct discrimination as being treated 'unfavourably'[120] rather than *less* favourably.)

A fundamental challenge, too, arises from the requirement that claimants show that their treatment was 'because of',[121] on the grounds of,[122] or 'on the basis of'[123] age

110. Resigned: *Gosling v. Harding* [2019] UKET 2501261/2018; *Ayree v. Langridge Organic Products Ltd* [2017] UKET 2301647/2016; *Mhlanga v. Kendrick* [2017] UKET 2300280/2017, ¶35; *Wallace v. KPI Bridge Oil London Ltd* [2017] UKET 227596/2016, ¶120; *Ellis v. Henley Media Group Ltd* [2017] UKET 2208129/2016; *Cheney v. MS Amlin Corporate Services Ltd* [2017] UKET 2207640/2016; *Ali v. Virgin Active Ltd* [2018] UKET 2206652/2017; *Taylor v. Dr Kelpie and Partners (A Partnership)* [2017] UKET 1401375/2016, ¶24.
111. *Wilson v. Wilson Devonald Griffiths John Ltd* [2017] UKET 1600416/2016, ¶36.
112. *Astor v. Ministry of Defence* [2017] UKET 2404378/2016, ¶33.
113. [2019] UKET 2207111/2017.
114. *Ibid.*, ¶51.
115. Though note the shifting burden in the ACT: Human Rights Commission Act, §53CA (2005). Queensland has also adopted a shifting burden of proof following the Respect at Work and Other Matters Amendment Act (Qld), §47A (2024).
116. A3; A5; A103; A107; A108; A109; A112; A113; A115; A118; A150; A155; A158; A160; A164; UK80; UK161; UK84. *See* further Blackham, *Reforming Age Discrimination Law, supra* n. 4, Chapter 6.
117. *See* Anna Chapman, Kathleen Love & Beth Gaze, *The Reverse Onus of Proof Then and Now: The Barclay Case and the History of the Fair Work Act's Union Victimisation and Freedom of Association*, 37 U. N. S. W. L. J. 471 (2014).
118. Belinda M. Smith, *From Wardley to Purvis: How Far Has Australian Anti-discrimination Law Come in 30 Years?*, 21 Austl. J. Lab. L. 3 (2008) https://doi.org/10.2139/ssrn.1005528.
119. Shreya Atrey, *Comparison in Intersectional Discrimination*, 38 Legal Stud. 379 (2018) https://doi.org/10.1017/lst.2017.17.
120. Equal Opportunity Act (Vic), §8(1) (2010); Discrimination Act (ACT), §8(2) (1991); Equal Opportunity Act (SA), §85A (1984).
121. EqA, §13 (2010); FWA, §351(1) (2009); ADA, §14 (2004); Equal Opportunity Act (Vic), §8(1) (2010); Equal Opportunity Act (SA), §85A (1984); Discrimination Act, §8(2) (1991).
122. Anti-Discrimination Act (NSW), §49ZYA (1977); Equal Opportunity Act (WA), §66V (1984).

to successfully bring a claim of age discrimination. While age does not need to be the only, sole, or dominant reason,[124] in some jurisdictions, it must be 'a substantial reason'.[125]

In practice, it appears fairly straightforward for respondents to deny or defend a claim of discrimination on the basis that the treatment was for some other reason. For example, in the UK, so long as respondents genuinely (even if not fairly) acted based on the claimant's perceived (mis)conduct,[126] or poor performance,[127] then this is sufficient to discharge their burden of proof. This reflects the focus on the actual mental processes of the respondent in causation in discrimination law.[128]

For example, in *Mundin v. Beal Developments Ltd*,[129] the claimant was dismissed with notice from his position after refusing to agree to a 'succession plan' that would reduce his working hours and pay. During the claimant's notice period, he was summarily dismissed following an altercation with the managing director. The respondent did not conduct a full investigation of the issue in accordance with its own policies before commencing disciplinary proceedings. The unfair dismissal claim in relation to the summary dismissal was successful, but the ET held that the summary dismissal did not constitute age discrimination.[130] Despite the procedural deficiencies of the summary dismissal, it was driven by a 'genuine belief in [the claimant's] misconduct',[131] even though a proper investigation would have revealed that the instigating issue – the claimant's use of an external hard drive – was not actually contrary to company policy or practice.[132]

This focus on the decision-makers' 'minds and thought processes' implies a semi-subjective test for causation, though the UK courts have expressly rejected any focus on or consideration of motive or intention.[133] This reliance on 'belief' and perception would not be acceptable if raised in an unfair dismissal claim, but age discrimination law is not directed to addressing what is 'unfair', but rather treatment 'because of' age. This is the case even if the respondent's treatment of the claimant is incompetent,[134] harsh,[135] or involves mistakes;[136] indeed, in one case in this sample,

123. Anti-Discrimination Act (Tas), §14(2) (1998); Anti-Discrimination Act (NT), §20(1) (1992); Anti-Discrimination Act (Qld), §10(1) (1991).
124. Equal Opportunity Act (Vic), §8(2) (2010); Anti-Discrimination Act (NT), §20(3) (1992); Anti-Discrimination Act (Tas), §14(2) (1998).
125. *See, e.g.*, Equal Opportunity Act (Vic), §8(2) (2010); Anti-Discrimination Act (Qld), §10(4) (1991).
126. *Fenton v. Pennine Acute Hospitals Trust* [2017] UKET 2414119/2012, ¶109; *Mundin v. Beal Developments Ltd* [2017] UKET 1800455/2017, ¶84.
127. *Astor v. Ministry of Defence* [2017] UKET 2404378/2016, ¶95; *Fairclough v. Allen* [2018] UKET 2403288/2017, ¶50; *Toner v. L F Fasthouse Ltd* [2019] NIFET 06955/18IT, ¶82.
128. *Ladele v. London Borough of Islington* [2009] ICR 387, 396, ¶40.
129. [2017] UKET 1800455/2017.
130. Though the dismissal with notice and imposition of a 'succession plan' was held to be age discrimination.
131. *Mundin v. Beal Developments Ltd* [2017] UKET 1800455/2017 ¶84.
132. *Ibid.*, ¶¶67, 85–87.
133. *R v. Governing Body of JFS* [2010] 2 AC 728, 748, ¶20 (Lord Phillips).
134. *Cassidy v. Quest Vitamins Ltd* [2017] UKET 2401277/2017, ¶¶87, 94.
135. *Amu v. Department for Work and Pensions* [2018] UKET 1600465/2017, ¶223.23.

the treatment was held to be due to the respondent's incompetence rather than the claimant's age, meaning causation was not established.[137]

Unreasonable treatment, or treatment for unreasonable reasons, does not necessarily constitute discrimination.[138] Similarly, if all employees are treated equally, treatment of the claimant will not be 'because of' a protected characteristic.[139] Again, this is the case even if the treatment is unreasonable.[140] In the case sample, this is amply demonstrated by the harassment case of *Shirin v. Wilson Barca LLP*.[141] In that case, the claimant worked as a paralegal in a law firm. The senior partner 'had temper issues':[142] 'he shouts and swears at all his staff and also clients'.[143] This was supported by evidence of multiple witnesses, staff, and the partner himself. The issue for a harassment complaint, however, was that every member of staff was shouted at and abused; it was therefore not 'related to a relevant protected characteristic'.[144] This reflects the 'levelling down' concerns related to a formal understanding of equality or seeing equality as consistency:[145] treating all employees equally badly is not direct discrimination, as everyone is treated the same. While this is a core feature of current formulations of age discrimination law, it limits its practical utility in addressing poor and abusive HR practices. In *Shirin v. Wilson Barca LLP*,[146] however, there *were* some instances of harassment by a different staff member that related to age as a relevant protected characteristic.[147] Thus, the claim succeeded, but not in relation to the senior partner's 'boorish' behaviour.

Similar issues with causation emerge in the Australian case law under the FWA. Under the FWA, employers must not take adverse action 'because of' age.[148] Under section 360 of the FWA, 'a person takes action for a particular reason if the reasons for the action include that reason'. Further, under section 361:

> (1) If:
> (a) ... it is alleged that a person took, or is taking, action for a particular reason or with a particular intent; and
> (b) taking that action for that reason or with that intent would constitute a contravention ...
>
> it is presumed that the action was, or is being, taken for that reason or with that intent, unless the person proves otherwise.

136. *Kumar v. Guy's and St Thomas' NHS Foundation Trust* [2017] UKET 2302841/2015, ¶67; *Richardson v. B&Q plc* [2017] UKET 1401373/2016, ¶¶73, 74.
137. *Cassidy v. Quest Vitamins Ltd* [2017] UKET 2401277/2017, ¶¶87, 94.
138. *Ladele*, *supra* n. 128, 397, ¶40 (Elias J).
139. *McCalister v. South Eastern Health & Social Care Trust* NIIT 00741/16IT (2017), ¶4.34. *See also Ladele*, *supra* n. 128, 401, ¶53 (Elias J).
140. Though treating all employees the same way, and failing to accommodate difference, may found a case of indirect discrimination: *see Ladele*, *supra* n. 128, ¶53 (Elias J).
141. [2019] UKET 2208035/2016.
142. *Ibid.*, ¶9.
143. *Ibid.*, ¶11.
144. *Ibid.*, ¶¶63–64.
145. Sandra Fredman, *Equality: A New Generation?*, 30 Indus. L. J. 145, 155 (2001) https://doi.org/10.1093/ilj/30.2.145.
146. [2019] UKET 2208035/2016.
147. *Shirin*, *supra* n. 77, ¶¶67, 69.
148. FWA, §351(1) (2009).

However, if an employer can show that age is not a 'substantial and operative factor' in the adverse treatment, the claim will fail.[149] In the case sample, this affected a number of claims under the FWA.[150]

Following the High Court decision of *Board of Bendigo Regional Institute of Technical and Further Education v. Barclay* ('*Barclay*'),[151] which related to industrial activity, an employer's evidence as to the reason for their actions can be enough to show that age is not a reason for the treatment.[152] The court's task is to ascertain the actual reason for the treatment. For French CJ and Crennan J in *Barclay*:

> the central question remains 'why was the adverse action taken?'. This question is one of fact, which must be answered in the light of all the facts established in the proceeding. ... Direct evidence of the reason why a decision-maker took adverse action, which may include positive evidence that the action was not taken for a prohibited reason, may be unreliable because of other contradictory evidence given by the decision-maker or because other objective facts are proven which contradict the decision-maker's evidence. However, direct testimony from the decision-maker which is accepted as reliable is capable of discharging the burden upon an employer ... .[153]

While this implies that courts look to the *subjective* reason for the treatment, Gummow and Hayne JJ expressly rejected the distinction between subjective and objective reasons in *Barclay:* 'to engage upon an inquiry contrasting "objective" and "subjective" reasons is to adopt an illusory frame of reference. Such an inquiry into the "objective" reasons risks the substitution by the court of its view of the matter for the finding it must make upon an issue of fact'.[154] However, where an employer gives 'direct evidence ... as to [their] state of mind, intent or purpose',[155] that may well be decisive. Indeed, an employer's reason for acting will likely be accepted if the evidence is reliable, even if the reason itself is irrational. This makes causation a substantial and possibly determinative hurdle for claimants, which is nearly impossible to surmount.

This was noted in this study by the expert respondents as being a challenge in practice:

> the cases where it is blatant [age discrimination] and [respondents] just come up with some whacky other excuse, that has to fly, because that's what they say, and the evidence that we have, that sometimes that's actually genuine.[156]

149. *Board of Bendigo Regional Institute of Technical and Further Education v. Barclay* (2012) 248 CLR 500, 522–523 ¶¶57–59 (French CJ and Crennan J), 542, ¶127 (Gummow and Hayne JJ), 546, ¶146 (Heydon J) ('*Barclay*'). *See also General Motors-Holden Pty Ltd v. Bowling* (1976) 12 ALR 605, 619 (Mason J).
150. *Silver v. Rogers & Rogers* [2012] FMCA 674, ¶32 ('*Silver*'); *Vink v. LED Technologies Pty Ltd* [2013] FCA 443 ('*Vink* [2013]'); *Farah v. Ahn* [2012] FMCA 44 ('*Farah*').
151. Barclay, *supra* n. 149.
152. *Ibid.*, at 517, ¶¶44–45 (French CJ and Crennan J); *see also* at 542, ¶127 (Gummow and Hayne JJ).
153. *Ibid.*, at 517, ¶¶44–45 (citations omitted); *see also* at 542 ¶127 (Gummow and Hayne JJ).
154. *Ibid.*, at 540–541, ¶121; *see also* at 541 [126] (Gummow and Hayne JJ).
155. *Ibid.*, at 517, ¶¶44–45 (French CJ and Crennan J).
156. A110.

In practice, even though the burden of proof is meant to shift under the FWA, courts are 'so deferential to employers' evidence'[157] that causation has become an impossible hurdle.

The impact of *Barclay* is illustrated by *Vink v. LED Technologies Pty Ltd* ('*Vink*').[158] In that case, the employer 'categorically denied that age was a factor in his decision to dismiss the applicant'.[159] On appeal, the Federal Court accepted that denial as: '[i]t seems to me that, rightly or wrongly, Mr Ottobre believed that the applicant was incompetent when Mr Ottobre decided on 9 November 2011 to dismiss the applicant'.[160] Even if that belief was wrong, it would not affect the quality of the denial. In *Vink*, there was some evidence to support the employer's belief of incompetence – even if that evidence was later proven to be false.[161] While this:

> may well have weighed heavily in an unfair dismissal claim ... In a case such as the present, however, where what was alleged was a contravention of s 351 of the FW Act, the focus was on the substantial and operative reasons which motivated Mr Ottobre to dismiss Mr Vink. Provided that those reasons did not include Mr Vink's age, it mattered not that they were based on a mistaken assessment or were not supported by the weight of the evidence.[162]

This was the case even though Mr Vink was likely told that the employer wanted a 'youthful and vibrant' culture – the issue was what the employer actually (subjectively) intended:[163] 'it is probable that Mr Clerk (the general manager) did tell the applicant that Mr Ottobre wanted a vibrant and youthful culture. However, that is not to say that Mr Ottobre did want a vibrant and youthful culture or that that was his reason for dismissing the applicant'.[164] Thus, this indicates that any plausible explanation for dismissal – which does not include a protected ground – will be sufficient to exclude a claim under the FWA and that courts are willing to second-guess employer statements to look for their 'true' motivation. This will operate as a substantial bar to success for claimants under the FWA. Again, then, discrimination law is not aimed at achieving 'fairness' or 'reasonableness' at work: that is the purview of unfair dismissal law.

6.3 Justifying Limited Reasoning? Concurrent Claims

In some cases, having recourse to both age discrimination and unfair dismissal law might undermine or limit concurrent claims. Judges or tribunal members might limit their consideration of concurrent and overlapping claims, assuming that there is limited benefit in addressing all grounds of claim in depth. Indeed, some US studies

157. A5.
158. *Vink* [2013], *supra* n. 150.
159. *Ibid.*, ¶26.
160. *Ibid.*, ¶¶26, 47–49.
161. *Ibid.*, ¶45.
162. *Ibid.*
163. *Vink v. Led Technologies Pty Ltd*, [2012] FMCA 917, ¶35 ('*Vink* [2012]'). *See also Farah*, *supra* n. 150, ¶94.
164. *Vink* [2012], *supra* n. 163, ¶35.

have shown that putting forward multiple grounds of claim is less likely to lead to success.[165]

For example, in the UK case of *Vickers v. ABM Facilities Services UK Ltd*,[166] the Tribunal accepted the actual comparator put forward by the claimant being another (older, female) cleaner in the respondent's business.[167] While the claimant (age 36) and the comparator (age 60) were treated differently when similar concerns were raised about their recorded working hours, the Tribunal held that this was not due to age or sex:

> Mrs Bell's recorded and claimed for hours were indeed a matter of concern, which the Respondent wished to address with her; but ... it was prevented from doing so by the shopping centre's owners, the Respondent's client, who adopted an extremely protective attitude towards Mrs Bell and others who had like her been working at the site for many years. In other words, any difference in treatment of the Claimant and Mrs Bell was nothing to do with the Respondent and, if anything, against their wishes. ... the most likely reason for the Respondent's treatment of the Claimant, [was] the fact that he had lodged a formal complaint about Mr Aungier's recruitment of a friend of his to work at the shopping centre. Finally, it is also noteworthy that there is no mention by the Respondent in any of the documentation that we have seen to either the Claimant's gender or age. Overall, we are in no doubt that neither the Claimant's age nor his gender had anything at all to do with his treatment by the Respondent in being disciplined and dismissed. Accordingly, the complaints of age and sex discrimination must fail and be dismissed.

The claimant's unfair dismissal claim was successful, perhaps meaning the Tribunal placed less focus on the claimant's direct discrimination claims. That said, this passage in the Tribunal's judgment is rather extraordinary, implying that pressure imposed by a third party to protect long-standing staff (who are more likely to be older) is sufficient to absolve the respondent of any allegations of age discrimination. Indeed, the Tribunal held that retaliation against filing a complaint was a better (non-discriminatory) explanation for the claimant's treatment. This case illustrates the potential ease with which respondents might avoid a claim of discrimination.

7 CONCLUSION: STRENGTHENING EMPLOYMENT PROTECTION?

There are clear limits to the ability of age discrimination law to strengthen employment protection for older workers; issues of proof and causation can be catastrophic to individual claims. These issues go to the heart of the aims of discrimination law: discrimination law, as it is presently framed and drafted, is not aimed at achieving 'fairness' or 'reasonableness' at work. Rather, that is the purview of unfair dismissal law. Age discrimination law and unfair dismissal law are therefore important –

165. Minna J. Kotkin, *Diversity and Discrimination: A Look at Complex Bias*, 50(5) Wm. & Mary L. Rev. 1439 (2009); Rachel Kahn Best et al., *Multiple Disadvantages: An Empirical Test of Intersectionality Theory in EEO Litigation*, 45(4) L. & Soc'y Rev. 991 (2011) https://doi.org/10.1111/j.1540-5893.2011.00463.x.
166. [2017] UKET 3200556/2016.
167. *Ibid.*, ¶¶5, 40.

potentially complementary – legal regimes. This is evidenced by the significant number of age discrimination claims that also raise unfair dismissal.

What this study has shown, though, is that the advantages of age discrimination law – in adopting broader approaches to employment status; uncapping damages and allowing for compensation for injury to feelings; omitting any qualifying period of service; and adopting a flexible approach to time limits for claiming – can and should inform our critique of unfair dismissal law. Equally, the strengths of unfair dismissal law – in focusing on unfair or unreasonable treatment rather than the (semi-)subjective reasons for treatment – can and should inform our development of equality law. There is a need to strengthen both unfair dismissal law and age discrimination law to ensure employment security for older workers; there is significant scope for mutual learning across equality and labour law.

In drawing together doctrinal, empirical and comparative elements, this study also illustrates the significant potential of mixed-method studies to advance our understanding of law in practice. Considering cases as both doctrinal and empirical objects of study, capable of revealing both systematised legal rules and broader qualitative and quantitative trends in enforcement, offers innovative insights into both how law is deployed and how law is developing in practice. This study, then, offers a framework for future legal empirical studies, and a challenge to other legal scholars, to better realise the potential of multiple method studies that integrate both doctrinal and empirical elements.

CHAPTER 9

The Capability Approach, Compulsory Retirement, and the *Hörnfeldt* Case Revisited

Ann Numhauser-Henning

1 INTRODUCTION

Addressing older workers, active ageing, and the future of work brings to the fore the differential treatment of ageing individuals, or 'ageism', throughout society. Discriminatory behaviour, stereotyping, and prejudice are central elements in ageism. As work is a necessary and central 'good'– not only in an economic perspective but also for the achievement of individual well-being – working life hitherto has been 'the only area of social life where legal protection against unequal treatment is deeply institutionalised due to binding regulations'.[1]

In the EU, we find the relevant regulation in the Employment Equality Directive, prohibiting direct and indirect discrimination, harassment, and instructions to discriminate on grounds of age (among other grounds) in a working-life context.[2] The directive also grants some general exemptions from the ban on discrimination in terms of genuine and determining occupational requirements, legislative measures necessary for public security and public order and for the armed forces in relation to age and disability. Unlike other discrimination bans, however, the Employment Equality

1. Justyna Stypinska & Pirjo Nikander, *Ageism and Age Discrimination in the Labour Market: A Macrostructural Perspective*, in: Liat Ayalon & Clemens Tesch-Römer (eds), *Contemporary Perspectives of Ageism* 91–108 (Springer 2018) at 94.
2. Council Directive (EU) 2000/78/EC establishing a general framework for equal treatment in employment and occupation, OJ L 180, 19.7.2000.

Directive – in Article 6.1 – also opens up for the justification of direct age discrimination.[3] The scope for such justification is ultimately decided by the CJEU in its case law.

Non-discrimination law is a widely analysed subject within labour law and has also been widely criticized for its shortcomings.[4] Non-discrimination laws are designed in the liberal tradition in an individual-complaints-led manner. Already from the beginning a tension has existed between formal equality according to the Aristotelian principle, in which like shall be treated alike, and more substantive comprehensions of equality in terms of both opportunities and outcomes. Not least, the design of the ban on age discrimination and its application has been questioned, opening up – as it does – for the justification of direct discrimination.

The so-called capability approach, as developed by Amartya Sen and Martha Nussbaum,[5] has recently had a strong influence on labour law discussion. Early on, the Supiot report[6] used the concept of 'capabilities' to open up a new front in the debate about the role of social policy. More recently, the ILO 2019 'Centenary Declaration for the Future of Work' can be said to build on Sen's capability theory. A comprehensive book discussing 'the Capability Approach to Labour Law' is Brian Langille's anthology from 2019.[7] Various scholars have argued that the capability approach is especially relevant for discrimination law, not least the age-discrimination ban.[8]

A comprehensive body of case law specifically addressing age discrimination has now been built up by the CJEU. A significant – and at societal level exceptionally influential – exception from the ban on age discrimination is the continued acceptance of so-called compulsory retirement, i.e., an obligation on the individual to leave his or her employment at a certain age. An illustrative case in this line of case law is the *Hörnfeldt* case, illustrating the Swedish legal system in place at that time.[9]

3. Thus, 'differential treatment on the grounds of age shall not constitute discrimination, if, in the context of national law, they are objectively and reasonably justified by a legitimate aim, including legitimate employment policy, labour market, and vocational training objectives, and if the means of achieving that aim are appropriate and necessary'.
4. Alysia Blackham, *Reforming Age Discrimination Law, Beyond Individual Enforcement* (Oxford University Press 2022).
5. Amartya Sen, *Development as Freedom* (Anchor Books 1999), Amartya Sen, *The Idea of Justice* (Harvard University Press 2009) and Martha Nussbaum, *Women and Human Development: 'The Capabilities Approach'* (Cambridge University Press 2000) and *Creating Capabilities: The Human Development Approach* (Harvard University Press 2013).
6. A report on the transformation of work and the future of labour law in Europe, presented to the European Commission in 1999 by a group of experts under the leadership of Alain Supiot. Compare also Catherine Barnard, Simon Deakin & Richard Hobbs, *Capabilities and Rights: An Emerging Agenda for Social Policy?*, Industrial Relations Journal 32: 52 (2001) https://doi.org/10.1111/1468-2338.00212.
7. Brian Langille (ed.), *The Capability Approach to Labour Law* (Oxford University Press 2019).
8. Rosie Harding, *Equality, Social Justice and Older People*, in: Issi Doron & Nina Georgantzi (eds), *Ageing, Ageism and the Law, European Perspectives on the Rights of Older People* 15–36 (Edward Elgar Publishing 2018) and Pnina Alon Shenker, *Capabilities and Age Discrimination*, in: Langille, *supra* n. 7.
9. European Union Court of Justice, case C-141/11, *Torsten Hörnfeldt v. Posten Meddelande AB* EU:C:2012:421. Other Important cases are case C-411/05, *Palacios de la Villa v. Cortefiel* EU:C:2007:604, case C-388/07 *Age Concern England v. Secretary of State for Business, Enterprise and Regulatory Reform* EU:C:2009:128 and case C-45/09 *Rosenbladt v. Oellerking Gebaudereinigungsges mbH*, EU:C:2010:601.

After providing a brief introduction to the capability approach, *Hörnfeldt* and recent Swedish legal reforms, I will continue to scrutinize the justification of compulsory retirement in *Hörnfeldt* and recent Swedish reforms in terms of the capability approach. Does the capability approach lend itself to a better understanding of the age-discrimination ban and its interpretations?

2 THE CAPABILITY APPROACH

Amartya Sen is the originator of the capability theory, which has been described as an attempt to identify the institutional preconditions for meaningful social development in terms of economic self-sufficiency on the part of individuals.[10] In traditional economics, individual rewards are seen as a combination of native endowments and the financial and other resources made available. Sen identifies an additional category, a set of 'functionings', valued by the individual, which are necessary for meaningful self-sufficiency: basic capabilities. Real freedom of choice to meet one's valued goals is a combination of available resources and conversion factors in terms of a person's ability to convert these resources into capabilities. Resources can be found and discussed at macro-, meso-, and micro-levels. At macro-level, we find institutionalized capabilities. The right to non-discrimination is such a right. Conversion factors are also divided into three levels: personal, social, and environmental.

Martha Nussbaum has taken the theory further by offering a list of core capabilities when building a more general theory on social justice from a constitutionalist perspective. These central capabilities are: Life, Bodily Health, Bodily Integrity, Senses, Imagination and Thought, Emotions, Practical Reason, Affiliation (entailing rights to non-discrimination), Other Species, Play, and Control over One's Environment. Nussbaum distinguishes between basic (native, such as seeing and hearing), internal (developed, such as the ability to play and make a political choice), and combined capabilities (internal ones in combination with suitable external conditions to exercise the function chosen). Nussbaum herself has described this as a minimalist approach, and she holds a threshold view on these capabilities and freedoms. The 10 freedoms should be secured up to a level where equality and adequacy are key notions.

It is obvious then that the capability theory does not really offer a more precise view of what permanent institutional structures (i.e., laws) are needed to secure the basic elements of justice in a society.[11] It is a goal-based theory of maximizing individual freedom. The capability approach can only adjudicate issues of justice on an ad hoc basis. Redistributive justice competes with individual rights. 'Sen's capability theory is always willing to consider making trade-offs between rights and goals, or between institutional structures and policy considerations. Unlike traditional human rights, social and economic rights are not generally regarded as fully imperative rights. It is generally said that social and economic rights can be realized progressively and do not have to be met absolutely. For that reason, ..., capability theory may provide a way

10. Barnard et al., *supra* n. 6, at 465.
11. Hugh Collins, *What Can Sen's Capability Approach Offer to Labour Law?*, in: Langille, *supra* n. 7, at 32.

of balancing these competing considerations by evaluating measures against the standard of the goal of positive freedom.'[12] The capability approach allows for justification of legal entitlements but that is as a piecemeal justification of legislative and substantive standards, much in the spirit of the ILO agenda on decent work.

It is also obvious that the central role for adequacy in Nussbaum's theory opens for piecemeal considerations of both a rights-based and a political nature. Nevertheless, Blackett sees the capability approach – especially as theorized by Nussbaum – as a way to lend to the notion of decent work an inherently distributional character: 'it would encompass substantive equality as both a process and a goal, substantive equality as inherent to an understanding of work itself as decent'.[13] She continues: 'The decent work mandate ... enable meaningful prioritizations on the basis of human capabilities, is potentially transformative.'[14,15]

Thus, there is already a vivid debate on the ability of the capability approach to form a justification of labour law as such.[16] Here, I will limit myself to addressing the issue of the suitability of the capability approach when analysing/applying the age-discrimination ban in the case of compulsory retirement.

3 THE *HÖRNFELDT* CASE

The *Hörnfeldt* case C-141/11 concerned compulsory retirement and the Swedish legal system then in place. Together with other cases on compulsory retirement as a general rule – this case has been perceived as representing a particularly 'loose' proportionality test.[17]

Mr Hörnfeldt had been working part-time for the Swedish *Postverket* since 1989. When he reached the age of 67 on 15 May 2009, the employment contract was

12. *Ibid.*, at 36 f.
13. Adelle Blackett, *Situated Reflections on International Labour Law, Capabilities, and Decent Work: The Case of Centre Maraicher Eugene Guinois*, Revue québécoise de droit international (Hors-série 2007), at 243.
14. *Ibid.*, at 244.
15. Compare also Doron's application on ageing of Nancy Fraser's theory on social justice in terms of both redistribution and recognition, Issi Doron, *Ithaka: On the Journey to a New International Human Rights Convention for the Rights of Older Persons*, in: Ralph Reubner, Teresa Do & Amy Taylor (eds), *International and Comparative Law on the Rights of Older Persons* 18–34 (Vandeplas Publishing 2018).
16. Langille, *supra* n. 7, and Collins, *supra* n. 11. Among later writings are David Cabrelli, *The Capabilities Approach: A Panacea for Labour Law's Ills?*, University of Toronto Law Journal, 70(4): 572–591 (Fall 2020) https://doi.org/10.3138/utlj.2019-0130 and Nicolas Bruno, *From Productive Work to Capability-Enhancing Work; Implications for Labour Law and Policy*, Journal of Human Development and Capabilities, 23(3): 354–372 (2022) https://doi.org/10.1080/19452829.2021.1951186, both addressing especially the collective dimension of the capability approach.
17. Monika Schlachter, *Mandatory Retirement and Age Discrimination under EU Law*. IJCLLIR, 27: 287–299 (2011) https://doi.org/10.54648/ijcl2011019, Claire Kilpatrick, *The Court of Justice and Labour Law in 2010: A New Anti-Discrimination Law Architecture*, Industrial Law Journal, 40(3): 280–301 (September 2011) https://doi.org/10.1093/indlaw/dwr011 and Elaine Dewhurst, *Intergenerational Balance, Mandatory Retirement and Age Discrimination in Europe: How Can the ECJ Better Support National Courts in Finding a Balance Between the Generations?*, CML Rev, 50: 1333–1362 (2013) https://doi.org/10.54648/cola2013134.

terminated on the last day of that month, according to the Swedish '67-year rule' and the collective agreement covering the contract. His monthly retirement pension amounted to SEK 5,847 net (approx. EUR 680), quite a low pension by Swedish standards. Mr Hörnfeldt claimed that this constituted unlawful discrimination on grounds of age.

At the centre of the *Hörnfeldt* case was the then-extant Swedish rule in section 33 of the (1982:80) Employment Protection Act (EPA, *Anställningsskyddslagen)* on the right of an employer to freely terminate an employment contract at the end of the month in which the employee reaches the age of 67. The employer only had to give the employee at least one month's written notice, and the 'normal' requirement for just cause did not apply. If, however, the employer did not use this possibility, the permanent employment continued with a limited employment protection - only one month's notice and no right to priority in accordance with the seniority rules or rules on re-employment in redundancy situations. At the same time, according to section 32a EPA, employees had an unconditional right to work until the age of 67 unless just cause was found for dismissal.

The core question in *Hörnfeldt* was whether the Swedish 67-year rule was compatible with Article 6 of the Employment Equality Directive - transposed into Swedish law by the (2008:567) Discrimination Act (*Diskrimineringslagen*). It was clear from the CJEU's earlier case law that termination of an employment contract on the basis of an employee reaching retirement age amounts to differential treatment based on age.[18] The question was whether the rule could be regarded as objectively and reasonably justified by legitimate aims and whether it was appropriate and necessary in order to achieve those aims. The CJEU responded to this question in the affirmative.

According to the referring court, the 67-year rule was established to give individuals the right to work longer and increase the amount of their retirement pension. At the same time, it reflected a balance between considerations relating to budgetary concerns, employment policy, and labour market policy. No such explicit aims were expressed in the EPA itself or in the *travaux préparatoires*, but the Swedish Government introduced multifaceted arguments for the 67-year rule, including the goal of avoiding humiliating dismissals and facilitating the entry of young people in the labour market.[19]

These aims were acceptable to the CJEU because 'the automatic termination of the employment contracts for employees who meet the conditions as regards age and contributions paid for the liquidation of their pension rights has, for a long time, been a feature of employment law in many member states and is widely used in employment relationships. It is a mechanism which is based on the balance to be struck between political, economic, social, demographic and/or budgetary considerations and the choice to be made between prolonging peoples working lives or, conversely, providing for early retirement'.[20]

18. Compare *Palacios de la Villa* and *Age Concern England.*
19. The judgment, §26.
20. The judgment, §28.

The 67-year rule was also found to be both appropriate and necessary. The 'distribution between generations' argument had long been accepted, and the CJEU also addressed the avoidance of humiliating dismissals for older workers as appropriate.[21]

In *Palacios de la Villa*, the CJEU noted that the Spanish rule on compulsory retirement was 'not based only on a specific age, but also takes account of the fact that the persons concerned are entitled to financial compensation by way of a retirement pension ... the level of which cannot be regarded as unreasonable'.[22] From *Hörnfeldt* it is now clear that the existence and application of a reasonable system of rights and pensions are sufficient, even if the pension in the specific case is quite low.[23]

4 SWEDISH REFORMS FOLLOWING HÖRNFELDT

The CJEU thus confirmed the Swedish 67-year rule and its method for designing continuous compulsory retirement. Nonetheless, this very rule and its context have undergone various reforms in recent years.

The most obvious change meant that as of 1 January 2020, the 67-year rule in section 33 EPA turned into a 68-year rule and then into a 69-year rule as of 1 January 2023. This was a consequence of the 2017 Pension Agreement, which also makes important changes concerning the pension system as such. A so-called *riktålder* (guiding age) for 'normal' pension age was introduced (to be applied only in 2026), and the lowest age for retirement as well as the right to a 'guarantee' pension was raised. The minimum age for retirement from 2020 was 62 years of age; this minimum increased to 63 in 2023 and, later, would automatically become the *riktålder* by subtracting three years. Guarantee pension is paid out only from the age of 66 since 2023 (earlier 65), later to coincide with the *riktålder*. The age limit in the systems for sick-leave benefits and unemployment benefits also became dependent on an age equal to the *riktålder*.

Less obvious - and equally important - is that the design of the EPA rule on compulsory retirement has changed. Earlier, the employer's possibility to terminate an employment was restricted to the very month the employee reached 67 years of age. Afterwards, this 'window' was closed, and the general rule on just cause for dismissal applied once again - accompanied, however, by a somewhat limited employment protection (shorter period of notice, no seniority rules, etc.). Now, the rule has changed: employees who are 69 years or older are exempted altogether from the requirement on just cause for dismissal. As before, after now 69, only one month of notice is required, and the right to priority in accordance with the seniority rules and rules on re-employment in redundancy situations no longer apply. This has also led to a reform of the rules on fixed-term employment. The special rules on free access to fixed-term employment after 67 years of age were omitted; they are no longer needed because any employment can be terminated with only one month of notice and without

21. The judgment, §34.
22. The judgment, §73.
23. Cf., *also Rosenbladt*.

just cause. Even so, the rule that fixed-term employment automatically turns into open-ended employment after a certain time still does not apply to employees 69 years of age or older.

This new design tends to create certain doubts about whether open-ended employment really is the 'normal' mode of employment in Sweden and, in principle, it certainly weakens the scope of the just-cause requirement protection against arbitrary dismissals. In a more provocative way, it also makes the difference in the treatment of older workers even more 'clear-cut' than before. However – and from a more practical point of view – it is possible that this new design may work to actually postpone retirement in many individual cases, a consequence pinpointed already in the preparatory works. Now, the employer does not need to act at a certain moment in time; termination can occur at any point in time after the employee has reached 69. Nevertheless, 'while these measures might increase participation, they may not be dignity enhancing'.[24] It is also important to note that in *Hörnfeldt*, the CJEU did not bring our attention to the arbitrariness of the old 67-year rule – the employer could freely use the possibility to terminate the employment or not.[25]

In 2022, the Swedish rules on compulsory retirement underwent some additional marginal changes as a consequence of a major reform to the EPA. The reform – in terms of 'a labour law for flexibility, transition and security' – is based on an agreement between some of the major social partners on the Swedish labour market following the delicate political negotiations after the 2018 elections in Sweden. This reform implies a reorientation of the just-cause requirement within the framework of a partly deregulatory reform of employment protection; a new semi-mandatory mandate for social partners at cross-sectoral level; a weakening of the seniority rules at lay-offs; and an 'increased balance' between employees in different categories of employment. The reform also includes new rules on general and collectively bargained benefit rights to facilitate the transfer to new jobs (*anställningsstöd*). As regards the 69-year rule, this reform implies only consequential, formal changes.[26]

In general, this latest reform implies a somewhat late 'flexicurity' reform of Swedish employment protection law, weakening employment protection in general. To this end, the post-*Hörnfeldt* reforms of the 67-year rule can be said to go 'hand in hand': despite increasing the age for compulsory retirement, these rules omit the relevant employees altogether from employment protection.

24. Blackham, *supra* n. 4.
25. It is difficult to predict what the CJEU will say regarding the new Swedish 68/69-year rule. In C-46/17 *John* ECLI:EU:C:2018:131 – which can be said to concern the 'borderline' between compulsory retirement and successive fixed-term employment – a German rule permitted the employer and the employee to 'postpone' compulsory retirement by agreement on one or several occasions. What is this other than a rule on compulsory retirement with the possibility to postpone it month by month – and it is not unlike the workings of the new Swedish rule?
26. On the 2022 EPA reform, *see further* Mia Rönnmar's chapter to this book.

5 THE AGE-DISCRIMINATION BAN AND COMPULSORY RETIREMENT

Robert Butler coined the concept in the late sixties of ageism as 'a process of systematic stereotyping of and discrimination against people because they are old, just as racism and sexism accomplish this with skin color and gender'.[27] A more recent and elaborated definition is the following:

> Negative or positive stereotypes, prejudices and/or discrimination against (or to the advantage of) elderly people on the basis of their chronological age or on the basis of a perception of them as being 'old' or 'elderly'. Ageism can be implicit or explicit and can be expressed on a micro-, meso- or macro-level.[28,29]

Discrimination – or discriminatory behaviour – is thus an integrated part of the very definition of ageism, going hand in hand with prejudice and stereotyping.[30] The concept of ageism may well cover both beneficial and negative differential treatment.

Non-discrimination regulation is an important tool to come to terms with ageism from the legal point of view.[31] When a ban on age discrimination was introduced in EU law, it was made age-neutral. However, policy documents adopted by the EU on workforce active ageing in the wake of population ageing refer to workers in their 50s as a special concern.[32,33]

In a human rights perspective, non-discrimination has been recognized as a fundamental right in itself – axiological to the equal rights of every person. Let us call this an individual-oriented or human rights approach. Shiek thus cites age-related

27. Rober Butler, *Age-ism: Another Form of Bigotry*, Gerontologist, 9: 243–246 (1969) https://doi.org/10.1093/geront/9.4_part_1.243 and Robert Butler, *Why Survive? Being Old in America* (Harper & Row 1975).
28. Iversen et al., *A Conceptual Analysis of Ageism*, Nordic Psychology 61(3): 14, 15 (2009) https://doi.org/10.1027/1901-2276.61.3.4.
29. For a broad and multidisciplinary analysis of ageism, *see* Liat Ayalon & Clemens Tesch-Römer (eds), *Contemporary Perspectives of Ageism* (Springer 2018). *See also* Sarit Okun & Liat Ayalon, *Ageism: The Importance of the Linguistic Concept for the Construction of the Experience*, Ageing & Society 1–15 (2022).
30. This has been described by Levy as ageism being reflected in three main ways: stereotypes or a cognitive element, predjudices or an emotional element, and discrimination or the behavioural element, Becca R. Levy, *Eradication of Ageism Requires Addressing the Enemy Within*, The Gerontologist 41: 578–580 (2001) https://doi.org/10.1093/geront/41.5.578.
31. Speaking of capabilities, the concept of ableism and its relation to ageism is of interest. In a recent article, van der Horst and Vickerstaff suggest that a part of ageism is actually ableism and that it is important to distinguish between those two concepts. What they suggest is a narrower definition of ageism, meaning differential treatment based on age and not based on impairments. 'Differential treatment based on (real or expected) impairments would be ableism' (pp. 1980 f.). Mariska van der Horst & Sarah Vickerstaff, *Is Part of Ageism Actually Ableism?*, Ageing & Society 42: 1979–1990 (2022) https://doi.org/10.1017/s0144686x20001890.
32. Commission Communication, Europe 2020, A Strategy for Smart, Sustainable and Inclusive Growth, COM(2010) 2020 final and the document Guiding Principles for Active Ageing and Solidarity Between Generations, Decision No. 940/2011/EU, 14 September 2011, OJ 23.9.2011 No. 246/5.
33. A ban on age discrimination was first introduced in the US through the Age Discrimination in Employment Act (ADEA), in 1967, modelled on title VII of the 1964 Civil Rights Act and covering ages 40–65. In 1986, mandatory retirement age was abolished in the US, thus eliminating the upper threshold.

stereotypes and prejudices that undermine the individual's dignity as an important rationale for age-discrimination bans.[34]

However, there is also another important rationale behind the age-discrimination ban. Apart from the individual dignity approach - easily applied to all ages - the differential treatment of older workers involves more material concerns; 'age issues' are rooted to a considerable extent in physical materiality[35] and economic considerations, making chronological age an important traditional social stratifier. The associated stereotyping evolves within a certain context, reflecting the need to legitimize differential treatment by age in terms of the requirements of real life. A collective-interest rationale of a more instrumental kind appears at a societal level. We are talking here about economic/distributive concerns and a collective or economic approach. These two main rationales behind the EU's ban on age discrimination - the individual approach and the collective approach - have been referred to as 'the double bind' of age discrimination, distinguishing it from other discrimination bans.[36,37]

In EU law - as we have seen in *Hörnfeldt* - the scope for justified differential treatment is ultimately decided by the CJEU in its interpretations of Article 6(1) in the Employment Equality Directive. For a better understanding of the interests at play here - and especially as regards compulsory retirement - we must take a closer look at the issue in the light of labour law more generally.[38] The 'ageing' worker must thus be understood in relation to work as the dominant distributive order in society, as well as in relation to the various institutions and developments associated with work: i.e., pension systems, the standard employment contract, and compulsory retirement; and, later, employment protection, the flexibilization of work, and anti-discrimination

34. Dagmar Schiek, *Age Discrimination Before the ECJ: Conceptual and Theoretical Issues,* CML Rev. 48: 777–799 (2011) https://doi.org/10.54648/cola2011032.
35. Judy Fudge & Ania Zbyszewska, *An Intersectional Approach to Age Discrimination in the European Union: Bridging Dignity and Distribution,* in: Ann Numhauser-Henning & Mia Rönnmar (eds), *Age Discrimination and Labour Law: Comparative and Conceptual Perspectives in the EU and Beyond* (Wolters Kluwer 2015), at 142. *Compare also supra* n. 31.
36. Frank Hendrickx, *Age and European Employment Discrimination Law,* in: Frank Hendrickx (ed.), *Active Ageing and Labour Law: Contributions in Honour of Professor Roger Blanpain* 3–30 (Intersentia 2012) and Ann Numhauser-Henning, *Labour Law, Pension Norms and the EU Ban on Age Discrimination, Towards Ultimate Flexibilisation?,* in: Ann Numhauser-Henning & Mia Rönnmar (eds), *Age Discrimination and Labour Law. Comparative and Conceptual Perspectives in the EU and Beyond* 115–140 (Wolters Kluwer 2015) and Alon Shenker, *supra* n. 8, at 279.
37. This double bind is why the ban on age discrimination in EU law has been given a weaker format than other non-discrimination bans. Also in an international setting, an uncertainty of its 'wrongness' is said to characterize age-discrimination bans, age-based distinctions not seen as historically embedded patterns of group subordination and thus not to have a negative impact on human dignity to the same degree as differentiation based on, for instance, gender and race. *See further, for example,* Colm O'Cinneide, *Constitutional and Fundamental Rights Aspects of Age Discrimination,* in: Ann Numhauser-Henning & Mia Rönnmar (eds), *Age Discrimination and Labour Law. Comparative and Conceptual Perspectives in the EU and Beyond* 51–70 (Wolters Kluwer 2015).
38. Numhauser-Henning, *supra* n. 36.

regulation. Social-security arrangements – including pension systems – have developed successively as a social order complementary to wage work, accompanied by labour law developments reflective of 'the standard employment contract'.[39]

A broadly contextualized old-age concept for achieving a deepened understanding of the rules in this area is needed. 'Old' age is but part of a larger – or externalized – story.[40] The story itself has its special impact on what is perceived as 'old'. The larger story is shaped by assumptions about what constitutes a typical working-life trajectory and about what 'ideal' workers – those closely fitted to the needs of production over time – require. Any 'solution' to an ageing society requires a deep understanding of these systems.[41]

One of the characteristics of the standard employment model is seniority wage-setting. That is, the worker's wage does not fluctuate throughout his career in response to actual productivity; rather, it tends to rise successively until retirement. This is what led the influential American economist Edward Lazear to launch his life-cycle theory of mandatory retirement as an implicit part of the standard employment contract. Employers pay their employees a wage premium towards the end of their career on the assumption that the employment relationship will cease at a predictable, fixed point in time specified in a bargained or statutory pension scheme.[42] The implicit contract, as Lazear describes it, depends on employment protection devices to maintain the inherent promise of a wage premium.

Already early on in industrialized society, production requirements typically led – despite the implicit contract identified by Lazear –to a marginalization of old and less productive workers. To some extent, it is true that the implicit contract could be maintained by means of severance-pay arrangements and bargained early retirement schemes. In more recent decades, technological evolution, the growth of service society and globalization have led to what is generally known as the flexibilization of work. Flexibilization has been pictured as a new trade-off between the pronounced need for flexibility on the one hand and traditional standard employment and pension solutions on the other. The growing importance of anti-discrimination regulation is held to be related to this trend – offering protection in an era when employment

39. Mark Freedland, *Burying Caesar: What Was the Standard Employment Contract?*, in: Katherine Stone & Harry Arthurs (eds), *Rethinking Workplace Regulation: Beyond the Standard Contract of Employment* 81–94 (Russell Sage Foundation 2013). The standard employment contract entails continuous full-time employment with a single employer, with accompanying expectations of remuneration and benefits. It is also grounded in a male-breadwinner model, with a wife and children economically dependent on the male breadwinner. *See also* Katherine Strauss, *Equality, Fair-Mutualisation and the Socialisation of Risk and Reward in European Pensions*, in: Nicolas Countouris & Mark Freedland (eds), *Resocialising Europe in a Time of Crisis* (Cambridge University Press 2013), at 337.
40. Ann Numhauser-Henning, *Elder Law and Its Subject: The Contextualized Ageing Individual*, Ageing & Society 41: 516–535 (2021) https://doi.org/10.1017/s0144686x19001284.
41. For a broad overview, *see also* Geoffery Wood, Adrian Wilkinson & Mark Harcourt, *Age Discrimination and Working Life: Perspectives and Contestations – A Review of the Contemporary Literature*, International Journal of Management Reviews 1468–2370 (2008) https://doi.org/10.1111/j.1468-2370.2008.00236.x.
42. Edward Lazear, *Why Is There Mandatory Retirement?*, Journal of Political Economy 87(6): 1261–1284 (1979) https://doi.org/10.1086/260835.

standards are being replaced by individualization. The deregulation of employment protection is now being accompanied, namely, by an increase in labour market segmentation and the spread of part-time and short-term employment.

It is clear from the CJEU's case law that differential treatment on grounds of age is often justifiable, and the practice of compulsory retirement especially so.[43] At the same time, inducing people to work beyond pensionable age is a core concern of active-ageing policies. If people are to be persuaded to do this, however, they must have both the practical and the legal possibility of doing so. Here, of course, the acceptance of compulsory retirement is a key concern. How can this continued practice be understood?

First, compulsory retirement is to be regarded as part and parcel of the standard employment contract and standard pension arrangement described earlier. Accepting compulsory retirement in line with the findings of the CJEU basically implies a defence of the traditional standard employment contract and existing employment protection devices. The Court's reasoning can also be cited in support of the view that upholding the ban may lead to the humiliating dismissal of older workers in terms of presumed 'incapacity'. Upholding the ban on age discrimination would even threaten to weaken employment protection altogether.[44] A stronger stress on capacity as an employment requirement would have the effect of undermining not only active-ageing strategies but also employment protection well before retirement age.[45]

Nonetheless, defending the standard employment contract can seem rather senseless, given the fact that the battle has apparently already been lost to flexibilization. Anti-discrimination regulation as such has been seen, as already indicated, as a natural companion to flexible work and the decline of the standard employment contract. Somek has gone so far as to label anti-discrimination regulation in general 'a neoliberal forerunner'.[46] Upholding the ban on age discrimination – and thus outlawing compulsory retirement – does imply a threat per se to traditional employment

43. Notwithstanding, compulsory retirement is far from being a general norm in EU Member States. *See further* Declan Dempsey & Anne Beale, *Age and Employment, Report from the Network of Legal Experts in the Non-discrimination Field to the European Commission* (Brussels 2011). Cf., *also* Stuart Goosey, *A Pluralist Theory of Age Discrimination* (Hart 2020) arguing a special theory of age discrimination for the UK setting when distinguishing justified from unjustified differential treatment on the grounds of age.
44. Ann Numhauser-Henning, *Labour Law in a Greying Labour Market: In Need of a Reconceptualisation of Work and Pension Norms. The Position of Older Workers in Labour Law,* European Labour Law Journal, 4(2): 84–100 (2013) https://doi.org/10.1177/201395251300400202, and Numhauser-Henning, *supra* n. 36.
45. Compare Catherine Barnard & Simon Deakin, *Age Discrimination and Labour Law in the UK: Managing Ageing,* in: Ann Numhauser-Henning & Mia Rönnmar (eds), *Age Discrimination and Labour Law, Comparative and Conceptual Perspectives in the EU and Beyond* 297–318 (Wolters Kluwer 2015). Thus, the abolition of the statutory compulsory retirement scheme in the UK is assumed to lead to an increased use of performance management: i.e., regular review, consultation, and documentation for monitoring the performance of the employee, and to build up a case for either voluntary retirement or a dismissal that will hold up against the UK's unfair dismissal legislation. Cf., *also* David Wainwright et al., *Extending Working Life and the Management of Change: Is the Workplace Ready for the Ageing Worker?*, Ageing & Society 39: 2397–2419 (2019) https://doi.org/10.1017/s0144686x18000569.
46. Alexander Somek, *Engineering Equality* (Oxford University Press 2011).

protection and would thus go hand in hand with the dominant trend towards flexibilization. To the extent active ageing comes about in this perspective, it is likely to be in the form of even more flexible employment. Dismissing an elderly worker from a permanent position can be expected to be a difficult process, making a fixed-term contract even more attractive from the perspective of the employer. Nevertheless, it should be said here that accepting compulsory employment seems as well to support 'active ageing' beyond pension age precisely in flexible contractual forms.[47] The use of fixed-term employment is often more generous beyond 'normal' pensionable age – i.e., following compulsory retirement. The conclusion is that both moves – accepting compulsory retirement and upholding the ban on age discrimination – basically enhance the flexibilization of work.[48]

6 DISCUSSION AND CONCLUDING REMARKS

Whereas ageism is a general concern and foundation within elder law, age discrimination is a manifest effect of this phenomenon. Despite this, the EU ban on age discrimination has thus been designed to continuously permit direct age discrimination to a considerable extent. The hitherto quite general acceptance of compulsory employment as a traditional way to end employment is an important expression of this.

In section 5, I have tried to explain the phenomenon of compulsory retirement only through 'the outer story' of labour law. However, it is also true that working-life conditions are changing. The flexibilization of working life may well call for a change in the CJEU's view on compulsory retirement.

Flexibilization has long since worked its way into the conditions under which large groups of workers (including older ones) carry out their labour; and pension-scheme reforms have 'flexibilized' pensions, making them increasingly precarious.[49] Policies allowing for direct age discrimination in terms of compulsory retirement may continue to work best for certain groups and for 'the logic' of general labour law in terms of traditional (standard) employment. However, these policies do not match the social and economic needs of everyone; there is no 'one solution fits all'. New realities in working life and economic inequalities mandate a reconsideration of justice between and within age groups.[50] For the growing number who have never had a standard employment contract, continued employment beyond pensionable age may well be necessary to compensate for reduced pension benefits. There are thus more or less strong arguments in favour of both continued acceptance of compulsory retirement in

47. *See Rosenbladt* and also cases C-250/09 and 268/09 *Georgiev v. Technischeski Universittet Sofia* EU:C:2010:699 and cases C-159/10 and 160/10 *Fuchs and Köhler v. Land Hessen* EU:C:2011:508.
48. Compare Araki's chapter in this book. Early on, Japan brought the standard employment contract to its extreme in terms of so-called lifetime employment. Mandatory (!) fixed-term re-employment has now become the solution, following still relatively early compulsory retirement in order to combine tradition with active ageing and increased pensionable age. In Japan, however, there is no ban yet on age discrimination – instead the country applies an 'active employment promotion approach'.
49. Strauss, *supra* n. 39.
50. Compare Anne L. Alcott, *The New Inequality of Old Age: Implications for Law*, Theoretical Inquiries L. 111 (2017).

the age range of 65 to 70 and the upholding of the ban on age discrimination later in life, in a labour law functional perspective. In addition, we must add to this the aspects of work as an indication of being part of society (Nussbaum) and work as a goal that the individual has reason to value (Sen) – aspects of growing importance in a society built on knowledge and individualism/self-development. The scope for compulsory retirement thus comes into play with the need for a sustainable pension system, an available and effective workforce, and welfare/dignity/agency for older workers.

Continued compulsory retirement may thus be perceived as *both* needed in view of a defence for labour law traditions and unjustifiably discriminatory because different groups of workers have different needs/demands.[51] It may also appear that over-simplification – as the practices of the CJEU and their 'loose' proportionality test may be perceived – is not the recommendable way forward.

Here, the capability approach has something to offer, focusing as it does on an individualistic perspective and substantive rather than formal rights. The capability approach is thus a theory on social development as individual freedom with capability at its centre. This model emphasizes – especially in the terms of Nussbaum – the role of the context (such as laws and pension systems) in facilitating or impeding a good life.[52] There is also, however, the pursuit of differentiated goals of value and the freedom of choice in view of the individual.

Simon Deakin argues for the capability approach to be seen as a methodological approach rather than a freestanding theory in relation to labour law.[53] The capabilities approach can thus be used as a normative framework in order to discuss both the understanding of labour law and labour law reform.[54] In relation to anti-discrimination law – in itself a conversion factor to the development of capabilities – the capability approach has been seen as having the potential to offer a more coherent and persuasive conceptual basis for normative development than traditional equality arguments.[55] The substantive character of capabilities arguments thus has new potential in relation to positive-action measures and issues of intersectionality as compared to traditional non-discrimination law and also in reconciling dignity and distributional concerns more generally.[56]

51. There is broad agreement within elder-law scholarship regarding the need to differentiate among ageing individuals and to avoid stereotyping. *See* Susan Sue Westwood, *I May Be Older, But I Ain't No Elder, Critique of Elder Law*, Temp., Pol. & Rts L, L. Rev. 21: 485 (2012), 302 ff. and Martha Fineman, *'Elderly' as Vulnerable: Rethinking the Nature of Individual and Societal Responsibility*, Elder Law Journal 20(2): 71 (2012) https://doi.org/10.2139/ssrn.2088159.
52. Clemens Tesch-Römer et al., *Successful Ageing. Ambition and Ambivalence* (Oxford University Press 2022).
53. Simon Deakin, *The Capability Approach and the Economics of Labour Law*, in: Langille, *supra* n. 7, 143–158. Compare also Eva-Maria Svensson et al., *The Capabilities Approach and the Concepts of Self-Determination, Legal Competence and Human Dignity in Social Services for Older People*, in: Hanna Falk et al., *A Multidisciplinary Approach to Capability in Age and Ageing* (Springer 2022).
54. Deakin, *supra* n. 53, at 143.
55. Harding, *supra* n. 8. The article is an attempt to make the case for a new international convention on the rights of old persons using the capabilities approach.
56. Cf., Alon Shenker, *supra* n. 8, at 289.

In our context, the capability approach can thus be said to require a careful evaluation of the capabilities offered to ageing individuals in variable situations and as including an elaborated discourse on the adequate level of such capabilities and their substantive content. This is an exercise mainly at macro-level. We are using the capability approach as a normative framework, scrutinizing law on compulsory retirement as an institution interrelated with other social structures, but we also add the view on individual abilities in terms of agency and constraints. In the individual case, the approach may also include a potential analysis at meso- and micro-level, taking workplace and personal circumstances into account. This article does not lend itself to an in-depth analysis of these complex issues. Rather, it is a sketch of analysis in relation precisely to the *Hörnfeldt* case and within the realm of the legal setting and methods of argument as they now stand.[57]

An immediate conclusion is that the capability approach could be particularly apt when considering the double bind – which lives at the heart of compulsory retirement! The concept of adequacy helps to reconcile the concern for the individual worker's dignity/well-being/agency and broader societal goals. A relevant question is whether the balance struck is still justified/adequate. In addition, has the collective efficiency principle been given too much room?[58]

The CJEU's acceptance of compulsory retirement in *Hörnfeldt* implies a very principled stand. When applying the 'double bind', the CJEU has in the main given weight to the societal concerns at macro-level because this is where adequacy is deemed to exist. Individual and collective interests are balanced on a very general and aggregated level, as long as there is a system in place that is compatible with what can be understood as an adequate level of worker protection. 'Adequacy' here 'assume[s] the existence of long-term employment arrangements and adequate pension plans, assumptions that no longer reflect the reality of many workers and were never relevant to many disadvantaged workers (such as older female or racialised workers)'.[59] This can be said to meet the principle of equal opportunity (eventually applies equally to everyone at a certain age; the rationale of 'complete lives egalitarianism')[60] and – arguably, *see* above – societal efficiency. However, it does not meet the principles of agency/autonomy and respect in view of the individual ageing worker.[61] Despite some attention given to individual concerns in terms of humiliating dismissals and the freedom of keeping one's employment for three years beyond pensionable age, the

57. Cf., the autopoiesis theory on law as a self-referential system of communication, Gunther Teubner, *Autopoietic Law: A New Approach to Law and Society* (de Gruyter 1987), and Nils Luhmann, *A Sociological Theory of Law* (Routledge 1985).
58. Compare Goosey, *supra* n. 43, at 99.
59. Alon Shenker, *supra* n. 8, at 281.
60. *Ibid.*, at 280.
61. Compare Ann Numhauser-Henning, *The Elder Law Individual Versus Societal Dichotomy: A European Perspective*, in: Ann Numhauser-Henning (ed.), *Elder Law, Evolving European Perspectives* 86–122 (Edward Elgar Publishing 2017). The article contains a discussion on the tension between autonomy and paternalism, a central concern regarding the capability approach as applied in macro-level legal analysis and an individual-agency perspective. Generalized welfare solutions tend to conflict with autonomy and individual agency – a balance must be achieved.

evaluation was carried out at an aggregated macro-level. No weight was put on the more subjective interests of Mr Hörnfeldt and the arbitrariness of the Swedish 67-year rule. As the rule was designed, it was simply left to the employer to decide whether to make use of the possibility to let Hörnfeldt go or not. Such 'age-based distinctions are not merely wrong when they are based on stereotypes and prejudice; they are primarily wrong because they fail to treat older workers as real agents who are capable of making their own choices, and because they undermine their sets of capabilities'.[62]

What would it have taken for the CJEU to come to a different stance in a case like *Hörnfeldt*? I have already argued that a defence of the employment protection inherent in the standard employment contract is no longer very meaningful. In addition, both accepting the practice of compulsory retirement and upholding the ban on age discrimination seem to favour flexible employment. The choice of a middle way may seem the most adequate way forward in terms of the collective-interest approach. What we are talking about here, ultimately, is the application of a stronger proportionality test.[63]

In *Hörnfeldt*, the CJEU literally dismissed the referring court's question of whether there was a need for an individually framed exception rule to the 67-year rule.[64] The Court kept their considerations at an aggregated systems level, referring to support systems in place. This puts aside individual-agency arguments.

One way, however, of 'bridging' the gap between the age-discrimination ban and a continued acceptance of the tradition of compulsory retirement could be precisely the requirement of 'a savings clause' much like the Court introduced in the *Marschall* case.[65] In *Marschall*, we dealt with the application of the rule on positive action in a sex discrimination case - positive action is seen as an exemption from the ban on sex discrimination. Here, we deal with the scope for discriminatory age differentials as an exemption to the general principle of equal treatment on the grounds of age. It is not too hard to see the parallel - to 'automatically' consider using age as a reason to terminate an employment acceptable only as long as there is room, in the individual case, to consider the personal situation of the employee at stake. This could have saved an employee such as Mr Hörnfeldt - or Mrs Rosenbladt, for that matter - from losing their jobs had their personal conditions not amounted to an 'adequate' level of individual freedom. Such a solution might - as labour markets develop - also turn out to be more adequate at an overall societal level. Compulsory retirement is continuously accepted as long as there is a savings clause, permitting a careful consideration of the individual circumstances in the case at stake. There would be room to consider, for instance, the actual pension rights and other relevant ambitions of the individual. This could fit well under the requirements of 'necessary and appropriate' in Article 6.1. At the same time, it is worth noting that the capabilities approach does not really have a neoliberal basis building on a right to formal equality. There is no need to make an exception from a ban

62. Alon Shenker, *supra* n. 8, at 284.
63. Cf., Sophie Robin-Olivier's chapter to this book.
64. The judgment §§18.2 and 35–47.
65. C-409/95 *Hellmut Marschall v. Land Nordrhein-Westfalen* ECLI:EU:C:1997:533. *See also* Case C-158/97 *Badeck et al. v. Hessischer Ministerpräsident und Landesanwalt beim Staatsgerichtshof des Landes Hessen* ECLI:EU:C:2000:163.

on discrimination – a balancing act in terms of adequate protection can be made within the proportionality test.

An alternative is to consider compulsory/non-voluntary retirement within the application of just-cause requirements. Here, again, we are dealing with a balancing act – balancing employer interests against those of the individual employee. This is quite within the character of such a regulation. Within the application of a requirement of just cause for dismissal, even a principled acceptance of compulsory retirement at a certain age – potentially amounting to objective grounds – would easily make room for more individualized considerations. (A rule – as is now the case in Sweden – that explicitly omits workers above a certain age from just-cause requirements altogether would require a 'savings clause' as discussed above.)

So far, the proportionality test in cases on compulsory retirement may have been particularly loose in that the CJEU has accepted a high level of generalizations and abstract conceptions concerning both the capacities of older workers and the needs of the labour market. But, as Sophie Robin-Olivier puts it in her chapter to this book – anti-discrimination law is not static: legal reasoning can change.

There is no doubt that a development along these lines requires a change of view in relation to *Hörnfeldt*. However, already in *Palacios de la Villa,* the CJEU has seemingly taken into account the situation of the employee at stake (although possibly on an aggregated level, as in *Hörnfeldt*). In other cases, it is obvious that the CJEU has applied a slightly more individual-based assessment (although essentially still at an aggregated level) when interpreting Article 6.1 of the Employment Equality Directive. This is the case in a series of judgments regarding a change in pensionable age.[66] Another line of case law concerns employment conditions in relation to lay-offs. Here too, there has been room for scrutinizing the effects on the individuals at stake.[67] This is normally done when assessing whether a legitimate aim is appropriate and necessary. The *CO* case can also be mentioned. After rather a meticulous scrutiny of the aim (to promote the rejuvenation of the labour force) and its proportionality, the Court left for the referring court the matter of striking a balance between 'the desire to promote the access of young workers to employment and the respect for the right of older persons to engage in work'.[68] In the context of just-cause assessments, the case law concerning an eventual spread of reasonable accommodation requirements is of special interest.[69] It is obvious from the Court's judgment in *Tartu Vangla* that a thorough individual assessment of whether the worker at issue 'is capable of fulfilling his or her duties' is necessary.[70] Moreover, the intersectionality between disability and

66. *See, for instance,* C-286/12 *the Commission v. Hungary* ECLI:EU:C:2012:687, C-250/09 and C-268/09 *Georgiev*, C-341/08 *Petersen* ECLI:EU:C:2010:4 and C-159/10 and C-160/10 *Fuchs and Köhler*.
67. Cf., C-499/08 *Ole Andersen* ECLI:EU:C:2010:600, C-152/11 *Odar* ECLI:EU:C:2012:772, C-546/11 *Toftgaard* ECLI:EU:C:2013:602 and C-515/13 *Tekniq* ECLI:EU:C:2015:115, though with somewhat different outcomes.
68. C-670/18 *CO* ECLI:EU:C:2020:272, the judgment §45.
69. Cf., Sophie Robin-Olivier's chapter to this book.
70. C-795/19 *Tartu Vangla v. Justitsminister, Tervise-ja töötminsiter, Õlguskantsler* ECLI:EU:C:2021:606.

age is considerable, with reasonable accommodation being a way to weigh in age-management practices more generally.[71] These references reflect only the varying standards of the proportionality principle as applied by the CJEU. A tightening of these practices in relation to compulsory retirement more generally may not seem all that revolutionary.

Generally speaking, the quest for a specific human rights document for older people has been seen as a trend in which individual rights and autonomy are strengthened.[72] The work of the ILO has long since built on the principle that work is not a commodity. In its 2019 Declaration for the Future of Work, the ILO declares its commitment to develop 'a human-centred approach' to work in order to enhance workers' capacity to make use of the opportunities available for decent work.[73] Both the EU Charter of Fundamental Rights (CFR) and the European Pillar of Social Rights[74] and its related Action Plan[75] have been held to imply a potential for reinforcing social rights in the EU legal system.[76] Moreover, the CJEU has acknowledged that Article 21 of the CFR can be relied upon by individuals in legal proceedings in the same manner as directly effective provisions of the EU Treaties - also in legal disputes between private parties.[77] It is unlikely that EU law will change its labour law normative framework to embrace the capabilities approach altogether, but there may be a growing scope for social justice in more substantive terms in the coming years - and especially so within the interpretation/application of the proportionality principle.

However, there is no need to exaggerate the actual potential of a capability approach. It provides no immediate solution to the balancing of individual freedom with more societal efficiency considerations. Here, adequacy is key – requiring detailed evaluations on a case-by-case basis.[78] Hitherto, studies have pointed to the capabilities concept as relative, always depending on a large number of influencing factors across all societal levels, changing over time, and almost kaleidoscopic in nature.[79] And at the heart of this approach is the old conflict between autonomy in terms of liberal freedom and welfare solutions, or the conflict between the liberal model and the solidarity model also at the heart of EU policies/debate.[80]

---

71. Compare Ewa Wikström et al., *Organisational Capability for Delayed Retirement*, in: Falk et al., *supra* n. 53, 221–232.
72. Svensson et al., *supra* n. 53, at 184.
73. In the ILO's background report *Work for a brighter future*, this human-centred agenda is developed in terms of three pillars: increasing investment in people's capabilities (with direct reference to Sen and Nussbaum), increasing investment in the institutions of work, and increasing investment in decent and sustainable work.
74. Interinstitutional Proclamation on the European Pillar of Social Rights OJ C 428, 13.12.2017.
75. The European Pillar of Social Rights Action Plan COM/2021/102 final.
76. *See* Groussot and Loxas' chapter in this book. There, the capability approach is said to fit both the more neoliberal 'dignity model' in terms of individual freedom and 'the solidarity model' of change used to extend the protection of social rights within EU legal doctrine.
77. C-414/16 *Egenberger* ECLI:EU:C:2018:257, the judgment §78.
78. Compare Goosey and his complicated 'Pluralist Theory of Age Discrimination', *supra* n. 43.
79. Falk et al., *supra* n. 53, at 250.
80. Again, *see* the chapter by Groussot and Loxas in this book.

Moreover, whether designed as a rule on compulsory retirement with a savings clause, as a consideration within the concept of just cause or applying the proportionality principle more generally, it would mainly be for the national courts to make the estimation of adequacy in individual cases! This tends to shift the balancing act from the CJEU to national courts, with a risk of obscuring still prevailing ageing practices at societal level. Then again, as an alternative to a continued principled acceptance of compulsory retirement despite a general flexibilization of work, maybe there is not that much to lose. Whatever the case may be, we can look forward to a continuous adaptation to changing social circumstances and labour markets in the future implementation of Article 6.1 of the Employment Equality Directive at both EU and domestic levels.

Part IV Advancements in Active Ageing

CHAPTER 10

Slavery of Ageing Domestic Workers: An Analysis of the Policies in Brazil

Ana Virginia Moreira Gomes & Afonso de Paula Pinheiro Rocha

1 INTRODUCTION

In May 2022, an 84-year-old worker in Rio de Janeiro was rescued from a situation analogous to slavery after working for 72 years as a domestic servant for three generations of the same family. The worker had never received wages, and none of her other labour and social-security rights had ever been fulfilled. Domestic work is one of the activities carried out in conditions of greater precariousness and vulnerability. In Brazil, around 75 % of domestic jobs are informal.[1] This situation becomes more acute as these workers become older. In addition to age as a factor that interferes with the employability of the worker, as a discriminatory factor, age also accompanies cases of work in conditions analogous to slavery. Unlike other cases of modern slavery that last for the duration of the task, cases of domestic slavery accompany the long periods of the relationship between the worker and the employer's family. It is common for the worker to start her activity as a child, remaining in her adult life and old age working for the family. 'In Brazil, after the rescue of a worker in Minas Gerais in 2020, reports of domestic slavery to labour inspection have increased. Of those rescued by the special mobile inspection groups since the beginning of 2022, five women were in domestic-slavery. Of the 1,937 people in slavery rescued in the country in 2021, 27 victims were in domestic work. In 2020, there were only 3.'[2]

1. This chapter is based on research completed in 2022.
2. Leonardo Sakamoto & Daniel Camargos, *Mulher é resgatada após 72 anos de trabalho escravo doméstico no Rio*, Repórter Brasil (4 September 2023), https://reporterbrasil.org.br/2022/05/mulher-e-resgatada-apos-72-anos-de-trabalho-escravo-domestico-no-rio/. *See also* Lívia Mendes Moreira Miraglia, Maurício Krepsky Fagundes, O perfil das trabalhadoras domésticas resgatadas

Our chapter analyses the specific situation of enslaved domestic work of elderly women workers in the context of the recent fight against domestic slavery in Brazil. This fight faces difficulties due to the extreme vulnerability of workers in such situations, which is created by the long-term work relationship and the relative isolation of the worker and the workplace. In addition, domestic work with high rates of informality has made this category resistant to protection from the regulation under labour law. Hidden in informality, practices of extreme violation of workers' fundamental rights survive, as it is a case of slavery.

This chapter's analysis is divided into five parts – *plus* Introduction and Conclusion. The second section analyses the intersections between forced labour, informality, gender, and race. The third section describes cases of rescued workers to analyse the main characteristics of this form of exploitation. The fourth section describes Brazilian mechanisms for repression and prevention in domestic slavery. Next, the fifth section examines the norms to combat domestic slave labour internationally and in Brazil. In the last section, we reflect on what the World Health Organization's Active Ageing Policy Framework means in the context of domestic slave labour. We address the specific vulnerabilities of enslaved, elderly female domestic workers and identify the challenges in the fight against domestic slavery in Brazil with regard to labour inspection, remedy, and social reintegration of these workers in the post-rescue period. Even though We rely here on our research in Brazil, this situation involving domestic work has broader applications.

2 INTERSECTIONS BETWEEN SLAVERY AND INFORMALITY

As a type of work performed by a worker in or for a private residence (ILO Convention 189, Article 1), domestic work is carried out mostly by women, migrants, specific racial groups and, in general, by workers with a low level of education and limited professional qualifications. The atypicality of the workplace (a private residence) and isolated working conditions add to the low social and economic recognition that makes domestic work one of the most vulnerable forms of work.

Brazil accounts for 7.7% of the total number of domestic workers in the world[3] even though the country accounts for only 2.6% of the global population. In 2021, 5.7 million people were domestic workers in the country. This number was down from 6.2 million in 2019, as approximately 500,000 domestic workers lost their livelihood during the pandemic. Informality has also grown due to the economic crisis related to the pandemic. According to the IBGE, about 76% of domestic workers are informal; i.e.,

de trabalho escravo no Brasil, 117 Revista Lua Nova (2022), https://boletimluanova.org/o-perfil-das-trabalhadoras-domesticas-resgatadas-de-trabalho-escravo-no-brasil/.

3. International Labour Organization (ILO), *Making Decent Work a Reality for Domestic Workers: Progress and Prospects Ten Years after the Adoption of the Domestic Workers Convention, 2011 (No. 189)* (4 September 2023) ilo.org.

they do not have their labour card signed by the employer and thus do not contribute to social security.[4]

The informality of domestic work in Brazil has been out of tune with the legal protection that has been promoted by the promulgation of the Federal Constitution in 1988. Before then, domestic workers were entitled to only some of the rights of a typical worker. After the Constitution's entry into force, a constitutional amendment in 2013, and the enactment of a law in 2015 regulating the domestic work contract, domestic workers formally have the same rights as other workers. In 2018, Brazil ratified ILO Convention 189 on decent work for domestic workers. The protective labour legislation has not resulted in reduced informality. The basic elements that sustained the exploitation of domestic work remain largely unchanged: discrimination based on colour, gender, and economic situation, in addition to the non-responsibility of the State and men in general for domestic and care services.[5] Given this situation, it is not difficult to explain the ineffectiveness of labour laws. Informality conceals the worst forms of aggression against domestic workers: harassment, violence, child labour, and slavery.

In Brazil, the concept of slavery defined by law is broader than that of forced labour defined in ILO Convention 29.[6] The Brazilian Criminal Code uses the concept of working in conditions analogous to slavery, covering forced labour as well as excessive working hours, degrading working conditions, or debt bondage.[7] The inclusion of the crime of 'reduction to a condition analogous to that of slavery' in the Brazilian legislation is a significant step forward, as it extends beyond the previous definition of forced labour and encompasses contemporary forms of slavery practices in Brazil. The Superior Court of Justice has established a legal precedent which declares that because the work can take various forms and involve different aspects, commission of this crime does not rely solely on the restriction of the worker's freedom.[8]

According to the Observatory for the Eradication of Slave Labour and Human Trafficking, a collaboration between the Federal Labour Public Prosecutor and the ILO

4. Instituto Brasileiro de Geografia e Estatística (IBGE). Pesquisa Nacional de Amostra de Domicílio (PNAD) contínua (31 January 2023), https://www.ibge.gov.br/estatisticas/sociais/trabalho/17270-pnad-continua.html.
5. Adélia Buriti & Ana Virginia Moreira Gomes, *A Regulação do Trabalho Doméstico pelo Direito do Trabalho como um Processo Inacabado: um estudo de caso de demandas judiciais de trabalhadoras em Quixadá, Ceará*, 24 Revista da Faculdade Mineira de Direito, 113–141 (2021).
6. ILO, Convention 29. 'Article 2.1. For the purposes of this Convention, the term forced or compulsory labour shall mean all work or service which is exacted from any person under the menace of any penalty and for which the said person has not offered himself voluntarily.'
7. Reduction to a condition similar to that of a slave: 'Art. 149. To reduce someone to a condition analogous to that of a slave, or to subject that person to forced labour or to arduous working days, or to subject them to degrading working conditions, or to restrict, in any manner whatsoever, their mobility by reason of a debt contracted in respect of the employer or a representative of that employer.'
8. *Superior Tribunal de Justiça (STJ)*: Recurso Especial No. 1.843.150 – PA (2019/0306530-1), 26/5, 2020, https://processo.stj.jus.br/processo/revista/documento/mediado/?componente=ITA&sequencial=1946514&num_registro=201903065301&data=20200602&formato=PDF.

Brazil, 60,251 Brazilian workers were found to be in conditions analogous to slavery between 1995 and 2022. Furthermore, from 2003 to 2022, over 55,000 workers in conditions analogous to slavery were rescued throughout Brazil. The industries with the highest incidence of slave labour include agriculture, civil construction, and mining.[9] Although most of the affected workers were male, there were cases of women and children being subjected to slavery, especially in domestic work. These statistics represent only a fraction of the actual situations, as many cases of slavery remain unreported, and countless workers continue to be exploited without the ability to report their employers or even to identify that their situation is slavery as such. Therefore, combating work analogous to slavery is an ongoing challenge for the Brazilian authorities and society.

Although these types of exploitation are also found among formal workers, it is in the informal sector that these practices are more common, especially slavery. The correlation between slavery and informality is not necessary; it is rare but possible to find formal workers in conditions analogous to slavery.[10] In the case of domestic workers, however, this correlation is common.

As noted earlier, informality is massive among domestic workers. The persistence of precariousness and informality in domestic work is linked to inequalities that stem from gender and racial division of paid reproductive work. The regulation of labour law, although protective of employees, perpetuates the bases of power rooted in the colonial era that were structured around a patriarchal and racialized society.[11] Labour law actively participates in this process, determining who deserves protection and the form that protection will take. Domestic work in Brazil is performed mostly by women (92%), of which 65% are black women.[12] The work of these women has never had its true economic and social value recognized.

Brazil has a history of 388 years of slavery of black workers: 'the most efficient, violent, merciless and dehumanizing system of recruiting, conserving and exploiting work'.[13] Slavery left deep marks on the country's society, economy, and labour relations. It was a fundamental basis for the construction of the Brazilian economic system, resulting in the concentration of wealth in the hands of a privileged elite.

9. *Observatório da Erradicação do Trabalho Escravo e do Tráfico de Pessoas*, Ministério Público do Trabalho (MPT) (4 September 2023), https://smartlabbr.org/trabalhoescravo/localidade/0?dimensao=perfilCasosTrabalhoEscravo.
10. Mauro O. Nogueira & Sandro S. de Carvalho, *Trabalho precário e informalidade: desprecarizando suas relações conceituais e esquemas analíticos*, Instituto de Pesquisa Econômica Aplicada (Ipea) (December 2021), https://repositorio.ipea.gov.br/bitstream/11058/10948/1/td_2707.pdf.
11. Flávia Souza Máximo Pereira & Pedro Augusto Gravatá Nicoli, *Os segredos epistêmicos do direito do trabalho*, 10 Revista Brasileira de Políticas Públicas, 10, 519–544, n. 2 (2020).
12. Instituto Brasileiro de Geografia e Estatística (IBGE). Pesquisa Nacional de Amostra de Domicílio (PNAD) contínua (31 January 2023), https://www.ibge.gov.br/estatisticas/sociais/trabalho/17270-pnad-continua.html.
13. Luiz Aranha Corrêa Lago, *Da escravidão ao trabalho livre. Brasil, 1550–1990*, 9 (Companhia das Letras 2014).

Enslaved women, in addition to working in agriculture, were responsible for household activities, such as cooking, washing, ironing, and cleaning[14] and suffered all types of violence. The formal abolition of slavery happened only in 1888. Black enslaved workers were freed but received no compensation or support to integrate into society and into the labour market. This perpetuated the social and economic exclusion of these workers, who were relegated to precarious and poorly paid jobs. Is it the past that explains why, in today's Brazil, 64% of workers rescued from conditions analogous to slavery are black or brown?[15] It is not just the past; unfortunately, power structures still make possible the exploitation of human labour, social inequality, and discrimination based on colour. The perpetuation of this mentality is accountable for the invisibility of domestic slave labour. Otherwise, how can we explain that such exploitation goes unnoticed by neighbours, relatives, and friends of the family responsible for the enslavement?

In the specific case of black women enslaved in domestic work, when they formally left slavery at the end of the 19th century, labour law placed them in informality, making the economic and social role and importance of domestic work all but invisible. For most of the 20th century, Brazilian labour law excluded domestic workers from the same legal protection of other workers.[16] In this system, it is almost natural that the domestic work performed mostly by black women is still informal and precarious.

This context also explains the permanence of slavery in domestic work. To enslave people is to use their labour without assigning value to their work. In the case of Brazil, this practice also incorporates discrimination against people of colour. Long after the abolition of slavery, prejudice, stigma, discrimination, and exploitation of domestic workers remained in the world of work.

3 CASES OF RESCUED WORKERS

From 2017 to 2022, 45 domestic workers were rescued from work in conditions analogous to slavery.[17] As mentioned earlier, in one case, a domestic worker was rescued from slavery after almost 40 years of working for a family without payment of wages or paid leave. In 2021, after this story came out in the press, the number of both complaints and rescued workers surged (*see* Figure 10.1). This form of publicity given to high-profile cases is essential if we are to uncover more cases of abuse. Labour inspection and the Public Ministry of Labour can act only if such complaints are filed.

14. Lenara Giron de Freitas; Freitas, Rodrigo de. A evolução da regulamentação do trabalho doméstico: principais diferenças entre o trabalhador doméstico e o trabalhador urbano e suas complexidades. *Revista de Direito do Trabalho*, vol. 209, 179–199, jan. 2020.
15. *Observatório da Erradicação do Trabalho Escravo e do Tráfico de Pessoas*, Ministério Público do Trabalho (MPT) (4 September 2023), https://smartlabbr.org/trabalhoescravo/localidade/0?dimensao=perfilCasosTrabalhoEscravo.
16. Adélia Buriti & Ana Virginia Moreira Gomes, *A Regulação do Trabalho Doméstico pelo Direito do Trabalho como um Processo Inacabado: um estudo de caso de demandas judiciais de trabalhadoras em Quixadá, Ceará*, 24 Revista da Faculdade Mineira de Direito, 113–141 (2021).
17. Ministério Trabalho e Emprego (MTE), Portal da Inspeção do Trabalho (4 September 2023), https://sit.trabalho.gov.br/radar/.

Figure 10.1 Number of Rescued Workers in Conditions Analogous to Slavery in Brazil Domestic Services

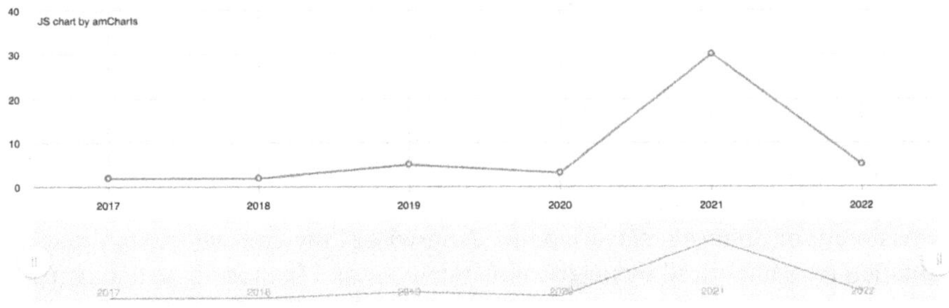

Source: https://sit.trabalho.gov.br/radar/.

According to the ILO, a total of 17.3 million people are considered to be in forced labour; 1.4 million adults (or 8%) are in domestic work around the world.[18] Globally, 17% of women victims of forced labour exploitation are domestic workers.[19] The organization estimates that the slave-like labour lasts an average of 18 months before the worker is rescued or escapes.[20] However, this time estimate is much longer in the case of women and girls in domestic work. The cases reported in Brazil confirm this conclusion. The long periods of slavery in the case of domestic work add to one more peculiarity of the problem: many of these workers are exploited until old age.

The case of the 84-year-old black female domestic worker rescued after 72 years of being exploited as a slave in 2022 in Rio de Janeiro is sadly illustrative. She worked for three generations of the same family without rest or payment of wages. She started working in the home of her employer at the age of 12; when the couple who owned the house died, the worker moved in with one of the children of the employer, continuing to provide domestic services. She started out as a caregiver for children, and at the time of the rescue, she was caring for her employer – an elderly woman like her:[21]

> For more than seven decades, the worker had no contact with any other type of social relationship, she had no role in her life, receiving tasks and orders from third

18. International Labour Organization (ILO), *Global Estimates of Modern Slavery: Forced Labour and Forced Marriage.* International Labour Organization (ILO), *Walk Free, and International Organization for Migration (IOM)* (2022), https://www.ilo.org/global/topics/forced-labour/publications/WCMS_854733/lang--en/index.htm.
19. International Labour Organization (ILO), *Global Estimates of Modern Slavery: Forced Labour and Forced Marriage.* International Labour Organization (ILO), *Walk Free, and International Organization for Migration (IOM),* 34 (2022), https://www.ilo.org/global/topics/forced-labour/publications/WCMS_854733/lang--en/index.htm.
20. International Labour Organization (ILO), *Global Estimates of Modern Slavery: Forced Labour and Forced Marriage.* International Labour Organization (ILO), *Walk Free, and International Organization for Migration (IOM)* (2022), https://www.ilo.org/global/topics/forced-labour/publications/WCMS_854733/lang--en/index.htm.
21. Leonardo Sakamoto & Daniel Camargos, *Mulher é resgatada após 72 anos de trabalho escravo doméstico no Rio,* Repórter Brasil (4 September 2023), https://reporterbrasil.org.br/2022/05/mulher-e-resgatada-apos-72-anos-de-trabalho-escravo-domestico-no-rio/.

> parties. Her life became a 'shadow', as analysed by a labour inspector. 'Given this, the world "outside" can be challenging. People rescued after long periods often ask to return to their employers because that is the only life they have ever known. This has been used by employers as a justification that the relationship between them was normal and healthy. The 84-year-old worker told the inspection that she was worried about her employer, who would be alone and without anyone to take care of her. She, who did not see herself as someone who was enslaved, even asked to return. Yasmim França, who is following the worker's case, says that the post-rescue period is a time for victims to think about life projects and strengthen family and community ties. A long walk.'[22]

A common narrative in such cases is that of a child abandoned by the family or whose family is too poor to raise her, who is then 'given' to the employer's family. Usually, the work relationship is not recognized and the child is said to be 'almost like family'. This label hides long working hours without payment of wages and no access to school and/or to other social relations. In addition, the worker does not have proper accommodation and is subject to violence, abuse, and harassment. A 63-year-old domestic worker was found sleeping in a room without electricity and with her belongings stored in a cardboard box. She had been enslaved for 38 years.[23] In some cases, the employer also used fraudulent methods to receive social benefits in the name of the worker but kept the money for their own personal use, essentially stealing from both the state and the domestic worker.

Another aspect of long-term slavery is a form of psychological kidnapping of the worker. After decades of exploitation, an aged worker has not built her own emotional and social relations, and the family that subjected her to slavery is her only emotional reference in life. Wyzykowski and Ribeiro's analysis of a case involving a black female worker forced into a relationship of extreme exploitation from the age of 4 elucidates how 'enslavement devastated her life for 40 years. Olivia's identity was erased, social and intellectual growth repressed, and subjectivity destroyed under the guise that she was almost part of the family'.[24] In some cases, the worker would not (or could not) even recognize the exploitation that she was subjected to.

The analysis of these cases indicates that in order for older domestic workers subjected to slavery to be able to rebuild their lives after rescue, public policies and regulations must recognize and increase awareness of the specific conditions and needs of these workers.

22. Free translation. Leonardo Sakamoto & Daniel Camargos, *Mulher é resgatada após 72 anos de trabalho escravo doméstico no Rio*, Repórter Brasil (4 September 2023), https://reporterbrasil.org.br/2022/05/mulher-e-resgatada-apos-72-anos-de-trabalho-escravo-domestico-no-rio/.
23. Ministério Público do Trabalho (MPT), *Mulher que manteve empregada doméstica idosa em regime de trabalho análogo à escravidão por 38 anos é condenada a pagar indenização de R$500 mil à vítima, além de outras verbas trabalhistas* (2 May 2022), https://www.prt1.mpt.mp.br/informe-se/noticias-do-mpt-rj/1549-mulher-que-manteve-empregada-domestica-idosa-em-regime-de-trabalho-analogo-a-escravidao-por-38-anos-e-condenada-a-pagar-indenizacao-de-r-500-mil-a-vitima-alem-de-outras-verbas-trabalhistas.
24. Adriana Brasil Vieira Wyzykowski & Thaís Lima Ribeiro, *A (in)visibilidade do trabalho doméstico análogo ao de escravo: um estudo casuístico da trabalhadoradoméstica resgatada em Elísio Medrado/BA*, V Laborare, 249 230–252, n. 9 (Jul-Dez/2022), https://revistalaborare.org/index.php/laborare/article/view/142.

4 SPECIFIC MECHANISMS FOR REPRESSION AND PREVENTION IN DOMESTIC SLAVERY AND ANALOGOUS CASES

The main agencies in Brazil responsible for addressing work analogous to slavery are the Federal Labour Inspection (Auditoria Fiscal do Trabalho) and the Federal Labour Public Prosecutor (Ministério Público do Trabalho - MPT). These agencies work in conjunction with one another. The process of identifying situations that constitute domestic slavery is carried out through a formal procedure known as the rescue of enslaved workers (resgate do trabalho escravo), which is regulated by federal ruling n° 3.484/2021. During this process, labour authorities impose administrative penalties and may terminate the labour relationship if a worker's rights have been violated by the employer.

This procedure typically concerns individual workers, but the Labour Public Prosecutor can initiate a collective lawsuit seeking punitive damages or other forms of reparation. Additionally, the Labour Public Prosecutor may employ a special legal agreement called a 'Termo de Ajustamento de Conduta' with employers who are identified as or suspected of exploiting domestic slavery; this is similar to a plea-bargain agreement. Through these agreements, labour situations can be regulated, and consensual reparations can be established for workers, or funding can be provided for awareness campaigns and other forms of societal reparation.

Precarious work often precedes slavery and is still prevalent in Brazil. Cases of domestic quasi-slavery that do not cross the legal threshold are not a specific statistical group; instead, these fall within the usual violations of labour rights, such as unregistered work, long working hours, and harassment. As a result, identifying cases of slavery can be challenging for inspection agencies.

Agencies working to eliminate these forms of work also encounter difficulties because most cases of domestic slavery occur within households, and the inviolability of households is guaranteed by the Federal Constitution. Therefore, entering a residence to collect evidence of domestic slavery requires a judicial warrant based on a robust denunciation. Often, the first line of evidence is a vague report from neighbours or friends of the domestic worker, but judicial authorities do not grant warrants based solely on such evidence. Moreover, the absence of surprise inspections provides employers with the opportunity to tamper with the evidence, produce false documents, and even persuade the victim to deny any wrongdoing. The Labour Public Prosecutor takes a particular position due to the circumstances, which requires a special balance in evaluating the initial evidence while taking into account the specific vulnerabilities of domestic workers.

Additionally, the MPT employs 'promotional procedures' as an important complementary strategy. These procedures aim to investigate public policies related to prevention practices and continuous training of social workers, teachers, and other professionals to enable effective social control in identifying cases of domestic slavery. Increasing awareness of these policies leads to a higher probability of reported cases.

In Brazil, the exploitation of work analogous to slavery leads to various types of punishment, including fines and criminal charges. Article 149 of the Penal Code provides the penalty for this crime of reduction to a work condition analogous to slavery: from two to eight years of imprisonment and a fine, in addition to the penalty corresponding to violence.

The big flaw in the system, however, is that there are very few criminal convictions. Research from the Federal University of Minas Gerais reveals that from 2008 to 2019, 2,679 individuals were accused of violating Article 149 of the Penal Code.[25] However, only 4.2% (112) of them were convicted. Among those convicted, only 1 % would face imprisonment because the rest would be subject to sanctions that restrict rights. These findings suggest a significant gap in the enforcement of laws against slave labour.

5 NORMS AGAINST DOMESTIC SLAVE LABOUR AND THE SPECIFIC VULNERABILITIES OF ENSLAVED DOMESTIC WORK OF ELDERLY FEMALE WORKERS

As we mentioned before, there has been some progress in adopting protective legislation for domestic work in Brazil. Nonetheless, precarity and informality still prevail. The rise in the number of reported cases of enslaved domestic work in 2021 indicates the need for a more innovative approach to labour regulation. We need a new conversation about how labour law should relate to domestic work in an effective way that goes beyond marginal improvements.

Specifically, regarding slavery, the Brazilian system offers three important contributions – this system still lacks some essential measures. First, the system has improved the effectiveness of inspection of domestic work by introducing anonymous whistleblowing through a hotline (*Disque Denúncia*), the Public Labour Prosecutor's app or website. In 2020, complaints regarding slave labour were centralized on the Ipê System digital platform.[26] The platform enables easy, anonymous, and secure reporting of incidents. Additionally, all reports are confidential and protected by law ensuring that whistle-blower information remains undisclosed. The anonymous report triggers a process through which the Labour Inspector can obtain judicial authorization to enter the home of the employer's family to investigate working conditions and, if there is evidence of abuse, to rescue the worker.

Second, the measures to fight violence against domestic workers have been strengthened through Law nº 11.340/2006, better known as *Maria da Penha Law*, which aims to combat domestic violence. The Maria da Penha Law covers violence against female domestic workers. According to the Law, in Article 5, 'it configures domestic and family violence against a woman any act or omission based on her gender that causes her death, injury, physical, sexual or psychological suffering and moral or property damage', covering those people 'in the scope of the domestic unit, understood as the space of permanent coexistence of people, with or without family ties, including those sporadically aggregated' (Article 5, I). Domestic Workers' Contract Law LC 150/2015, in its Article 27, sole paragraph item VII, recognizes the scope of the Maria

25. Carlos H.B. Haddad et al., *Trabalho escravo na balança da justiça* 496 (IEPEL 2021).
26. The Sistema Ipê is a tool to receive, collect, and handle reports of alleged slavery: https://ipe.sit.trabalho.gov.br/#!/. The Labour Public Prosecutor app is 'MPT Pardal'.

da Penha Law, by identifying, among the causes for indirect termination in the domestic work contract, when 'the employer practices any form of violence domestic or family against women referred to in art. 5 of Law No. 11,340, of August 7, 2006'.

Third, there are measures aimed at enabling the rescued worker to receive economic assistance and sue the employer for unpaid wages, benefits, and moral harm. For example, domestic workers who have been rescued from slavery have the right to three unemployment insurance payments as immediate economic aid. In the case of a worker who had been enslaved for 38 years, the Labour Court ordered the employer to pay a USD 95,000 indemnification for moral damages and compensation for material damages in the monthly amount equivalent to that which would be owed to the victim for retirement by age, between 22 December 2017 and the final judgment.[27]

Despite these improvements, some elements to help victims are lacking. For example, the longer the period of exploitation, the greater the need for social and psychological aid after the rescue. Often, the worker has no social or family relations outside the employer's family. In such cases, it is important to provide a safe place for the worker where she can rebuild her life for independent living.

6 WHAT DOES ACTIVE AGEING MEAN IN THIS CONTEXT?

Domestic workers who have been rescued after extended periods of time of being enslaved by a family often express a desire to return to their employers because this is the only life these workers know.[28] This highlights the significance of the State's post-rescue actions in providing crucial assistance and protection to enable rescued workers to integrate into society and rebuild their lives.

In addition to the emotional destabilization they suffer, rescued workers lose a place to live. In the case of elderly domestic workers who have been subjected to slavery, they might find themselves seeking refuge in public shelters, where they can begin to rebuild their social ties and their own identity as a free person. As a way of guaranteeing compensation and making this reconstruction possible, the Public Ministry of Labour has been requested to secure compensation for moral damages on a case-by-case basis. This compensation not only serves to redress the serious harm inflicted on the individual but also provides them with the material means to move forward. In addition, these persons have the right to three instalments of unemployment insurance, equivalent to one monthly minimum wage.[29] Financial stability is

27. Ministério Público do Trabalho (MPT), *Mulher que manteve empregada doméstica idosa em regime de trabalho análogo à escravidão por 38 anos é condenada a pagar indenização de R$500 mil à vítima, além de outras verbas trabalhistas* (2 May 2022), https://www.prt1.mpt.mp.br/informe-se/noticias-do-mpt-rj/1549-mulher-que-manteve-empregada-domestica-idosa-em-regime-de-trabalho-analogo-a-escravidao-por-38-anos-e-condenada-a-pagar-indenizacao-de-r-500-mil-a-vitima-alem-de-outras-verbas-trabalhistas.
28. Leonardo Sakamoto & Daniel Camargos, *Mulher é resgatada após 72 anos de trabalho escravo doméstico no Rio*, Repórter Brasil (4 September 2023), https://reporterbrasil.org.br/2022/05/mulher-e-resgatada-apos-72-anos-de-trabalho-escravo-domestico-no-rio/.
29. Fernanda Brigatti, *Trabalho escravo: a difícil jornada depois do resgate, Políticas públicas ainda esbarram em falta de acompanhamento e estrutura para proteger e reinserir trabalhador*

central to enabling rescued workers to regain some control over their lives, given the loss of social and familial ties that frequently occurs, but this is not enough.[30]

The National Flow of Assistance to Victims of Slave Labour, which is organized by the National Commission for the Eradication of Slave Labour (Conatrae), provides a policy framework for assisting those who have been rescued from work in slavery-analogous conditions.[31] The Flow comprises the following three distinct stages of action: Complaint to Planning, Rescue, and Post-rescue. The Flow explains the Post-rescue as follows:

> Following the worker's rescue and receipt of emergency care, the focus shifts to providing ongoing assistance and follow-up support. This phase heavily relies on the services of social assistance bodies to play a crucial role in addressing the needs of victims. Public agencies involved in the operation are responsible for ensuring that other relevant entities and agencies involved in post-rescue activities are engaged in monitoring the victims and their families. This will enable them to overcome their social vulnerabilities and rebuild their lives.[32]

In this context, the World Health Organization's Active Ageing Policy Framework might be a useful mechanism to inform the existent public policies if this framework can be adapted to the specific needs of this very vulnerable group of workers. The framework can serve as a useful guide for policymaking aimed at protecting elderly domestic workers, particularly with regard to the security pillar. This entails the enactment and enforcement of laws that safeguard women against domestic and other forms of violence as they age, as well as providing social-security measures such as income support to older women who lack pensions or have meagre retirement incomes due to having worked in the home or informal sector for most of their lives.[33] It is worth noting that this framework refers to the needs of informal caretakers.[34] Therefore, additional research and policy initiatives may be required to address their specific needs and challenges.

7 CONCLUSIONS

Elderly workers in situations of extreme vulnerability should be a primary focus of ageing-related policies. In this chapter, we explore a particular case among vulnerable elderly workers, namely domestic workers who often also provide caregiving services

submetido à exploração, Folha de Sao Paulo (28 January 2023), https://www1.folha.uol.com.br/mercado/2023/01/trabalho-escravo-a-dificil-jornada-depois-do-resgate.shtml.

30. Fernanda Brigatti, *Trabalho escravo: a difícil jornada depois do resgate*, *Políticas públicas ainda esbarram em falta de acompanhamento e estrutura para proteger e reinserir trabalhador submetido à exploração*, Folha de Sao Paulo (28 January 2023), https://www1.folha.uol.com.br/mercado/2023/01/trabalho-escravo-a-dificil-jornada-depois-do-resgate.shtml.
31. Governo Federal, *Portaria nº 3.484, de 6 de outubro de 2021. Fluxo Nacional de Atendimento às Vítimas de Trabalho Escravo no Brasil*, www.gov.br.
32. Governo Federal, *Portaria nº 3.484, de 6 de outubro de 2021. Fluxo Nacional de Atendimento às Vítimas de Trabalho Escravo no Brasil*, https://www.in.gov.br/en/web/dou/-/portaria-n-3.484-de-6-de-outubro-de-2021-350935539.
33. World Health Organization, *Active Ageing: A Policy Framework*, 53 (2002), who.int.
34. World Health Organization, *Active Ageing: A Policy Framework*, 49 (2002), who.int.

and are held in slavery by their employers. This type of slavery differs from contemporary forms in two ways. First, workers may endure these conditions for extended periods, spanning up to 50, 60, or even more than 70 years, starting from childhood. Second, residing within the employers' family home leads to emotional attachment to the enslaving family, resulting in the destruction of familial and social bonds outside the household.

We investigated how Brazilian legislation criminalizes this practice and the increasing ease for the population to report suspected cases, including digital complaint systems. However, two significant challenges persist: the low number of cases in which employers are effectively punished by a criminal court and the lack of sufficient policies addressing post-rescue needs so that rescued workers can establish emotional and social connections and rebuild their lives and their dignity.

CHAPTER 11

Japan's Elderly Employment Promotion Policy Without Anti-age Discrimination Law: Experiments in a Most Rapidly Ageing Country

Takashi Araki

1 INTRODUCTION

Japan is the fastest-ageing country in the world. Unlike the US and EU countries, Japan does not have age-discrimination laws, yet it is far ahead of other countries in employing elderly people. This chapter examines this unique Japanese policy of promoting elderly employment in the following four sections.

First, this chapter overviews the rapid ageing of Japan's population, the decline in the number of working people, and the inevitable increase in the age at which pension benefits begin to be paid (pensionable age) and confirms that these circumstances have necessitated policies to promote employment of older people. Second, it compares two different legal policies designed to address the problems of an ageing society. In many developed countries, age-discrimination laws have been introduced, and mandatory retirement has been outlawed (non-discrimination approach). In Japan, by contrast, anti-age discrimination has not been adopted. Instead, Japan utilized the mandatory retirement age to promote elderly employment by raising the retirement age from 55 to 60, and then obliged employers to take one of three optional measures (extending the mandatory retirement age to 65, re-employment, or abolishing the mandatory retirement system) for continued employment from 60 to 65 (policy-responsive approach). Third, the developments of Japanese elderly employment policies over the past five decades will be reviewed. These policies have been quite successful as far as the quantity of elderly employment is concerned. Fourth, however, regarding the quality of elder employment, several lawsuits have been filed challenging as illegal the decline in wages and job content. Finally, several comparative comments will be made on the uniqueness of age discrimination, differences between the non-discrimination approach and Japan's policy-responsive approach, and the prospects of elderly employment.[1]

2 AGEING POPULATION IN JAPAN

2.1 Rapid Ageing, Declining Productive Population, and Extended Pensionable Age

Japan is experiencing the most rapidly ageing society in the world. Not only has the life expectancy been extended[2] but also the fertility rate has generally been declining.[3] As a result, the number of 'productive-age' persons (20–64) who are to support one older person (over 65) was dramatically reduced from 5.8 in 1990 to 2.1 in 2020 and is estimated to be 1.3 in 2070.[4]

Therefore, to sustain the social-security and pension system, the 1994 revision of the Employees' Pension Insurance Act raised the pensionable age for Basic Pension (flat-rate) from 60 to 65 every three years from 2001 through 2013. Then, by the 2000 revision, the pensionable age for Earnings-Related Pension was planned to be extended from 60 to 65 every three years from 2013 through 2025 (*see* Table 11.1).[5]

1. This chapter relies in part on Takashi Araki, *Age Discrimination and Labour Law in Japan: An Alternative Approach to Age Discrimination Law in a Most Rapidly Ageing Country?* in *Age Discrimination and Labour Law: Comparative and Conceptual Perspectives in the EU and Beyond*, 337 (Ann Numhauser Henning & Mia Rönnmar eds, Wolters Kluwer 2015), but deepens its discussion in light of subsequent legislative and case law developments.
2. Life expectancy for males was 50.06 years in 1947 and 63.6 years in 1955; in 2021 it was 81.47 years for males and 87.57 years for females. *See* Cabinet Office [Naikaku-fu], *2023 White Paper on Ageing Society [Reiwa 5 Nenban Kourei Shakai Hakusho]*, 6 (2022).
3. The fertility rate was 3.65 in 1950 and 1.30 in 2021.
4. Cabinet Office, *supra* n. 2, 5.
5. The Japanese public pension for elderly basically consists of two systems: National Pension, which provides the Basic Pension for all residents of Japan (the so-called first layer); and Employee's Pension, which provides the Earning-Related Pension for the employed in addition to the Basic Pension (the so-called second layer). In addition to these two public pensions, private companies – especially large corporations – often establish corporate pension schemes as the third layer.

Table 11.1 Extension of Pensionable Age for Men

	1973 – 2000	*2001*	*2004*	*2007*	*2010*	*2013*	*2016*	*2019*	*2022*	*2025*
Basic Pension (Flat Rate) Decided in 1994	60	61	62	63	64	65	65	65	65	65
Earnings-Related Pension Decided in 2000	60	60	60	60	60	61	62	63	64	65

The extension of the pensionable age inevitably triggers the question of how to fill the gap between the mandatory retirement age (mostly 60 years of age) and the extended pensionable age. As explained below, Japan dealt with this problem by obliging employers to raise the mandatory retirement age and/or promote re-employment.

Furthermore, the declining fertility rate results in a decrease in the productive population. Such labour-shortage concerns also necessitated the promotion of older persons' employment.

2.2 High Employment Rate of Older Persons Without Harming Youth Employment

The employment rate of older persons in Japan is higher than in other industrialized countries. In 2021, the labour-force participation rate for men aged 65 and over was much higher in Japan, at 34.9%, compared to 23.4% in the United States, 18.8% in Canada, 13.2% in the United Kingdom, 10.1% in Germany, and 4.4% in France.[6]

In Japan, older people's desire to work is quite high. In 2020, 40.2% of people 60 and over wanted to continue working with income (*see* Figure 11.1).

6. Japan Institute for Labour Policy and Training, *Databook International Labour Comparisons 2023*, 52 (Japan Institute for Labour Policy and Training, 2023). https://www.jil.go.jp/kokunai/statistics/databook/2023/documents/Databook2023.pdf.

Figure 11.1 Older Persons' Desire to Continue Working in the Future

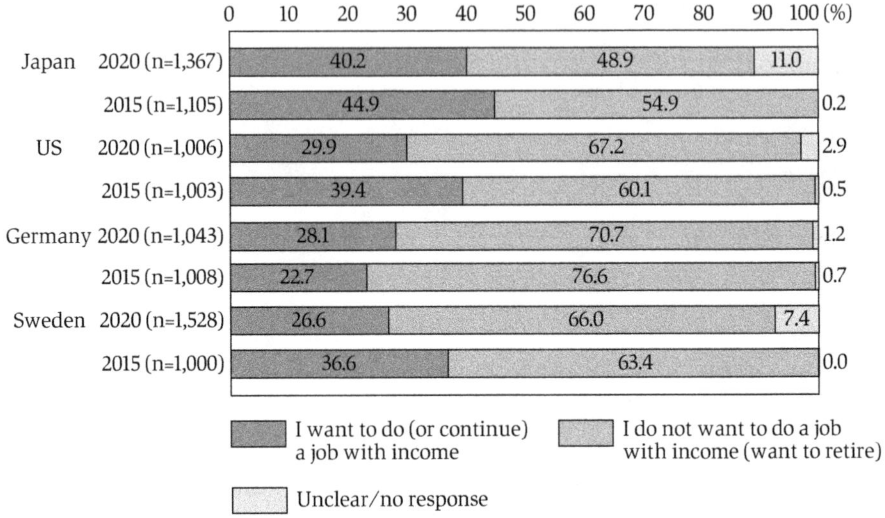

Source: Cabinet Office, 2021 White Paper on Ageing Society, https://www8.cao.go.jp/kourei/english/annualreport/2021/pdf/2021.pdf.

However, the high employment rate of older people does not harm the youth employment in Japan. Japan's youth unemployment rate (ages 15–24) as of 2021 is 4.6%, which is much lower compared to the rates of 9.7% in the US, 12.6% in the UK, 6.9% in Germany, 18.9% in France, 29.7% in Italy, and 24.8% in Sweden.[7] According to the OECD survey in 2018, Japan's ratio of NEET (Not in Education, Employment, or Training) between 15 and 29 years of age is 9.8%, which is also lower compared to the rates of 12.7% in the US, 12.6% in the UK, 16.1% in France, 23.9% in Italy, although slightly higher than the rates in Germany (9.2%) and Sweden (8.9%).

3 JAPAN'S ELDERLY EMPLOYMENT PROMOTION POLICY DIRECTLY ADDRESSED EMPLOYERS

Owing to these developments, Japan's policies to promote elderly employment have been relatively successful and have not had a negative impact on youth employment. From a comparative perspective, the Japanese approach stands in stark contrast to those of other industrialized nations that have adopted anti-age discrimination laws.

7. Japan Institute for Labour Policy and Training, *supra* n. 6, 160.

To promote the employment of older employees, the US and the EU have introduced anti-age discrimination regulations (non-age discrimination approach). Because the rules prohibiting age discrimination – which consider age as one of the prohibited grounds – make it illegal to treat employees differently based on their age, employers are required to adopt 'age-blind' measures as a principle. Non-discrimination law requires the discriminated persons to take action to challenge the discriminatory treatment. In other words, the effectiveness of non-discrimination regulations depends on the victim's actions.

In contrast, Japan adopted a policy directly obligating employers to promote elderly employment rather than waiting for action by the victims. First, the government imposed a *duty to endeavour* on employers to hire elderly persons as a certain percentage or more of their workforce (the elderly employment rate). Companies not meeting this ratio were ordered to draw up a specific employment plan to achieve this goal. Then, Japan abolished the elderly employment ratio system and switched to new regulations requiring an increase in retirement age from 55 to 60. Employers were then obligated to continue to employ workers who had reached age 60 until age 65, the age at which pension payments begin (*see* section 4).

To promote elderly employment, Japan utilized 'age-conscious' measures, such as setting the elderly employment rate and raising the mandatory retirement age. These measures would have been impossible if Japan had adopted anti-age discrimination regulations. The employment promotion policy directly approaching the employers has been thought to be more effective than anti-discrimination regulations in Japan, where litigation is exceptionally rare.[8]

4 DEVELOPMENT OF JAPAN'S 'AGE-CONSCIOUS' ACTIVE EMPLOYMENT PROMOTION POLICY

4.1 Phase 1: Duty to Endeavour to Hire 55+ Persons as More Than 6% of Regular Employees (1976–1986)

In 1976, Japan first set the goal employment rate for older persons (55 and older). Under the government guidelines for the elderly employment rate, employers were supposed to hire more senior employees over 55, with a goal of employing 55+ persons as more than 6% of the regular employees in the workplace in question. However, this regulation remained a *duty to endeavour* or make a good-faith effort and lacked legally binding effect.

8. In 1991, only about thousand labour lawsuits were filed in district courts (courts of first instance) throughout Japan, a country with a population of 124 million.

The government took measures to make this moral obligation effective, such as issuing an order to employers who had not achieved the employment rate to draw up an employment-rate achievement plan and advising to ensure the plan's proper implementation.

4.2 Phase 2: Duty to Endeavour to Extend the Mandatory Retirement Age from 55 to 60 (1986–1994)

Next, in the mid-1980s, Japan shifted focus from the elderly employment rate to new measures to extend the mandatory retirement age. Under Japan's well-known practice of lifetime or long-term employment, coupled with the mandatory retirement system, employees have been expected to enjoy employment security until they reach the mandatory retirement age. Until the 1980s, the typical age of compulsory retirement in Japanese firms was 55.

To promote older people's employment, the 1986 OPESA (Older Persons' Employment Security Act) introduced the employers' duty to endeavour to set the mandatory retirement age at 60 years or older when they established the mandatory retirement system.

Violation of this endeavour provision was not sanctioned by civil or criminal penalties. However, it gave the government the administrative power to request employers whose mandatory retirement age was below 60 to make a concrete plan to raise the retirement age to 60. The government could publicize the name of the employer if this employer failed to follow the administrative order.

In contrast, employers whose employment rate of 60 and over exceeded 3 % of their regular workforce were given a subsidy for their active elderly employment from the Employment Stabilization Project under the Employment Insurance System. The Employment Stabilization Project was funded by the employers' contribution (0.3 % of employers' total wages).

By applying such a '(soft) stick-and-carrot' strategy – on the one hand by assigning the moral duty to employers, accompanied by administrative guidance, and publicizing information about firms that failed to comply, and by giving the subsidy incentives on the other – the government vigorously implemented the policy of promoting older-person employment. Under this administrative campaign, the ratio of firms setting mandatory retirement age at 60 or older dramatically increased in the 1980s and reached 84.1 % in 1994 (*see* Figure 11.2).

Figure 11.2 Ratio of Firms by Mandatory Retirement Ages

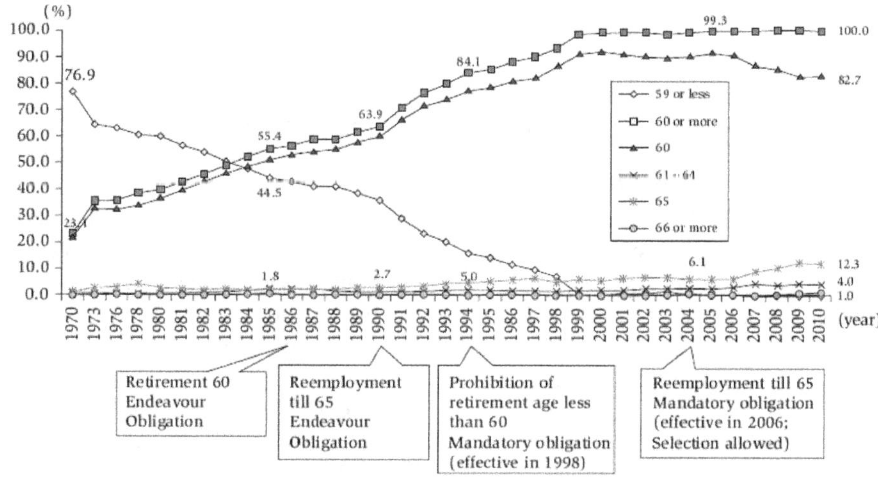

Source: Based on the annual surveys conducted by the Ministry of Welfare and Labour.

4.3 Phase 3: Prohibition of Setting Mandatory Retirement Age Below 60 (1994 [Effective 1998] to Date)

Given the spread of the mandatory retirement age of 60, the 1994 Revision of the OPESA changed the endeavour obligation to make the 60-and-over retirement age mandatory. In other words, setting the compulsory retirement age below 60 was prohibited and invalid. When this revision was implemented in 1998, below-60 retirement ages disappeared (*see* Figure 11.2).

4.4 Phase 4: Continued Employment from 60 to 65 (Pensionable Age) by Three Options (2004 [Effective 2006]–2020)

4.4.1 Continued Employment Through Selective Re-employment Measures (2006–2013)

By the end of the 1990s, Japan had succeeded in ensuring employment until age 60 by raising the mandatory retirement age. In the 2000s, however, elderly employment after 60 became a new policy issue because of the extension of the pensionable age.

Until 2000, the pensionable age for both the Basic Pension and the Earnings-Related Pension was 60. However, under a 1994 amendment to the law, the pensionable age for the Basic Pension was to be raised by one year every three years starting in 2001, and from 2013, it would be 65 (*see* Table 11.1). As a result, further measures were thought necessary to fill the gap between mandatory retirement and pensionable age.

This time, Japan gave employers three options: (1) extend the mandatory retirement age to pensionable age (ultimately 65), (2) re-employ the person who quit the job at the mandatory retirement age (usually 60) until they reach pensionable age (ultimately 65) [re-employment measures], and (3) abolish the mandatory retirement system. Employers were obliged to secure older people's employment by taking one of these three options. This was no longer a duty to endeavour – it was a legal obligation.

Among the three options, (2) re-employment has been the most popular. According to the statistics in 2013, 81.2% of the adopted measures were re-employment, whereas 16% were extensions of mandatory retirement age and 2.8% abolished mandatory retirement.[9] Thus, the primary vehicle to attain employment until 65 was not extending the retirement age but the re-employment of those reaching the 60-year mandatory retirement age.

The re-employment measures under the 2004 OPESA Revision had several features. First, an employer was allowed to select re-employable persons by concluding a labour-management agreement on the selection criteria with a majority union in the establishment; if no such union representation was in place, an employee was elected as the majority representative of employees. Those who did not meet the selection criteria, such as good performance, sufficient skills, and good health, were legally excluded from re-employment.

Second, under the re-employment scheme, the former employer and former employee who retired from the firm at the retirement age (60) usually concluded a fixed-term contract for a year (and sometimes on a part-time basis), and they renew their contracts until pensionable age or 65. The terms and conditions of employment are usually much more limited than before retirement because re-employment is a new employment relationship insulated from pre-retirement employment (see section 5).

Third, the discrepancy arising from reduced wages under re-employment can be covered by two social-security benefits: Zaishoku Rorei Nenkin (Pension for the Employed), paid from the Public Pension, and Korei Koyo Keizoku Kyufu (Re-employment Benefit for the Older Persons), paid from the Employment Insurance System. In other words, after retirement at age 60, livelihood until age 65 was expected to be supported by both wages from re-employment and benefits from the social-security system.

4.4.2 Continued Employment for All until 65 (2013–2020)

Until 2013, the earnings-related pension was paid from age 60, although the pensionable age for basic pension was extended. However, starting in 2013, the pensionable age for the earnings-related pension was raised to 61 and scheduled to be raised by one

9. Ministry of Health, Labour and Welfare, Koreisha no Koyo Jokyo Chosa [Survey on the Employment Situation of Older Persons] in 2013.

year every three years until 2025, ultimately reaching 65 (*see* Table 11.1). This meant that if those who reached the retirement age of 60 were not employed, they would have no income until they reached the extended pensionable age. There was concern that the existing re-employment measures, which allowed the selection of those eligible for re-employment through labour-management agreements, would create a significant social problem for older people without jobs and pensions.

Therefore, the 2012 Revision of the OPESA prohibits such selection based on the agreements with the majority representative. As a result, under the current law, employers with a mandatory retirement age below the pensionable age must re-employ all employees if they desire to be re-employed and until they reach the official pensionable age.

Because the revision would impose severe employment obligations on employers, the 2012 Amendments simultaneously provided that the re-employment obligation could be fulfilled not only by the former employer but also through re-employment in its affiliate companies.[10]

4.5 Phase 5: Endeavour Duty to Secure Work until 70 (2020 [Effective 2021] to Date)

With Japan facing the further ageing of society, the 2020 revision of the OPESA introduced an endeavour duty for employers to take measures to ensure the employment or work of older people up to the age of 70. The unique feature of this revision is that the content of the duty to endeavour is not limited to the employment of workers (extending the retirement age to 70, re-employment, and abolishing the mandatory retirement system); it also includes financial support for older persons to start businesses as self-employed, and measures ensuring that they can engage in paid activities in projects that contribute to society.

Under this endeavour duty, according to the 2022 statistics,[11] 40.7 % of Japanese companies have a system allowing people to work until age 66 or older, and 39.1 % have a system allowing them to work until age 70 or older.

5 RECENT LEGAL ISSUES

5.1 Quantitative and Qualitative Issues of Elderly Employment

As we have seen in this chapter, Japan has succeeded in promoting elderly employment in quantitative terms by encouraging or requiring employers to adopt measures to employ older people instead of embracing the anti-age discrimination law. However, problems have been pointed out about the qualitative aspect of elderly employment,

10. Even under the 2004 Revision, employment by such an affiliate company was regarded as one form of re-employment by interpretation. The 2012 Revision endorsed such an interpretation and made it an explicit provision in the OPESA.
11. Ministry of Health, Labour and Welfare, Reiwa 4 nen Korei-sha Koyo Jokyo tou Hokoku [2022 Report of the Employment Situation of Older Persons].

and lawsuits have been filed. The quality of elderly jobs has been particularly problematic in the case of re-employment through fixed-term contracts.

5.2 The Problem of Diminished Working Conditions in Re-employment

As mentioned, among the three employment-securing options imposed on employers starting in 2006, the re-employment measure was the most utilized.[12] Because the retirement age is 60, and from the day after an employee turns 60 or after the end of the fiscal year in which he or she turns 60, the employee is re-employed by the same employer, 60 is no longer a mandatory retirement age but merely the point at which the regular employment relationship ends. Rehired elderly employees usually sign a one-year, fixed-term contract and renew it until they reach the pensionable age. Rehiring is not done out of employers' desire to do so; it is an obligation imposed on them by law as a countermeasure to income decreases for older people due to the development of the state's pension policy of raising the pensionable age. In particular, since 2013 – when it became prohibited for companies to select those eligible for rehiring – [13] it has become a significant burden for companies.

Considering the fact that employers did not necessarily want to re-employ retiring employees but were compelled to do so by a re-employment obligation designed to deal with the aftermath of the government's pension-policy reform, both the government and labour scholars took the view that the content of the re-employment contract could be flexibly determined in light of a company's current situation, as long as it did not contradict the purpose of the scheme.[14]

Under these circumstances, the lawsuits raised the following questions. The first matter was whether the disparity between working conditions as a regular employee before retirement and those as a fixed-term contract employee after retirement was illegal because it constituted an 'unreasonable difference', prohibited by Article 20 of the Labour Contract Act (hereinafter 'LCA'); the second question was whether the re-employment conditions offered by the employer were illegal because they did not qualify as 'continuous employment' as defined by the OPESA.

---

12. As of 2022, although the ratio of the firms adopting an increase in the mandatory retirement age (25.5%) and elimination of the mandatory retirement system (3.9%) increased, 70.6% of the firms nevertheless adopted re-employment measures.
13. Until 2013, labour and management agreements could exclude poor performers and others from rehiring, but now all employees have the right to be rehired if they wish, except those who are in a situation where they can be legally dismissed.
14. Kazuo Sugeno, *Rodo-Ho [Labour Law]* 757 (Kobundo, 12th ed., 2019); Takashi Araki, *Rodo-Ho [Labour Law]* 371 (Yuhikaku, 5th ed., 2022); Ministry of Health, Labour and Welfare, *Kounen-reisha Koyo Antei-Ho Q&A [Q& A of OPESA]*, Q1-9.

5.3 Are Disparities in Working Conditions of Pre-retirement and Post-retirement Contracts Unreasonable?

Article 20 of the LCA prohibited unreasonable differences in working conditions between employees on permanent contracts (regular employees) and those on fixed-term contracts, taking into consideration the following three factors: (1) job content (nature of work and degree of responsibility), (2) scope of changes in the job content and personnel assignment, and (3) other circumstances.[15] Based on this provision, truck drivers in the *Nagasawa Un-yu* case who were rehired by the same company after retirement at age 60 filed a lawsuit claiming that because their work was the same both before and after retirement, the 20%–24% reduction in wages compared to their pre-retirement wages was an unreasonable difference. The Supreme Court[16] recognized the unreasonableness of the portion of some allowances that were not paid after re-employment but held that the disparity in basic wages was not unreasonable and emphasized that the rehiring of these employees after retirement should be considered as 'other circumstances'.

According to 2016 statistics, wages in Japan in the case of post-retirement re-employment were on average 73.5% of pre-retirement wages.[17] This could be difficult for foreigners to understand without assuming that seniority-based wages have been widely adopted under Japan's practice of lifetime or long-term employment. Under the Japanese employment system, employers have hired new graduates with no work experience,[18] educated and trained them on the premise of long-term employment, and developed a wage system where wages generally increase as the employee's ability to perform the work increases. In other words, the basic wage is determined not by the value of the job that the employee performs but by the employee's ability or potential to carry out the work as individually determined by the employer's evaluation. This is a crucial difference between the Japanese wage system and other countries' systems, where the value of the duties or jobs determines wages.

Because objective and individual assessment of employees' ability to perform work is difficult, employers have tended to evaluate their employees based on the length of service, assuming that their ability will increase in proportion to their years of service. Thus, the Japanese ability-based wage system has become similar to a seniority-based system.[19] As a result, pre-retirement employees in Japan are generally paid considerably higher wages than their market value (*see* Figure 11.3).

---

15. Article 20 of the LCA was introduced by the 2012 Revision and entered into force in April 2013. This provision has now been moved to Art. 8 of the Part-Time and Fixed-Term Work Act, as a result of the 2018 Amendment.
16. *Nagasawa Un-yu* Case, Supreme Court, 1 June 2018, 72 Minshu 202.
17. Japan Institute for Labour Policy and Training, *Konenrei-sha no Koyo ni Kansuru Chosa (Kigyo Chosa) [Survey on Employment of Older Workers*] (company Survey on employment of older workers (company survey)), 29 (2016). https://www.jil.go.jp/institute/research/2016/documents/156.pdf.
18. As a result, the youth unemployment rate in Japan is extremely low compared to other countries; *see* section 2.3 of this chapter.
19. This is ironic given the history of ability-based wage systems, which were introduced to overcome the age-based and seniority-based pay system employed in the past.

Figure 11.3 Seniority-Based Wage and Mandatory Retirement

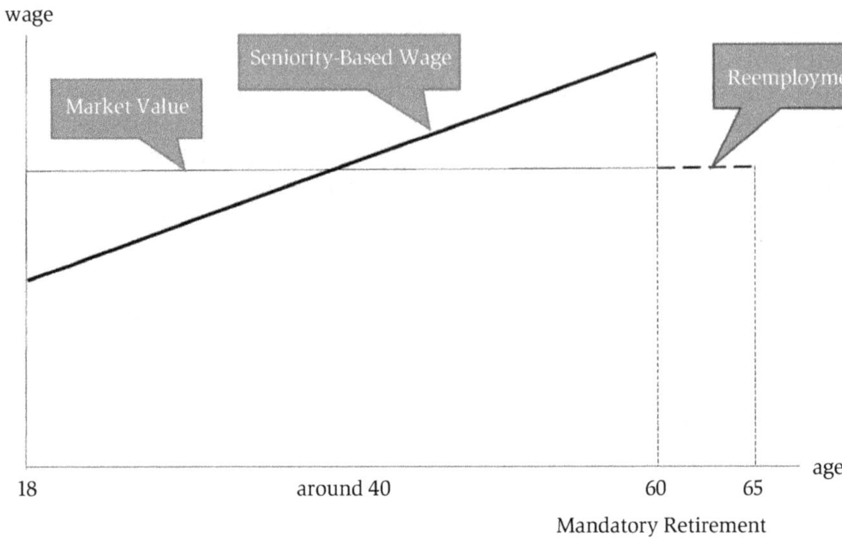

As Edward Lazear pointed out in his article 'Why Is There Mandatory Retirement?',[20] under a seniority-based wage system, if the employment relationship is not terminated when the total amount of below-market wages received by employees at a young age and the total amount of above-market wages received by them at the middle and older ages reach an equilibrium, the employer will continue to pay above-market wages and suffer losses. This is why the seniority wage system requires a mandatory retirement.

Japan's long-term employment system with seniority-based wages has also been based on the assumption that the total wages paid from the hire date until retirement are balanced for both labour and management. Therefore, when government policy mandates re-employment after retirement age, the rational response for employers from an economic perspective is to rehire at market value (*see* Figure 11.3). The fact that wages at the time of post-retirement rehiring are 26.5% lower on average than wages at the time of retirement reflects this situation.

However, because a significant decrease in wages upon re-employment is a major problem for employees, the government has developed policies to guarantee employees' livelihood by providing measures that could supplement income, such as Continued Employment Benefits for Older People[21] from employment insurance and payment

20. Edward Lazear, *Why Is There Mandatory Retirement?*, 87 Journal of Political Economy 1261 (1979) https://doi.org/10.1086/260835.
21. If an employee between the ages of 60 and 65 has his/her wages reduced to less than 75% of the pre-retirement level, a system called Continued Employment Benefits for Older People is available to compensate for the difference up to 75%, paid by unemployment insurance. For example, if a rehired employee's wages decrease to 65% of the pre-retirement level, the 10% difference will be paid from unemployment insurance.

of the Old-Age Pension for the Employed from the pension system. The Supreme Court probably considered these circumstances of fixed-term contract employees who were rehired after retirement as 'other circumstances' and did not regard the disparity in their basic wages before and after retirement as 'unreasonable'.

5.4 The Illegality of Re-employment Proposals with More Limited Working Conditions

Since 2013, employers have been obligated to hire all employees after 60 if they desire to be rehired. This is a potentially burdensome system for employers. As the OPESA does not stipulate working conditions for rehiring, the government and scholars have interpreted the law to give employers broad discretion in determining terms and conditions of re-employment.

However, when working conditions offered by the employer were so poor that the employee did not accept the proposal and the re-employment contract was not concluded, lawsuits were filed against the employer, claiming that the re-employment proposal was illegal and seeking compensation for damages.

First, the proposed duties of re-employment were at issue in the *Toyota* case.[22] The employer offered the employee, who had worked as a white-collar employee until retirement, simple labour tasks such as office cleaning and mail distribution. The employee did not accept the offer, and thus no re-employment contract was concluded. He sued for damages for tort, claiming that the employer's proposal for rehiring could not be evaluated as a proposal for 'continuous employment' as required by the OPESA. The Nagoya High Court accepted the claim for emotional distress damages because the company's re-employment proposal was unacceptable in light of socially accepted norms, and it could not be said to have given the employee a substantial opportunity for continued employment.

Second, the issue of the substantial reduction in wages in the proposed rehiring was raised in the *Kyushu Souzai* case.[23] In this case, the employer offered to hire the employee as a part-time employee with a 75% wage reduction on a monthly income basis. The Fukuoka High Court, finding no reasonable justification for such a proposal and deeming it contrary to the purpose of the continuous employment system, ruled it illegal and granted the claim for emotional distress damages.

Thus, the qualitative aspect of rehiring has become an issue, and cases are beginning to arise in which employers are obligated to pay damages if their rehiring proposals are contrary to the intent of the OPESA. It is important to note, however, that judicial review of such issues in Japan is not conducted as an age-discrimination matter but rather in light of the legislative intent of regulations to redress the unreasonable disparity between regular and non-regular employees and whether rehiring proposals are contrary to the legislative purpose of the OPESA.

22. Toyota Case, Nagoya High Court, 28 September 2016, 1146 Rodo Hanrei 22.
23. *Kyushu Souzai* Case, Fukuoka High Court, 7 September 2017, 1167 Rodo Hanrei 49.

6 CONCLUSION: COMPARATIVE ANALYSIS AND PROSPECTS

As home to one of the most rapidly ageing populations in the world, Japan has responded to this situation by implementing a diverse range of policy measures, such as raising the mandatory retirement age and imposing obligations on employers to rehire retired employees until age 65, rather than introducing age-discrimination regulations. This provides material for the following discussion from a comparative legal perspective.

6.1 Concept of Age Discrimination

First, Japan's approach to addressing the elderly employment offers the perspective that the age-discrimination prohibition is of a different character than the universal (traditional) prohibition of human rights discrimination based on sex, colour, race, religion, or national origin.[24] The US – the first country in the world to enact an age-discrimination law (Age Discrimination in Employment Act of 1967, ADEA) – initially restricted regulatory coverage for age discrimination to individuals aged 40 to 65. Subsequently, the upper age limit of 65 was eliminated, but the current law maintains the lower limit of 40. Thus, ADEA prohibits only discrimination based on age over 40 and not all forms of age discrimination. In contrast, the 2000 EU Directive on General Framework for Equal Treatment prohibits age discrimination alongside other forms of discrimination without limiting effect to those aged 40 and above. In addition, while a mandatory retirement age is prohibited in the US as typical age discrimination, a mandatory retirement age combined with the pensionable age tends not to be considered illegal in the EU.[25] Thus, the prohibited age discrimination varies among countries with age-discrimination laws.

While the issues of reverse discrimination are typically addressed in traditional human rights discrimination regulations, the reverse discrimination (such as favouring older individuals or those with longer years of service in lay-offs or severance payments vis-à-vis younger ones) in the age-discrimination law is not deemed illegal.[26]

In this context, the following description from the Report of Secretary of Labor Wirtz, which was the starting point for the ADEA legislation in the US, is still instructive today:

24. Ann Numhauser-Henning, *Elder Law and Its Subject: The Contextualized Ageing Individual*, 41 Ageing & Society 516 (2021) observes that the prohibition against age discrimination has been given a weaker format than prohibitions against other kinds of discrimination, and the ban on ageism has failed to achieve a clear legal status.
25. Unlike other discrimination bans, the EU Employment Equality Directive Art. 6.1 explicitly provides justification for direct age discrimination. The Directive Art. 6.2 also stipulates exemption concerning age for admission or entitlement to retirement benefits. As to CJEU decisions allowing compulsory retirement combined with pension eligibility, *see* Numhauser-Henning, *supra* n. 24, 522ff.
26. For a case in the US that explicitly rejects reverse discrimination regarding being young, *see* General Dynamics Land Systems, *Inc. v. Cline*, 540 U.S. 581 (2004).

> The development of responsible and effective public policy regarding discrimination based on age requires as steadfast and unfearing confrontation of reality as did the development of a national policy opposed to discrimination based on race, colour, religion, sex, or national origin. But there is an essential difference.
>
> The Nation has faced the fact – rejecting inherited prejudice or contrary conviction – that people's ability and usefulness is unrelated to the facts of their race, or colour, or religion, or sex, or the geography of their birth. Having accepted this truth, the easy thing to do would be simply to extend the conclusions derived from it to the problem of discrimination in employment based on aging, and be done with the matter. This would be easy – and wrong.[27]

6.2 Japan's Policy-Responsive Approach

Second, if age differs from other universal human rights discrimination grounds, it would be permissible to approach age issues differently from universal anti-discrimination regulations. All people age equally each year. Therefore, in Japan, age is considered an objective standard that is not arbitrary.[28] The mandatory retirement age in the Japanese employment system has been regarded as a socially valuable arrangement, strengthening job security for employees until retirement, preventing youth unemployment by filling positions left by retirees with young people, and facilitating organizational rejuvenation. Thus, Japan has opted not to introduce an age-discrimination law that deems mandatory retirement and other age-based treatment illegal. Instead, the country has applied the mandatory retirement system and other age-conscious measures to promote elderly employment.

Not adopting an age-discrimination law does not preclude in general the introduction of age-discrimination regulations in certain situations. In fact, Japan has introduced age-discrimination regulations specifically for recruitment and hiring processes[29] while maintaining the legality of the mandatory retirement age. Such a flexible policy response has been possible because Japan has viewed age differently from other prohibited grounds of human rights discrimination. In contrast to the human rights-based 'non-discrimination approach', Japan's policy can be called the 'policy-responsive approach', which gives legislators broad discretion and allows for diverse legislative measures to deal with older people's employment.

6.3 Elderly Employment Policy in the Era of 100-Year Life Expectancy

Third, however, the measures adopted under Japan's policy-responsive approach have been based only on the evaluation of the mandatory retirement system in the

27. Report of the Secretary of Labor, *The Older American Worker: Age Discrimination in Employment, Introduction* (1965).
28. Incidentally, Art. 79, para. 5 of the Japanese Constitution recognizes a mandatory retirement age for Supreme Court judges, stating that they 'shall retire from office when they reach the age prescribed by law'.
29. Article 9 of the Law for the Comprehensive Promotion of Labour Measures stipulates, with various conditions, that 'employers ... shall ... in recruiting and hiring employees ... provide equal opportunities regardless of their age'.

employment system from that era. Therefore, if the times and the employment environment change, and the social benefits attributed to the retirement age system diminish, policies will naturally need to be reconsidered.

As discussed in section 5, it has become clear that the system of rehiring employees with fixed-term contracts until the pensionable age, while maintaining the retirement age at 60, is problematic in terms of the quantitative aspects of elderly employment. In Japan, which has no law prohibiting age discrimination, the worsening of wages and working conditions after age 60 is not discussed as an age-discrimination matter. Judicial review is conducted from the perspective of whether the situation violates the law's intent to redress unreasonable differences between regular and non-regular employees or to ensure older people's continuous employment.

The decline in elderly employment quality has become apparent only during the relatively limited period between ages 60 and 65. However, as we enter the era of 100-year life expectancy, the quality of employment of older people could become a more serious social issue. Expanding elderly jobs is essential for sustaining the pension system. Japan has already enriched the policy menu by imposing the endeavour duty on employers to support continued employment and supporting the establishment of businesses for self-employed work until age 70. If this employment of the elderly is to continue for an even longer period, there will be an ever-stronger demand for appropriate working conditions for them. Regulating this issue from the perspective of age discrimination would be one option.

Still, whether it is reasonable to handle this issue entirely through anti-age discrimination requires careful consideration. The problem of elderly employment after age 60 in Japan stems from the state's pension reform of raising the pensionable age. In dealing with this shift in state policy, it is unlikely that simply ordering individual employers to prohibit age discrimination is a reasonable and sustainable approach. It will be necessary for the state to mobilize various measures to assist both employers and employees in coping with the pension policy change.

Japan's approach to addressing the elderly employment issue by combining diverse policies tailored to specific circumstances, rather than relying solely on age-discrimination regulations, seems to stem from such considerations. However, the policy-responsive approach does not preclude age-discrimination regulations; where the age-discrimination approach can more reasonably address the problem, Japan may adopt age-discrimination legislation in such situations – just as it did for recruitment and hiring.

In any event, Japan's policy-responsive approach is free from the fixed idea that age must be deemed one of the prohibited grounds. It seeks to find better policies, considering the changing environment surrounding working and retiring people, and consistency with evolving industrial, social, and employment policies. Japan's unique approach to ageing society may be one social experiment that can serve as a reference for other countries.

CHAPTER 12

Telework, Sustainability of Pensions, and Synergies with Markets Institutions: Constructing a Theory of Fundamental Rights

Julia López López, Núria Pumar Beltrán & Eusebi Colàs-Neila

1 INTRODUCTION

For decades, the sustainability of pensions has been a major objective – and challenge – for both actors and institutions in a multilevel scenario within and beyond the European Union. Demographic dynamics, the segmentation of professional careers, and economic crises have challenged the viability of welfare systems, thus accentuating the urgency of research on ways to guarantee pensions. A central assumption of many analyses of this question has been that strictly economic calculations should take priority over other considerations, including social sensibilities and rights, in the interest of achieving pension sustainability. Our approach is quite different. We argue that the guarantee and full development of fundamental rights – and related social objectives – can actually contribute to the sustainability of pensions. A key component of our analysis is the consideration of implications of the voluntary nature of both part-time work and telework; this factor underpins the importance of motivating workers to use these employment options, resulting in increased numbers of people in the labour force and thus diminishing reliance solely on pensions.

More concretely, this chapter presents an approach to enhancing the economic sustainability of pensions by *leveraging synergies* – instead of presuming the existence of tensions or conflict – between this sustainability objective and other elements of the sustainability perspective, namely the pursuit of social inclusion and the reinforcement of fundamental rights. Concretely, we seek to specify ways in which continued employment of retirement age workers – typically through part-time telework – can be enhanced by structuring certain crucial labour market arrangements in ways that protect the fundamental rights of relatively older workers who might otherwise be forced to rely exclusively on retirement pensions for their incomes. Our specific focus centres on telework arrangements and ways to inform the regulation of this type of work through a reading of fundamental rights that fosters social inclusion and, as a result, continued labour market involvement by workers who might otherwise rely exclusively on retirement pensions. In our analysis, key synergies between labour institutions and the principles present in the regulation of part-time work and telework can be developed by emphasizing the principles of voluntary work and non-discrimination.

Strategies and policies to maintain the sustainability of pensions take account of the combination of public and private systems in retirement pensions[1] and other factors such as the extension of working careers and the simultaneous combination of pension and work. Our contribution analyses the combination of pension and work and the possible extension of professional lives, centring the pursuit of these objectives on the frame of fundamental rights – including equality and non-discrimination – as well as the interaction of the sustainability of pensions with labour institutions. We emphasize remote work and part-time employment, identifying approaches to their regulation designed to reinforce principles that affirm labour rights and develop social principles that have been linked to an expansive understanding of sustainable development and thus policies of inclusive solidarity,[2] within the general context of post-industrial welfare capitalism.[3]

A world with equitable and universal access to quality education at all levels, to health care and social protection, where physical, mental, and social well-being are assured is defined in the Resolution of the UN 2030 Agenda for Sustainable Development as a main goal. Sustainability, in this sense, involves not only the continued economic viability of pensions but also the pursuit of social protection and well-being. The construction of this model of global development has far-reaching implications for the legal system: it points to the relevance of a cosmopolitan legal order[4] to guarantee, through both hard- and soft-law regulation, the right to be entitled to social protection.

The general goals at play here are very important. As the Green Paper (2010) points out, an adequate and sustainable retirement income for EU citizens, now and in the future, is a priority for the European Union. A subsequent green strategy, the 2021

1. Isabel Oriz, Fabio Durán-Valverde, Stefan Urban & Veronika Wodsak, *Reversing Pension Privatizations: Rebuilding Public Pension Systems in Eastern Europe and Latin America* (Isabel Ortiz, Fabio Durán-Valverde, Stefan Urban & Veronika Wodsak eds, ILO 2018). ILO, FAO & UNICEF, *UN Collaboration on Social Protection: Reaching Consensus on How to Accelerate Social Protection Systems-Building* (Geneva 2022).
2. Julia López López, *Inscribing Solidarity in Labour Law: Promise and Limitations*, in *Inscriptions of Solidarity: Labor Law and Beyond*, 1–23 (Julia López López ed., Cambridge University Press 2022).
3. Gøsta Esping-Andersen, *Social Foundations of Postindustrial Economies* 145–169 (Oxford University Press 1999).
4. Alec Stone Sweet & Clare Ryan, *A Cosmopolitan Legal Order: Kant, Constitutional Justice, and the European Convention on Human Rights* (Oxford University Press 2018).

Green Paper in Ageing,[5] articulated the challenges posed by an ageing population and opportunities to respond to growing necessities – including matters of health care, long-term care mobility, connectivity and well-being, the promotion of lifelong learning, and active ageing. Successfully addressing these matters can promote voluntary extension of working life and thus the sustainability of fair pension systems.

Practical application includes the combination of the regulatory framework of the subsidiarity principle with soft- and hard-law instruments, thus creating a complex panorama with a wide variety of results at the national level and a strong impact on equality and non-discrimination policies.[6] Other actors, such as the European Trade Union Confederation (ETUC), have adopted the 2017 European Social Partners' Autonomous Framework Agreement on Active Ageing and An Inter-Generational Approach, an important instrument implemented by the Member States.[7] These initiatives underscore the fact that, to guarantee active ageing, Member States must address the labour market institutions' interaction with digitalization and the increasing relevance of new skills.[8] The agreement focuses on the role of social partners in designing and enhancing active-ageing policies through the lens of fundamental rights.

The perspective that we adopt to study sustainability of retirement pensions links the promotion of this sustainability goal to several fundamental rights, including dignity,[9] equality and non-discrimination, and participation. We see this framing as a way to promote solidarity.[10] This includes freedom from age discrimination, a phenomenon that Freeland characterizes as discrimination against both older and the youngest workers as well as discrimination surrounding issues of retirement.[11]

In the context of sustainability and fundamental rights, the construction of regulatory policies of solidarity – understood as inclusive solidarity – must be accepted in the terms proposed by the ILO conventions and related regulatory instruments along with the EU Charter of Fundamental Rights. In essence, these documents offer well-developed tools for pursuing inclusive solidarity.[12]

---

5. European Commission, Directorate-General for Economic and Financial Affairs, Directorate-General for Employment, Social Affairs and Inclusion, Directorate-General for the Internal Market and Services, *Towards Adequate, Sustainable and Safe European Pension Systems: Green Paper* (Publications Office, 2010).
6. *See* Veronika Lemeire & Patrizia Zanoni, *Beyond Methodological Nationalism in Explanations of Gender Equality: The Impact of EU Policies on Gender Provisions in National Collective Agreements in Belgium (1957–2020)*, 28(1) European Journal of Industrial Relations 47–64 (2022) https://doi.org/10.1177/09596801211027400.
7. Final Report, adopted at the virtual Executive Committee Meeting of 22–23 March 2021.
8. *Ibid.*, 45.
9. *See* Judy Fudge, *Dignity, Disadvantage, and Age: Putting Constitutional and Fundamental Rights to Work for Older Workers*, in *Elder Law: Evolving European Perspectives*, 55–86 (Ann Numhauser-Henning ed., Edward Elgar Publishing 2017).
10. *See* Jenny Julén Votinius & Mia Rönnmar, *Intergenerational Aspects of Elder Law: Conflict, Solidarity: Or Ambivalence*, in *Elder Law: Evolving European Perspectives*, 113–132 (Ann Numhauser-Henning ed., Edward Elgar Publishing 2017).
11. *See* Mark Freedland & Lucy Vickers, *Age Discrimination and EU Labour Rights Law*, in *Research Handbook on EU Labour Law*, 527–546 (Alan Bogg, Cathryn Costello & Anne Davies eds, Edward Elgar Publishing 2016).
12. López López, *supra* n. 2.

2 WORK AND PENSIONS: PART-TIME WORK AND TELEWORK AND THE EMBEDDEDNESS OF FUNDAMENTAL RIGHTS

The sufficiency and economic support basis of retirement pensions and the compatibility of benefits and work constitute the terrain for one of the main debates about sustainability. The approach in this chapter is to study how retirement pensions – and the goal of guaranteeing their sustainability – can be compatible with part-time telework, thereby identifying the advantages of combining regulatory frameworks through an emphasis on fundamental rights. For this purpose, it is important to specify certain features shared by part-time regulation and telework. This allows us to underline a series of synergies present in the regulatory combination of work extension and labour market institutions. A first synergy between the institutions regulating part-time work and telework concerns multilevel regulation and how this regulation recognizes collective bargaining as a key instrument for developing part-time work based on the principle of subsidiarity. In the European Union, framework agreements on part-time work and telework regulate these aspects. Clause 1 of the Framework Agreement on Part Time Work provides for the removal of discrimination against part-time workers; improving the quality of part-time work; facilitation of the development of part-time work on a voluntary basis; and contribution to the flexible organization of working time in a manner that takes into account the needs of employers and workers.

A second synergy refers to telework regulation. In the European Union, the framework agreement on telework sets out the main principles of telework regulation; it refers to the *voluntary* nature of teleworking and equality and non-discrimination in telework arrangements. Furthermore, privacy, data protection, and health and safety guarantees are recognized among other rights as being crucial for those engaged in telework.

Our central contribution is to identify how the compatibility of part-time work and telework carries significant implications for pension sustainability, thus embedding the debate on voluntary compatibility between work and pensions within the examination of sustainability. In this way, we emphasize the agency of pension recipients and the importance of guaranteeing recipients' freedom from discrimination – two considerations of relevance due to their implications for elderly workers[13] and also for gender factors within the contours of employment.[14] Paid employment of women and people who have reached retirement age increases labour-force contributions to pensions, thereby enhancing the sustainability of pensions. This approach allows us to understand the complexity of pension sustainability in a way that looks beyond the purely economic and financial debate. Placing the debates about sustainability in a context of equality and non-discrimination permits us to introduce this

13. Julia López López, *Age as Factor of Discrimination and Collective Dismissals*, in *Festskrift Till Ann Numhauser-Henning* (Mia Rönnmar & Jenny Julén Votinius eds, University of Lund 2017).
14. Gøsta Esping-Andersen, *The Incomplete Revolution: Adapting to Women's New Roles* (Polity Press, 2009).

fundamental social objective - equality - in a new legal framework that holds significant practical implications.[15]

3 GUARANTEES OF SUSTAINABLE PENSION SYSTEMS FOR HARD-LAW REGULATION

It is useful to underscore that the pension regulation offers a complex panorama including both hard- and soft-law approaches in a multilevel layering of the protection models. A main reference at the EU level is the constitutional framing of pensions as a mechanism of protection in the Charter of Fundamental Rights,[16] which integrates these social rights in the chapter on solidarity. Article 25 of the Charter declares that 'The Union recognises and respects the rights of the elderly to lead a life of dignity and independence and to participate in social and cultural life', and this is connected to social security and social assistance (Article 34) intended to combat poverty and social exclusion. The constitutionalization of pensions in this context is relevant because of its implications for equality and non-discrimination policies.

The Charter of Fundamental Rights of the European Union includes pensions as an element of the solidarity principle. This crucial document also formulates the policies of sustainability - under the subsidiarity principle - not only in economic and budgetary terms but also as a matter of fundamental rights. In this understanding, the synergies between labour market institutions and the sustainability of pensions help to produce a reading of this topic that extends beyond the economic approach. A fundamental building block in constructing the interaction and synergies between pension sustainability and labour market institutions is the regulation of remote work and part-time work in ways that simultaneously embody these goals and their interaction.

The extension of labour activity beyond current practice has been not only a goal in the EU but also a policy in the Member States. This broad objective holds numerous concrete implications, many of which concern part-time employment. The EU's regulation of part-time work establishes the principles of non-discrimination and the voluntary character of workers' decisions to not only move from full-time to part-time jobs but also do the opposite. The regulation of part-time employment, with its focus on non-discrimination and *voluntariness*, can be seen as the implementation and defence of fundamental rights in this form of work. Developing the voluntary element of part-time employment and defending equality and non-discrimination are crucial components of the approach that we advocate. The legal significance of these matters is reflected in a European Court of Justice (ECJ) decision, in which the Court found that Spain's national pension scheme for part-timers was in violation of the law owing to its impact on gender - thereby undercutting the right to non-discrimination. The fundamental right to non-discrimination is a principle that can improve conditions for

15. Bob Hepple, *Equality: The New Legal Framework* (Hart Publishing 2011).
16. C 364/16 Official Journal of the European Communities 18 December 2000.

workers and thus increase incentives to work, thereby enhancing the sustainability of pensions.

Another important set of interactions was set in motion by the COVID-19 pandemic, which increased telework, remote work, and hybrid approaches to work organization. This new context reconfigured the conditions for working from home and thus introduced several challenges for pension schemes; it also presented new opportunities to make continuing work more attractive for many older workers. We emphasize how the sustainability of pensions can be enhanced through forms of work characterized by technology and decentralization or de-localization of production systems - if those types of work are regulated in ways that offer workers positive motivation to continue work past previous pension-age levels. A good example can be found in the Telework agreement on remote work, which establishes the principle of equality and non-discrimination of teleworkers. As in the case of part-time employment, this telework is legally defined as non-compulsory, not only in the implementation of a telework arrangement but also in its reversibility - if the worker so wishes. Crucially, the regulatory framework for remote work promotes consensus as part of the implementation of such forms of work in firms. Many fundamental rights are relevant for the regulation of part-time and telework; these include privacy, dignity, equality and non-discrimination - all incorporating matters of health and safety.

At the same time, the regulation of remote work through the European Union Agreement also reinforces the rights to freedom of association and representation, including the role of collective bargaining. All of these guarantees and rights can enhance the attractiveness of optional forms of employment; for retirement age workers, these forms also result in lower employment costs than standard full-time and on-site employment. Thus, we argue that a strengthening of fundamental rights can extend the working life of many individuals and reduce the reliance of retirement age workers on pensions for economic support.

The symbiotic relationship between both remote and part-time work on the one hand and the sustainability of pensions on the other is conditioned by new complexities in the application of the subsidiarity principle. The Spanish case is emblematic of this process. The European Telework agreement, a form of soft regulation, has been implemented in a law at the Spanish national level, thus transplanting the agreement's contents on working time and conciliation (as well as other matters) into hard-law regulation.

The Charter of Fundamental Rights frames the sustainability of pensions as a constitutional matter extending beyond economic and budgetary plans. This crucial document articulates a discourse of solidarity linked with principles of equality and non-discrimination, as we have emphasized. Alongside this constitutionalization of the right to guaranteed retirement pensions, one encounters a broad range of relevant policies in the Member States, including those that seek to combine work and pension with a view to lengthening working lives. This extension of working life can be pursued by shifting the age of retirement or promoting the combination of work and pensions. Our proposal is to fortify this second pathway - i.e., combining some portion of continued work with a first stage of pensions - through the possibilities that remote and hybrid work offer, insofar as these work options are regulated in ways that accentuate their voluntariness and guarantee of equality and non-discrimination. This approach offers the promise of improving results in equality and non-discrimination by gender and age, life-cycle training, and healthy ageing. An EU policy document that pursues this approach is Council Directive 97/81/EC of 15 December 1997 concerning the Framework Agreement on part-time work.[17] Its purpose is to 'provide for the removal of discrimination against part-time workers and to improve the quality of part-time work' and 'facilitate the development of part-time work on a voluntary basis and to contribute to the flexible organization of working time'. We emphasize how synergies between part-time work and remote work – as well as the added support for these options provided by regulations that guarantee fundamental rights – can offer advantages for policies seeking to sustain retirement age pensions while simultaneously reaffirming rights such as equality and non-discrimination, voluntariness (and thus the agency of beneficiaries), participation, and training throughout life.[18]

The voluntary character of telework is clearly affirmed by the EU Framework Agreement when this agreement states that 'telework is voluntary for the worker and the employer concerned'. This principle is reaffirmed in all the social partners' transposition measures across Europe. The provision of the EU Framework Agreement has even been used by the Spanish Supreme Court in a case from 11 April 2005 as an interpretation criterion to highlight the importance of the worker's willingness to opt for telework if telework is not part of the initial job description.[19] The Framework Agreement stipulates that teleworkers are entitled to fundamental rights such as privacy, health and safety, the training of teleworkers, and collective rights. Recently, in its Work Program 2022–2024, the ETUC inserted a call for reviewing and updating this Autonomous Agreement and to develop a legally binding agreement implemented via a Directive.[20]

Linking both remote work and part-time work to a reduced reliance on retirement pensions through a regulatory reference to fundamental rights is an approach that holds special relevance for certain demographic groups of the population, including very large segments. For instance, the objective of eliminating systemic gender discrimination for women, especially older women,[21] could permit many retirement aged women to continue working part-time, or through telework arrangements, or both – thereby reducing their reliance on pensions. This avenue to pension-system sustainability would obviously also promote 'active ageing'. Training options also hold relevance for our approach. What we propose is a way of thinking about sustainability that holds numerous and concrete practical implications.

17. Directive concluded by UNICE, CEEP and the ETUC – Annex: Framework agreement on part-time work.
18. Frame agreement signed by ETUC, UNICE and UEPM and CEEP in Telework, 16 July 2002.
19. Joint implementation Report of Telework Frame Agreement, 28 July 2006, p. 15.
20. 28 July 2022.
21. About systemic discrimination for the youngest workers, *see* Julia López López, *Traineeships and Systemic Discrimination Against Young Workers*, in *Internships, Employability and the Search for Decent Work Experience*, 321–334 (Andrew Stewart, Rosemary Owens, Niall O'Higgins & Anne Hewitt eds, ILO & Edward Elgar Publishing 2021).

4 ACTIVE AGEING AND EUROPEAN LONG-TERM CARE POLICIES: A GENDER APPROACH

The growth in Europe's older population has increased the need for both formal and informal care, but as a result of demographic, economic, and cultural change, families increasingly find themselves less capable of meeting these needs. The current care model is beset by crisis, highlighting the unequal distribution of responsibilities of the state, companies, and families, as well as between women and men.[22] This explains why policies that seek to promote permanence at work cannot be dissociated from the challenge of the worsening care crisis and the progressive ageing of the population.[23]

Here, it is argued that respecting the fundamental right of older people – and by extension all dependents – to lead a life of dignity and independence while also remaining integrated in society facilitates the prolongation of working life and gender equality.

Care occupies a pivotal place in old age in two senses. With advancing years – for reasons of health and the loss of functional abilities – the elderly are more likely to need more care; yet, parallel to this, it is these older people, and above all older women, who find themselves dedicating a considerable amount of their time to caring for children and dependents. As a general rule, the work of older women who care for the elderly is neither recognized as such nor remunerated. This work tends to cause additional problems of health and social isolation for these women.

All in all, European women live longer than their male counterparts but are at greater risk of living in poverty and suffering social exclusion.[24] Income gaps between older women and older men indicate how consequences of past discrimination and structural inequalities, derived mainly from stereotypes and the unequal distribution of tasks, worsen in the ageing stage.[25] A survey conducted among workers in various OECD countries shows that older workers enjoy less flexibility when it comes to reconciling their work obligations with their care responsibilities for both children and dependent adults. Moreover, many active women who delayed the age of childbearing are likely to be subjected to greater pressure to leave the job market to care not only for their children, who are still minors, but also, and more especially, for their parents. This explains why policies of permanence at work aimed at older workers need to be framed within broader policies of the sustainability of care,[26] solidarity between

22. A. Pérez Orozco, *Del Trabajo Doméstico al Trabajo de Cuidados*, 49–67 (Cristina Carrasco ed., La Oveja Roja 2014).
23. *See* recommendations in order to implement transformative care policies in ILO, *Care at Work. Investing in Care Leave and Services for a More Gender Equal World of Work* (Geneva 2022).
24. Eurostat, *Ageing Europe: Looking at the Lives of Older People in the EU* 124–138 (Publications Office of the European Union 2020).
25. World Health Organization, *Active Ageing: A Policy Framework* 40–41 (2002).
26. *See, e.g.*, on the need to promote policies of the sustainability of care in the wider debate of achieving greater democracy and gender justice, Dolors Comas, *Cuidados y derechos. El avance hacia la democratización de los cuidados*, no. 49 *Cuadernos de Antropología Social* 13–29 (2019). *See also* Cristina Carrasco, *La economía feminista: ruptura teórica y propuesta política*, in *Con voz propia: La economía feminista como apuesta teórica y política* 25–47 (Cristina Carrasco ed., La Oveja Roja 2014).

generations, and active ageing, embodied very much in terms of basic rights and a careful consideration of gender issues. The promotion of flexible work formulas, which allow women and men to reconcile work with care responsibilities, needs to converge with the introduction of social policies that guarantee universal care and healthcare structures, as well as decent jobs in the care sector.

For many years, the European Commission opted to define active ageing as 'helping people stay in charge of their own lives for as long as possible as they age and, where possible, to contribute to the economy and society'.[27] Thus, while older people continued to work and stay healthy, and continued to pay their contributions into the system, they were contributing to state savings in terms of the pension pot and the provision of health and social services.

However, an analysis of this EU discourse on ageing highlighted the somewhat reductionist vision of this phenomenon, which diverged from the notion as understood by the World Health Organization. Moreover, it left outside its radius of action the right of older people to lead a life of dignity and independence, as provided for under Article 25 of the Charter of Fundamental Rights of the European Union.

In the face of this situation, the public powers had to coordinate their actions towards the targeting of employability, enhancement of lifelong skills, sustainability of pensions, and the provision of incentives that might facilitate older persons' delay of retirement age. However, one matter was conspicuous in its absence: Member States' assumption of responsibility for the provision of care for older people. Indeed, even when the European authorities provided the Member States with recommendations for the provision of care structures for young children, they failed to contemplate the need for care of the elderly or dependents.[28] The turning point in European discourse on ageing came with the publication of the EU's 2030 Strategy[29] for a socially stronger Europe in transition to a greener and more digital economy. Both the European Commission and the Council, in their programme for implementation of the European Pillar of Social Rights, have now placed the strengthening of health systems and accessibility to quality long-term care services within their social-policy objectives.

Although great disparities exist among the Member States in terms of the degree of coverage offered, most of the care needs of older people are not met by institutions; rather, these duties are assumed by family members.[30] In turn, long-term care policies, implemented primarily by regional and local governments, point to the strengthening of two trends: 'support for active ageing as a way to postpone care needs, and

27. European Commission, *The European Innovation Partnership on Active and Healthy Ageing* (2011), https://digital-strategy.ec.europa.eu/en/policies/eip-aha.
28. For this reason, one of the main innovations of the Directive on work-life balance was the provision of carers' leave. *See* Directive (EU) 2019/1158 of the European Parliament and of the Council of 20 June 2019 on work-life balance for parents and carers and repealing Council Directive 2010/18/EU, OJL 188 (12.7.2019).
29. European Commission, *A Strong Social Europe for Just Transitions*, COM (2022) 14 final.
30. European Commission and Social Protection Committee, *Long Term Care Report. Trends, Challenges and Opportunities in an Ageing Society*, Vol. I (European Commission 2021). *See also*, in this sense, European Institute for Gender Equality, *Gender Inequalities in Care and Consequences for the Labour Market*, 37–38 (EIGE 2022).

prioritising homecare and community-based care over residential care'.[31] Long-term care is the responsibility of the Member States and forms part of the open method of coordination in the field of social protection, but to date, the European Union has not laid down any strategies for Member States to adopt. A shift in EU discourse is apparent, however, as evidenced by the debate launched in the Green Paper on Ageing, while the Commission seems to have made a greater commitment in this policy area with the announcement of its European Care Strategy. Nevertheless, this initiative is unlikely to be truly transformative, given that it is not backed by numerical targets or the necessary financial support.

5 EXTENDING WORKING LIFE THROUGH TELEWORK AND THE RISKS OF EMPLOYEE DISCRIMINATION

Experiences of the past and present related to career paths and job prospects, employment precarity, and workplace health conditions can vary greatly from one person to another and, more particularly, according to gender and other factors, including qualifications and migrant status. These inequalities subsequently emerge in the latter stages of a person's working life so that career and retirement options differ enormously among those approaching retirement age. Here, the gender variable is once again very much present:[32] women are affected by the phenomena of horizontal and vertical segregation, double shifts, mental-health risks derived from work, and the tendency to have fewer career options and fewer choices when making the transition to retirement.

Individuals' work experiences over the course of working life are critical in their decision to prolong their professional activity.[33] Work organization and working conditions can greatly condition the decision of older workers to extend their working lives. Thus, health at work, career prospects, the possibility of reconciling professional life with personal and family life, and financial security act as obvious conditioning factors.[34]

The ILO[35] and Europe's social agents[36] recommend that companies manage their workforces in an inclusive manner, taking advantage of the synergies, skills, and

31. European Parliament, *European Care Strategy, Briefing of the European Parliamentary Research Service* 3–4 (2022).
32. Gérard Valenduc & Patricia Vendramin, *Genre, âge et conditions de travail* in *Genre, conditions de travail et santé. Qu'est-ce qui a changé?* 85–94 (Christelle Casse & Marianne De Troyer dir., ETUI, 2020).
33. A. Numhauser Henning, *Labour Law in a Greying Labour Market: In Need of a Reconceptualisation of Work and Pension Norms: The Position of Older Workers in Labour Law*, 4(2) *European Labour Law Journal* 84–100 (2013) https://doi.org/10.1177/201395251300400202.
34. Valenduc & Vendramin, *supra* n. 32.
35. ILO, *Una sociedad inclusiva para una población que envejece: el desafío del empleo y la protección social*, 37 Rev. Esp. Geriatr. Gerontol. 106–122 (2002). Also ILO, *Older Workers Recommendation* (23 June 1980, nº 162).
36. European Social Partners' Autonomous Framework Agreement on Active Ageing and an Inter-Generational Approach (8 March 2017), http://etuc.org.

competencies of workers in their different age groups and creating healthy, non-discriminatory work environments with decent working conditions.[37]

However, business practices that are common in personnel management – guided by short-termism, the constant search for cost reduction, and stereotypes concerning the work capacities of older workers – largely contradict these recommendations. The turnover and instability of workers is a growing trend, and it is common practice for companies to resort to rejuvenating the workforce through lay-offs or the marginalization of older workers in terms of training, job prospects, and more.

However, the ageing of the active population and the resulting shortage of available labour, especially in certain sectors, could change business policies with regard to older workers. In this respect, more flexible working arrangements such as working from home (teleworking) have considerable potential for promoting the employability and retention of older workers.[38]

In Europe, people who continue to work beyond the 'traditional' retirement age (65 +) do so mainly by means of flexible working arrangements and by working fewer hours than their younger counterparts.[39] In fact, they are two times as likely to work mostly from home as their younger colleagues.[40]

Figure 12.1 Employed Persons Usually Working from Home by Age and Sex in EU-27 (%), 2022

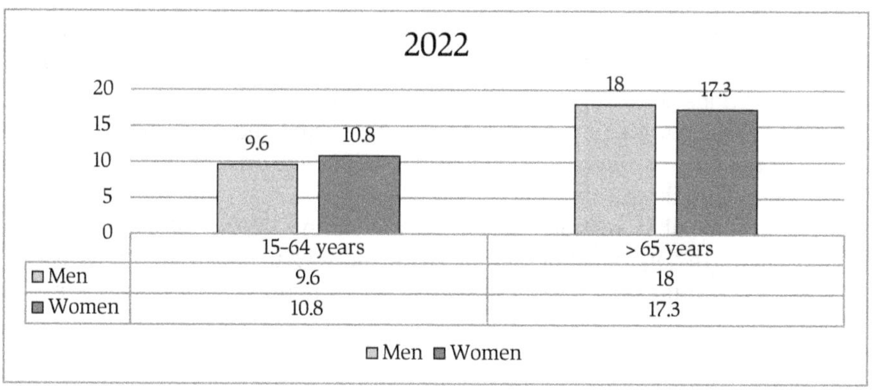

Source: Eurostat: Statistics | Eurostat (europa.eu).

37. Eurofound similarly, employs the concept of sustainable work. Eurofound, *Sustainable Work and the Ageing Workforce* (Publications Office of the European Union 2012).
38. Margaret Patrickson, *Teleworking: Potential Employment Opportunities for Older Workers?*, 23(8) International Journal of Manpower 704–715 (2002) https://doi.org/10.1108/01437720210453902.
39. Eurostat, *supra* n. 24, 96–97.
40. *Ibid.*, pp. 99–100.

In this age group, men who remain active at work far outnumber women and if we look at working conditions, older women work fewer hours and extend their working lives over shorter periods than do men.[41]

Based on the findings of the Eurofound surveys,[42] the vast majority of European workers would prefer hybrid working arrangements, a preference that has surely grown as a result of the widespread adoption of teleworking during the COVID-19 pandemic. The main advantages of being able to work from home are identified as the greater autonomy workers experience and a better work-life balance while avoiding other aspects, such as time spent commuting to and from the workplace. Among its social advantages, teleworking would improve employment opportunities and prolong the working life of older people and those with health problems. In this sense, teleworking can be seen as a key ally in policies to extend the active life of workers.

Teleworking makes it easier for workers to carry out their professional activity with greater autonomy: workers decide how, when, and where they work. This advantage is especially evident in how employees manage their work time because it facilitates the adaptation of the workday and working hours to workers' personal needs.

Yet in what many authors refer to as the 'autonomy paradox',[43] teleworking can sometimes lead to greater work demands or requirements, intensification of working hours and, in general, a greater immediacy or availability of workers that tends to blur the boundaries between personal and work life. Teleworking has been characterized as creating unstructured flexibility[44] which gives rise to greater conflicts between family and work, as well as health problems linked to stress and psychosocial risks. Such circumstances are most likely to manifest themselves in jobs with poorly regulated working conditions and unstructured working days.[45] In contrast, in sectors and professions where working conditions are strongly regulated by both legislation and collective bargaining, workers would likely appreciate the advantages afforded by the autonomy of teleworking.

In general, flexible work agreements should emphasize the autonomy of workers when it comes to the organization of their work and seek to ensure they have a greater margin for decision-making in relation to their working times. In fact, companies that

41. *Ibid.*, pp. 104–105.
42. According to its surveys, two-thirds of workers would prefer hybrid work arrangements. Eurofound, *Telework in the EU: Regulatory frameworks and Recent Updates* 7 (Publications Office of the European Union 2022).
43. *See*, in this sense, Paula Rodríguez-Modroño & Purificación López-Igual, *Job Quality and Work: Life Balance of Teleworkers*, Int. J. Environ. Res. Public Health 1–13 (2021) https://doi.org/10.3390/ijerph18063239.
44. I adopt the classification proposed by Colette Fagan in relation to types of flexibility. Colette Fagan, *Gender and Working-Time in Industrialized Countries: Practices and Preferences*, in *Working-time and Workers' Preferences in Industrialized Countries: Finding the Balance*, 108–146 (Jon Messenger ed., ILO, 2004).
45. Jaeseung Kim et al., *Workplace Flexibility and Worker Well-Being by Gender*, 82 J. of Marriage and Family 892–910 (2020) https://doi.org/10.1111/jomf.12633.

have adopted teleworking formulas report less absenteeism and a decrease in employee requests for reduced working hours and part-time jobs.[46] Although these data need to be examined in greater depth, they show that teleworking formulas have considerable benefits for work-life balance and appear to facilitate the transition to retirement. Still, it should be stressed that in the case of older workers, it is not enough to make the place and time of work more flexible; rather, the workload must be reduced by either rearranging tasks or resorting to part-time work.

At the same time and as with other measures that facilitate reconciliation, the risk emerges that teleworking reinforces traditional roles in the distribution of care and increases employment-related gender gaps.[47] In this regard, women's true degree of voluntariness when choosing this form of work is of obvious relevance insofar as they are not forced into it due to the unequal distribution of care.

Ultimately, it is a matter of seeking to avoid any discrimination within a company between home workers and office workers and, more specifically, between male and female employees[48] or between older and younger workers. In this sense, personnel policies that promote an age-friendly organizational culture would be welcome – i.e., policies that focus not only on the needs of older workers but also allow the entire workforce to benefit from the advantages of teleworking or other flexible work organization formulas, regardless of worker age and gender. Here, the participation of workers' representatives and collective bargaining at a range of levels are critical, without overlooking the importance that equality plans can have when evaluating the gender impact of such measures.

6 POLICY AND REGULATORY OPTIONS IN EUROPEAN COUNTRIES TO EXTEND WORKING LIFE

Retirement, as a situation protected by social-security systems, is traditionally defined by the confluence of two factors: reaching a certain age and leaving work. Its configuration has not been static; it has allowed for adaptation through the possibility of bringing forward or delaying access to retirement and the possibility of combining a pension and part-time work. However, in comparative law, both elements have become more flexible in recent years, and this has led to a significant blurring of the contours of the retirement contingency.

The ageing of European populations and the search for financial sustainability of pension systems, as stated earlier, has been one of the main arguments used by many legal systems to introduce wide-ranging pension reforms. This common trend is explained partly by the role played by the European Union which, through various

46. El País, *Los efectos del teletrabajo: bajan las reducciones de jornada* (7 March 2022), https://elpais.com/economia/negocios/2022-03-07/los-efectos-del-teletrabajo-bajan-las-reducciones-de-jornada.html.
47. ILO, *Achieving Gender Equality at Work* 248 (Geneve 2023) and also Rodríguez-Modroño & López-Igual, *supra* n. 43.
48. *See*, in this regard, Manuela Tomei, *Teleworking: A Curse or a Blessing for Gender Equality and Work-Life Balance?*, 5 Intereconomics 260–264 (2021) https://doi.org/10.1007/s10272-021-0995-4.

soft-law instruments, has influenced these reforms.[49] In fact, and especially since the publication of the White Paper 'An agenda for adequate, safe and sustainable pensions', the European Commission has been insisting on the need to face the challenges posed by ageing and sustainability.[50] The Union therefore considers it necessary for Member States to introduce mechanisms to increase the labour market participation of women and older workers or to seek a better balance between working time and retirement. To this end, the white paper offers some general recommendations, such as increasing the retirement age (considering longer life expectancy), making access to early retirement more difficult, providing incentives to postpone retirement age, or reducing gender differences in pensions. Reforms introduced in pension systems have been in line with these recommendations.

According to the 2021 Ageing Report,[51] most European countries are in a process of raising the ordinary retirement age; at the same time, as a logical consequence, they are raising the age from which early retirement can take place. Some, such as Luxembourg (65), Ireland (66) and Norway (67), have not modified this age parameter. Others offer some nuances instead: Poland maintains different retirement ages for men (65) and women (60); Romania maintains the standard retirement age for men (65) while gradually raising the age for women, but not to the same level (61.2 in 2019 and 63 in 2030); Slovenia also maintains the ordinary age for men (65) and increases it for women until they are equalized (64.5 in 2019 and 65 in 2030). Austria also keeps the retirement age for men unchanged (65) and gradually increases the retirement age for women to equalize them by 2030 (60 in 2019 and 63.5 in 2030). Spain is a special case: despite increasing the normal retirement age from 65 to 67, it maintains the possibility of retiring at 65 with a particularly high contribution. In connection with these policies extending the retirement age, many countries continue to allow access to early retirement – but they have tightened eligibility requirements and have introduced penalties (as in the case of Portugal and Spain). At the other extreme, bonuses for continuing to work and postponing retirement are common. However, there are significant differences between the effective age at which workers leave the labour market and the statutory retirement age; this gap is expected to widen in the future.

The other defining element of the retirement pension – termination of employment – is also becoming more flexible as well. In this sense, regulatory changes are making the classic idea of total withdrawal from the labour market more malleable, allowing and encouraging the reconciliation of pension and activity to varying degrees and in different configurations, with the idea of extending working life.[52] This is the

---

49. Eusebi Colàs-Neila, *Reconfiguring the Employment-Pension Connection in Times of Austerity*, 7(3) European Labour Law Journal 461–478 (2016) https://doi.org/10.1177/201395251600700309.
50. COM (2012) 55 final. This document contains the results of the consultation process on the subject that took place from the 2010 Green Paper on pensions. *See* European Commission, *Green Paper: Towards Adequate, Sustainable and Safe European Pension Systems* (European Commission, Publications Office, COM (2010) 365).
51. European Commission, *The 2021 Ageing Report. Economic & Budgetary Projections for the EU Member States (2019–2070)* (Publication Office of the European Union 2021).
52. *Social Security Programs and Retirement around the World: Reforms and Retirement Incentives* (Axel Börsch-Supan & Courtney C. Coile eds, University of Chicago Press 2018).

case in EU countries, where there are common rules on the compatibility of pensions and work, as an alternative to full retirement.

Despite the heterogeneity that characterizes these regulations, some common trends can be noted.[53] On the one hand, and in line with the above, it is common for rules to be more restrictive when access to retirement is sought below the ordinary age, and some countries do not even allow this possibility (such as Norway, Estonia, Ireland, Latvia, Lithuania, Luxembourg, and Poland). On the other hand, there is a certain convergence in the requirements that are usually set to combine work and pension. It is common to require certain minimum contribution periods, which in some cases correspond to those necessary to qualify for a full pension (France, Italy, Belgium, and Spain). Sometimes, income thresholds are also set, above which certain restrictions are imposed. Finally, though in varying degrees in different countries, the contributions of these workers, though maintained, are lower than those of other workers.

Certainly, transitions from working life to retirement have a significant impact on the sustainability of pensions. According to our view of sustainability that runs counter to the precarization of pensions deriving from the prevailing normative discourse, we argue that among the regulatory possibilities of pension policies mentioned here, it is necessary to reinforce those that make it possible to reconcile work and pensions. Strengthening this pathway can contribute to the economic sustainability of the system because it entails lower pension costs; it ensures a level (albeit reduced in many cases) of income through contributions; and at the same time, as stated, it reduces the exclusive dependence on pension income thus ensuring social sustainability as a manifestation of our fundamental rights approach. Making this formula more attractive may involve mechanisms that make it easier for the retirement age worker's total net income to be higher than the option of full retirement or continuing to work. However, in terms of working conditions, the possibility of part-time teleworking may be more attractive as an alternative to full retirement, as it makes it easier to combine the availability of free time and active ageing.

The combination of work and pension takes various forms; for example, in Spain, the 'contrato de relevo' (relief contact) combines part-time work and pension. This contract allows an unemployed worker to be hired to cover the part of the working day freed up by a worker who, with a long contribution record, can take early part-time retirement without penalty. In this way, in addition to serving as an instrument for integration into the labour market, the relief contract helps to offer alternatives to those who wish to retire gradually before the normal retirement age. It would be interesting to reformulate this contract by extending its time limits beyond the normal retirement age as a good practice to promote extension of working lives. From a perspective of inclusive intergenerational solidarity, it would allow older persons to contribute actively to the labour market in a way that is compatible with the incorporation of young unemployed workers. This can take place in two areas and in two different

53. Alfonso R. Sánchez Martín & Sergi Jiménez Martín, *La compatibilidad del trabajo y el cobro de pensión en España: análisis institucional en el contexto europeo*, 11 FEDEA – Estudios sobre la Economía Española (2021).

directions. In the labour sphere, the knowledge and experience of mature workers can be very useful in the training of younger generations. From a social-protection perspective, the incorporation of new generations of workers makes it easier for mature workers to take advantage of flexible retirement formulas that combine retirement with the continuity of working life. In addition, as an expression of this idea of solidarity, the establishment of quotas in companies for mature workers could be considered, guaranteeing these workers a certain presence in the labour market.

7 TELEWORK AND LIFELONG LEARNING AS MECHANISMS TO OVERCOME THE TECHNOLOGICAL GAP OF OLDER WORKERS

In the past 20 years, lifelong learning has emerged as one of the workers' rights requiring the most attention in order to ensure its effectiveness. Working practices, policies, and regulations, at both European and national levels, have pushed towards an employment relationship characterized by greater flexibility, fragmented careers, and demands to adapt to the changes imposed by digitalization. Flexicurity policies represent the contemporary paradigm, where traditional security based on the guarantee of employment stability has been replaced by protection in the transitions that take place in the labour market, at the level of unemployment benefits and, as far as we are concerned here, by offering training measures that allow workers to increase their employability. However, in many cases, neither the national authorities nor the employer can provide an effective guarantee through this training; this gives rise to 'flexiprecarity' models characterized by a complete imbalance between the elements of flexibility in favour of companies and security in favour of workers.[54] The main result is that when it comes to achieving employability levels that promote short transitions in the labour market and new employment, the responsibility lands squarely on the worker.

As we have seen, working-life extension is a common feature of European legal systems through the combination of various formulas in the field of social protection. In our opinion, choosing paths that not only allow the combination work and pension but also make it more attractive offers a range of beneficial effects for both the social-security system and the working individual.

However, mechanisms are needed to ensure effective lifelong learning; as noted earlier, these mechanisms have a significant impact on the lengthening of working life.[55]

This chapter attempts to argue that the facilitation of telework, as a voluntary option for workers, can promote compatibility between part-time work and pension and make such combinations an attractive choice for workers. Although this area of

54. Julia López, Alexandre de le Court & Sergio Canalda, *Breaking the Equilibrium between Flexibility and Security: Flexiprecarity as the Spanish Version of the Model*, 5(1) European Labour Law Journal 22-42 (2014) ttps://doi.org/10.1177/201395251400500104.
55. Baltic Sea Labour Forum for Sustainable Working Life, *Lifelong Learning to Extend Working Life. Participation in Education and Learning Among People in the Age Group 55+ in the Baltic Sea Region and How We Can Increase It*, Policy Brief #9 (2022).

study has not received much attention, some empirical research can be found showing the willingness of older people working with information and communications technologies (ICTs) to extend their working life if they could telework.[56]

However, this prolonged labour involvement may provide the worker with access to training, particularly in transversal digital skills, which can have a spillover effect and lead to greater autonomy in an increasingly digitalized life, thus narrowing the technology gap that may affect many older workers. Facilitating telework combined with the retirement pension means that companies continue to have an obligation to train these workers, in particular in ICT issues. This training, which is necessary to develop telework skills, may give older workers digital skills that can be useful beyond the employment sphere and provide autonomy in an increasingly digital world to carry out basic activities such as banking and administrative tasks or the purchase of public transport fares. This beneficial effect may be essential in reducing the digital exclusion of the elderly in developed countries,[57] thus increasing their agency.

Moreover, as a formula to provide employment for older workers, telework may facilitate their ability to maintain relationships with other workers and pensioners, creating important health impacts and increased visibility for this collective. In this sense, the Council Recommendation on Key Competences for Lifelong Learning,[58] based on a Commission Proposal, includes digital and technology-based competences among the eight key competences required for 'personal fulfilment, a healthy and sustainable lifestyle, employability, active citizenship and social inclusion'.

8 CONCLUSION

The debates about the sustainability of retirement pensions, from our perspective, should integrate the synergies of part-time contracts and telework as a way to extend working lives. The impact of pension systems on fundamental rights is a reason to reinforce mechanisms that improve equality and non-discrimination - principles present in the regulation of both part-time work and telework - thereby creating a continuous cycle for formalizing the discussion of sustainability in a normative form. The policies concerning: (1) care, with its direct impact on gender, and (2) training, with its clear impact on age and gender, should be integrated and visualized in the governance of pensions in the goal of achieving gender equality at work.[59]

56. René Arvola, Kaja Lutsoja, Ülo Kristjuhan & Piia Tint, *Telework as an Option to Postpone the Retirement for Ageing People?*, 8 Safety of Technology Environment 15–23 (2017) https://doi.org/10.1515/ste-2017-0003.
57. *See* Farooq Mubarak & Reima Suomi, *Elderly Forgotten? Digital Exclusion in the Information Age and the Rising Grey Digital Divide*, 59 INQUIRY: The Journal of Health Care Organization, Provision, and Financing 1–7 (2022) https://doi.org/10.1177/00469580221096272.
58. Council Recommendation of 22 May 2018 on key competences for lifelong learning, ST/9009/2018/INIT, OJ C 189, 4 June 2018, 1–13.
59. *See* Achieving gender equality at work. ILO Conferences 111th, session 2023.

Table of Cases

1 UN Committee on the Rights of Persons with Disabilities (CRPD)

Sahlin v. Sweden CRPD/C/23/D/45/2018 (2020)
Pending cases 98/2022 *Sweden* CRPD-4, CRPD-5, CRPD-24

2 The Court of Justice of the European Union

2.1 Judgments

Case C-80/70 (Defrenne I) ECLI:EU:C:1971:55
Case C-43/75 (Defrenne II) ECLI:EU:C:1976:56
Case C-33/76 *Rewe* ECLI:EU:C:1979:42
Case C-45/76 *Comet BV* ECLI:EU:C:1976:191
Case C-149/77 (Defrenne III) ECLI:EU:C:1978:130
Case C-409/95 *Hellmut Marschall v. Land Nordrhein-Westfalen* ECLI:EU:C:1997:533
Case C-249/96 *Grant v. South-West Trains Ltd* ECLI:EU:C:1998:63
Case C-158/97 *Badeck et al. v. Hessischer Ministerpräsident und Landesanwalt beim Staatsgerichtshof des Landes Hessen* ECLI:EU:C:2000:163
Case C-236/98 *Jämställdhetsombudsmannen* ECLI:EU:C:2000:173
Case C-173/99 *BECTU* ECLI:EU:C:2001:356
Case C-144/04 *Mangold* ECLI:EU:C:2005:709
Case C-411/05 *Palacios de la Villa v. Cortefiel* ECLI:EU:C:2007:604
Case C-303/06 *Coleman* ECLI:EU:C:2008:415
Case C-388/07 *Age Concern England v. Secretary of State for Business, Enterprise and Regulatory Reform* ECLI:EU:C:2009:128
Case C-555/07 *Kücükdeveci* ECLI:EU:C:2010:21
Case C-277/08 *Vicente Pereda* ECLI:EU:C:2009:542
Case C-499/08 *Ole Andersen* ECLI:EU:C:2010:600
Case C-45/09 *Rosenbladt v. Oellerking Gebaudereinigungsges mbH* ECLI:EU:C:2010:601
Case C-250/09 and 268/09 *Georgiev v. Technischeski Universittet Sofia* ECLI:EU:C:2010:699

Case C-155/10 *Williams and others* ECLI:EU:C:2011:588
Case C-159/10 and 160/10 *Fuchs and Köhler v. Land Hessen* ECLI:EU:C:2011:508
Case C-214/10 *KHS* ECLI:EU:C:2011:761
Case C-337/10 *Neidel* ECLI:EU:C:2012:263
Case C-141/11 *Torsten Hörnfeldt v. Posten Meddelande AB* ECLI:EU:C:2012:421
Case C-152/11 *Odar* ECLI:EU:C:2012:772
Joined Cases C-335/11 and C-337/11 HK Danmark, ECLI:EU:C:2013:222
Case C-426/11 *Alemo-Herron and others* ECLI:EU:C:2013:521
Case C-546/11 *Toftgaard* ECLI:EU:C:2013:602
Case C-81/12 *Asociaţia Accept* ECLI:EU:C:2013:275
Case C-176/12 *Association de médiation sociale (AMS)* ECLI:EU:C:2014:2
Case C-286/12 *Commission v. Hungary* ECLI:EU:C:2012:687
Case C-316/13 *Fenoll* ECLI:EU:C:2015:200
Case C-515/13 *Tekniq* ECLI:EU:C:2015:115
Case C-441/14 *Dansk Industri* ECLI:EU:C:2016:278
Case C-178/15 *Sobczyszyn* ECLI:EU:C:2016:502, paragraph 20
Case C-188/15 *Bougnaoui*, ECLI:EU:C:2017:204
C-236/98 *Jämställdhetsombudsmannen v. Örebro läns landsting* ECLI:EU:C:2000:173
Case C-414/16 *Egenberger* ECLI:EU:C:2018:257
Joined Cases C-569/16 and C-570/16 *Bauer* ECLI:EU:C:2018:871
Case C-684/16 *Max-Planck-Gesellschaft zur* Förderung *der Wissenschaften* ECLI:EU:C:2018:874
Case C- 46/17 *John* ECLI:EU:C:2018:131
Case C-396/17 *Leitner* ECLI:EU:C:2019:375
Joined Cases C-609/17 and C-610/17, *TSN* ECLI:EU:C:2019:981
Case C-670/18 *CO* ECLI:EU:C:2020:272
Case C-30/19 *Braathens* ECLI:EU:C:2021:269
Case C-795/19 *Tartu Vangla v. Justitsminister, Tervise-ja töötminsiter, Ölguskantsler* ECLI:EU:C:2021:606
Case C-485/20 *XXXX v. HR Rail SA*, ECLI :EU:C:2022:85
Case C-715/20, *K.L.*, 20.2.2024, ECLI:EU:C:2024:139
Case C-156/21 *Hungary v. Parliament and Council* ECLI:EU:C:2022:97
Case C-157/21 *Poland v. Parliament and Council* ECLI:EU:C:2022:98
Joined Cases C-257/21 and C-258/21 *Coca-Cola European Partners Deutschland* ECLI:EU:C:2022:529
Case C-356/21 *TP (Monteur audiovisuel pour la télévision publique)* ECLI:EU:C:2023:9

2.2 Opinions of Advocate Generals

Opinion of Advocate General Cruz Villalón in Case C-176/12 *AMS*, delivered on 18.7.2013, ECLI:EU:C:2013:491
Opinion of Advocate General Cruz-Villallon in Case C-426/11 *Alemo-Herron and others*, delivered on 19.2.2013, ECLI:EU:C:2013:82
Opinion of Advocate General Mengozzi in Case C-316/13 *Fenoll*, delivered on 12.6.2014, ECLI:EU:C:2014:1753

Opinion of AG Bot in Joined Cases C-609/17 and C-610/17 *TSN*, delivered on 4.6.2019, ECLI:EU:C:2019:459

3 The European Committee of Social Rights

Collective complaint No. 1/1998, *International Commission of Jurists (ICJ) v. Portugal*
Collective complaint No. 13/2002, *International association Autism-Europe (IAAE) v. France*
Collective complaint No. 39/2006, *European Federation of National Organisations Working with the Homeless (FEANTSA) v. France*
Collective complaint No. 50/2008, *Confédération Francaise Démocratique du Travail (CFDT) v. France*
Collective complaint No. 51/2008, *European Roma Rights Centre (ERRC) v. France*
Collective complaint No. 53/2008, *European Federation of National Organisations Working with the Homeless (FEANTSA) v. Slovenia*
Collective complaint No. 58/2009, *Centre on Housing Rights and Evictions (COHRE) v. Italy*
Collective complaint No. 74/2011, *Fællesforbundet for Sjøfolk (FFFS) v. Norway*
Collective complaint No. 145/2017, *International Federation of Associations of the Elderly (FIAPA) v. France*
Collective complaint No. 162/2018, International Federation of Associations of the Elderly *(FIAPA) v. France*

4 National Jurisdictions

4.1 Australia

Board of Bendigo Regional Institute of Technical and Further Education v. Barclay, (2012) 248 CLR 500
General Motors-Holden Pty Ltd v. Bowling, (1976) 12 ALR 605
Vink v. LED Technologies Pty Ltd, [2013] FCA 443
Wroughton v. Catholic Education Office Diocese of Parramatta, [2015] FCA 1236
Bayford v. MAXXIA Pty Ltd, [2011] FMCA 202
CFMEU v. Leighton Contractors Pty Ltd, [2012] FMCA 487
Farah v. Ahn, [2012] FMCA 44
Silver v. Rogers & Rogers, [2012] FMCA 674
Stephens v. Australian Postal Corporation, [2011] FMCA 448
Vink v. Led Technologies Pty Ltd, [2012] FMCA 917
Gutierrez v. MUR Shipping Australia Pty Limited, [2021] FedCFamC2G 56
Gladdish v. Queensland, [2012] QCAT 721
Lidis v. Top Dog Minders Pty Ltd, [2011] QCAT 232

4.2 Brazil

Superior Tribunal de Justiça (STJ): Recurso Especial No. 1.843.150 – PA (2019/0306530-1), 26/5, 2020

4.3 Japan

Nagasawa Un-yu Case, Supreme Court, 1 June 2018, 72 Minshu 202
Kyushu Souzai Case, Fukuoka High Court, 7 September 2017, 1167 Rodo Hanrei 49
Toyota Case, Nagoya High Court, 28 September 2016, 1146 Rodo Hanrei 22
General Dynamics Land Systems, *Inc. v. Cline*, 540 U.S. 581 (2004).

4.4 Spain

Spanish Supreme Court Decision of 11 April 2005 (ECLI:ES:TS:2005:2126)

4.5 Sweden

Swedish Supreme Court Judgment NJA 2006, p. 683
Swedish Supreme Court Judgment NJA 2021, p. 1093
Swedish Labour Court Judgment AD 1993 No. 61
Swedish Labour Court Judgment AD 1983 No. 107
Swedish Labour Court Judgment AD 1993 No. 101
Swedish Labour Court Judgment AD 1996 No. 4
Swedish Labour Court Judgment AD 2001 No. 13
Swedish Labour Court Judgment AD 2001 No. 76
Swedish Labour Court Judgment AD 2005 No. 32
Swedish Labour Court Judgment AD 2010 No. 3
Swedish Labour Court Judgment AD 2011 No. 37
Swedish Labour Court Judgment AD 2013 No. 78
Swedish Labour Court Judgment AD 2014 No. 26
Swedish Labour Court Judgment AD 2015 No. 51
Swedish Labour Court Judgment AD 2017 No. 51
Swedish Labour Court Judgment AD 2018 No. 76
Swedish Labour Court Judgment AD 2020 No. 58
Swedish Labour Court Judgment AD 2024 No. 12
Swedish Labour Court Judgment AD 2024 No. 49
Stockholm Administrative Court of Appeal, Judgment 20-12-2012, Case 1968-12

4.6 The United Kingdom

Jivraj v. Hashwani, [2011] UKSC 40
R v. Governing Body of JFS, [2010] 2 AC 728
Halawi v. WDFG UK Ltd, [2014] EWCA Civ 1387
Ladele v. London Borough of Islington, [2009] ICR 387
Ahmed v. Autism Consulting Ltd, [2017] UKET 3322728/2016
Ali v. Virgin Active Ltd, [2018] UKET 2206652/2017
Amu v. Department for Work and Pensions, [2018] UKET 1600465/2017
Astor v. Ministry of Defence, [2017] UKET 2404378/2016
Ayree v. Langridge Organic Products Ltd, [2017] UKET 2301647/2016
Cassidy v. Quest Vitamins Ltd, [2017] UKET 2401277/2017
Cheney v. MS Amlin Corporate Services Ltd, [2017] UKET 2207640/2016
Ellis v. Henley Media Group Ltd, [2017] UKET 2208129/2016

Fairclough v. Allen, [2018] UKET 2403288/2017
Fenton v. Pennine Acute Hospitals Trust, [2017] UKET 2414119/2012
Florian v. Adecco UK Ltd, [2018] UKET 3200082/2018
Fogarty v. Colman Greaves Fabrications Ltd, [2019] UKET 2410534/2018
Gosling v. Harding, [2019] UKET 2501261/2018
Hughes v. Rolls Royce plc, [2019] UKET 2601847/2018
Kopec v. BDW Trading Ltd, [2019] UKET 2207111/2017
Kumar v. Guy's and St Thomas' NHS Foundation Trust, [2017] UKET 2302841/2015
Law v. Wirral Golf Club Ltd, [2017] UKET 2405273/2016
Mhlanga v. Kendrick, [2017] UKET 2300280/2017
Mundin v. Beal Developments Ltd, [2017] UKET 1800455/2017
Ramzan v. Shop On Time Ltd, [2018] UKET 1304475/2017
Richardson v. B&Q plc, [2017] UKET 1401373/2016
Roberts v. Logo Design Grp Ltd, [2018] UKET 2404024/2017
Shirin v. Wilson Barca LLP, [2019] UKET 2208035/2016
Taylor v. Dr Kelpie and Partners (A Partnership), [2017] UKET 1401375/2016
Vickers v. ABM Facilities Services UK Ltd, [2017] UKET 3200556/2016
Wallace v. KPI Bridge Oil London Ltd, [2017] UKET 227596/2016
Warrilow v. Openwork Ltd, [2018] UKET 3329040/2017
Wilkinson v. Arnold Brickwork Ltd, [2019] UKET 1401376/2018
Wilson v. Wilson Devonald Griffiths John Ltd, [2017] UKET 1600416/2016
Winschief v. SRS Realisations 2017 Ltd (in administration), [2019] UKET 1402539/2018
Worboyes v. FDR Ltd, [2017] UKET 3200314/2017
McCalister v. South Eastern Health & Social Care Trust, (2017) NIIT 00741/16IT
Toner v. L F Fasthouse Ltd, [2019] NIFET 06955/18IT

4.7 The United States

Brown v. Board of Education, 347 U.S. 483 (1954)
General Dynamics Land Systems, Inc. v. Cline, 540 U.S. 581 (2004)
Roe v. Wade, 410 U.S. 113 (1973)

STUDIES IN EMPLOYMENT AND SOCIAL POLICY

1. W. Beck, L. van der Maesen & A. Walker (eds), *The Social Quality of Europe*, 1997 (ISBN 90-411-0456-9).
2. R. Blanpain, M. Colucci, C. Engels, F. Hendrickx, L. Salas & E. De Smyter, *Institutional Changes and European Social Policies after the Treaty of Amsterdam*, 1998 (ISBN 90-411-1018-6).
3. V. Lo: *Law and Industrial Relations: China and Japan after World War II*, 1998 (ISBN 90-411-1075-5).
4. A. Den Exter & H. Hermans (eds), *The Right to Health Care in Several European Countries*, 1998 (ISBN 90-411-1087-9).
5. M. Biagi (ed.), *Job Creation and Labour Law from Protection towards Pro- Action*, 2000 (ISBN 90-411-1432-7).
6. W. Beck, L. van der Maesen, F. Thomése & A. Walker (eds), *Social Quality: A Vision for Europe*, 2000 (ISBN 90-411-1523-4).
7. F. Pennings, *Introduction to European Social Law*, 3rd ed., 2001 (ISBN 90-411-1628-1).
8. J. Murray, *Transnational Labour Regulation: The ILO and EC Compared*, 2001 (ISBN 90-411-1583-8).
9. R. Blanpain & C. Engels (eds), *The ILO and Social Challenges of the 21st Century*, 2001 (ISBN 90-411-1572-2).
10. M. Biagi (ed.), *Towards a European Model of Industrial Relations? Building on the First Report of the European Commission*, 2001 (ISBN 90-411-1653-2).
11. J. Clasen (ed.), *What Future for Social Security? Debates and Reforms in National and Cross-National Perspective*, 2001 (ISBN 90-411-1671-0).
12. A. Numhauser-Henning (ed.), *Legal Perspectives on Equal Treatment and Non-Discrimination*, 2001 (ISBN 90-411-1665-6).
13. R. Blanpain (ed.), *Labour Law, Human Rights and Social Justice* 2001 (ISBN 90-411-1697-4).
14. M.-C. Kuo, H.F. Zacher & H.-S. Chan (eds), *Reform and Perspectives on Social Insurance: Lessons from the East and West*, 2002 (ISBN 90-411-1819-5).
15. P. Foubert, *The Legal Protection of the Pregnant Worker in the European Community*, 2002 (ISBN 90-411-1842-X).
16. M. Biagi (ed.), *Quality of Work and Employee Involvement in Europe*, 2002 (ISBN 90-411-1885-3).
17. F. Pennings, *Dutch Social Security Law in an International Context*, 2002 (ISBN 90-411-1887-X).

18. T. Carney & G. Ramia, *From Rights to Management: Contract, New Public Management and Employment Services*, 2002 (ISBN 90-411-1889-6).
19. R. Blanpain & M. Colucci, *European Labour and Social Security Law, Glossary*, 2002 (ISBN 90-411-1905-1).
20. I.U. Zeytinoglu (ed.), *Flexible Work Arrangements: Conceptualizations and International Experiences*, 2002 (ISBN 90-411-1947-7).
21. J. Berghman, A. Nagelkerke, M. Boos, R. Doeschot & G. Vonk (eds), *Social Security in Transition*, 2002 (ISBN 90-411-1969-8).
22. R. Blanpain, *The Legal Status of Sportsmen and Sportswomen under International, European and Belgian National and Regional Law*, 2003 (ISBN 90-411-1980-9).
23. R. Blanpain & M. Weiss (eds), *Changing Industrial Relations & Modernisation of Labour Law, Liber Amicorum in Honour of Professor Marco Biagi*, 2003 (ISBN 90-411-2008-4).
24. J. Malmberg (ed.), *Effective Enforcement of EC Labour Law*, 2003 (ISBN 90-411-2160-9).
25. M. De Vos (ed.), *A Decade Beyond Maastricht: The European Social Dialogue Revisited*, 2003 (ISBN 90-411-2163-3).
26. M. Sewerynski (ed.), *Collective Agreements and Individual Contracts of Employment*, 2003 (ISBN 90-411-2190-0).
27. R. Blanpain & M. Van Gestel, *Use and Monitoring of E-Mail, Intranet and Internet Facilities at Work: Law and Practice*, 2004 (ISBN 90-411-22-66-4).
28. A. C. Neal (ed.), *The Changing Face of European Labour Law and Social Policy*, 2004 (ISBN 90-411-2312-1).
29. E. Sol & M. Westerveld (eds), *Contractualism in Employment Services: A New Form of Welfare State Governance*, 2005 (ISBN 90-411-2405-5).
30. F. Pennings (ed.), *Between Soft and Hard Law – The Impact of International Social Security Standards on National Social Security Law*, 2006 (ISBN 978-90-411-2491-3).
31. L. Dickens & A. C. Neal (eds), *The Changing Institutional Face of British Employment Relations*, 2006 (ISBN 978-90-411-2541-5).
32. G. Sebardt, *Redundancy and the Swedish Model in an International Context*, 2006 (ISBN 978-90-411-2503-3).
33. A.M. Swiatkowski, *Charter of Social Rights of the Council of Europe*, 2007 (ISBN 978-90-411-2608-5).
34. M. Sargeant (ed.), *The Law on Age Discrimination in the EU*, 2008 (ISBN 978-90-411-2522-4).
35. G. Di Domenico & S. Spattini (eds), *New European Approaches to Long- Term Unemployment: What Role for Public Employment Services and What Market for Private Stakeholders?*, 2008 (ISBN 978-90-411-2614-6.)
36. C. Welz, *The European Social Dialogue under Articles 138 and 139 of the EC Treaty: Actors, Processes, Outcomes*, 2008 (ISBN 978-90-411-2744-0).
37. M. Rönnmar (ed.), *EU Industrial Relations v. National Industrial Relations: Comparative and Interdisciplinary Perspectives*, 2008 (ISBN 978-90-411- 2770-9).

38. F. Pennings, Y. Konijn & A. Veldman (eds), *Social Responsibility in Labour Relations: European and Comparative Perspectives*, 2008 (ISBN 978-90- 411-2783-9).
39. F. Pennings & C. Bosse (eds), *The Protection of Working Relationships: A Comparative Study*, 2011 (ISBN 978-90-411-3289-5).
40. S. Devetzi & S. Stendahl (eds), *Too Sick to Work?: Social Security Reference in Europe for Persons with Reduced Earnings Capacity*, 2011 (ISBN 978-90- 411-3426-4).
41. Ulrich Becker, Frans Pennings & Tineke Dijkhoff (eds), *International Standard Setting and Innovations in Social Security*, 2013 (ISBN 978-90-411-3233-8).
42. E. Ales (ed.), *Health and Safety at Work: European and Comparative Perspective*, 2013 (ISBN 978-90-411-4661-8).
43. F. Pennings, T. Erhag & S. Stendahl (eds), *Non-public Actors in Social Security Administration: A Comparative Study*, 2013 (ISBN 978-90-411-4917-6).
44. A. Neal (ed.), *Cross-Currents in Modern Chinese Labour Law*, 2014 (ISBN 978-90-411-4763-9).
45. B. Waas (ed.), *The Right to Strike: A Comparative View*, 2014 (ISBN 978-90-411-5007-3).
46. A. Ojeda-Avilés, *Transnational Labour Law*, 2015 (ISBN 978-90-411-5858-1).
47. A. Numhauser-Henning & M. Rönnmar, *Age Discrimination and Labour-Law: Comparative and Conceptual Perspectives in the EU and Beyond*, 2015 (ISBN 978-90-411-4979-4).
48. A. Perulli & T. Treu (eds), *Enterprise and Social Rights*, 2017 (ISBN 978-90-411-8234-0).
49. Dr F.C.A. van Haasteren, *Decent Flexibility: The Impact of ILO Convention 181 and the Regulation on Temporary Agency Work*, 2017 (ISBN 978-90-411-9236-3).
50. T. Dijkhoff & L.G. Mpedi (eds), *Recommendation on Social Protection Floors: Basic Principles for Innovative Solutions*, 2018 (ISBN 978-90-411-8623-2).
51. A. Perulli & T. Treu (eds), *Sustainable Development, Global Trade and Social Rights*, 2018 (ISBN 978-90-411-9235-6).
52. M. Mironi & M. Schlachter (eds), *Regulating Strikes in Essential Services: A Comparative 'Law in Action' Perspective*, 2019 (ISBN 978-90-411-8997-4).
53. A. Perulli & T. Treu (eds), *The Role of the State and Industrial Relations*, 2019 (ISBN 978-94-035-0661-6).
54. T. Gyulavári & E. Menegatti (eds), *The Sources of Labour Law*, 2020 (ISBN 978-94-035-0284-7).
55. V. Cagnin, *Labour Law and Sustainable Development*, 2020 (ISBN 978-94-035-2074-2).
56. A. Perulli & T. Treu (eds), *The Future of Work: Labour Law and Labour Market Regulation in the Digital Era*, 2021 (ISBN 978-94-035-2853-3).
57. A. Perulli & T. Treu (eds), *Labour Law and Climate Change: Towards a Just Transition*, 2023 (ISBN 978-94-035-0877-1).
58. A. Perulli & T. Treu (eds), *Labour Law in the Mirror: Categories, Values, Interlocutors*, 2025 (ISBN 978-94-035-2798-7).

59. J.J. Votinius & M. Rönnmar (eds), *Older Workers, Active Ageing, and the Future of Work: Discourses and Legal Advancements*, 2025 (ISBN 978-94-035-1047-7).

www.ingramcontent.com/pod-product-compliance
Lightning Source LLC
Chambersburg PA
CBHW071331230926
51849CB00002B/368
* 9 7 8 9 4 0 3 5 1 0 4 7 7 *